POSTCARD HISTORY SERIES

# *Cohoes*

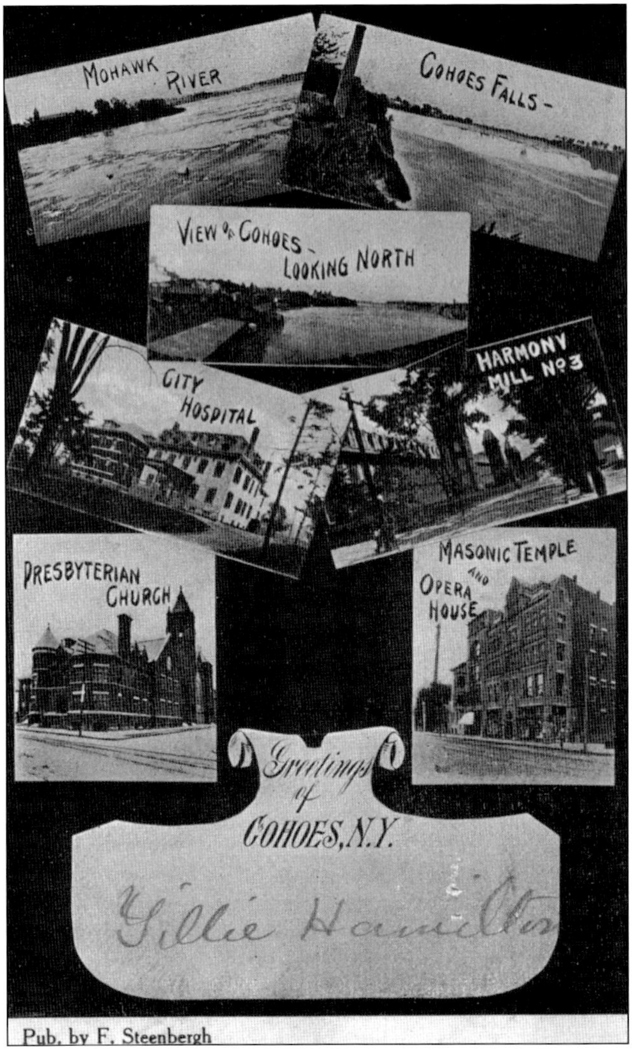


This photographic postcard reads, "Greetings of Cohoes, N.Y." It depicts the Mohawk River, the Cohoes Falls, a northern view of Cohoes, the city hospital, Harmony Mill No. 3, the Presbyterian church, the Masonic temple, and opera house. This book was written as a greeting from Cohoes and as a tribute to all that Cohoes represents to its residents, who are proudly known as Cohoesiers. (Spindle City Historic Society.)

**On the Front Cover:** This view of Ontario Street, looking east, shows the Manufacturers Bank, the Silliman Memorial Church, and city hall. On the right, at the corner of Remsen and Ontario Streets, is Granite Hall. Granite Hall was built in 1847 and was the Cohoes showplace of its day. The four-story building had storefronts at street level and a large hall on the top floor that hosted social events and lectures. (Spindle City Historic Society.)

**On the Back Cover:** This postcard view shows the Harmony Mills complex along the bank of the Mohawk River. The Cohoes Falls are in the distance. At its peak, in the late 19th century, the Harmony Mills Company had five large textile mill buildings, a picker house, a storehouse, a pump house, a company office building, and a full range of housing for various economic levels of mill workers in this section of Cohoes. (Spindle City Historic Society.)

POSTCARD HISTORY SERIES

# *Cohoes*

*Spindle City Historic Society*

ARCADIA
PUBLISHING

ISBN 978-1-4671-2129-3

Published by Arcadia Publishing
Charleston, South Carolina

Printed in the United States of America

Library of Congress Control Number: 2013946818

For all general information contact Arcadia Publishing at:
Telephone 843-853-2070
Fax 843-853-0044
E-mail sales@arcadiapublishing.com
For customer service and orders:
Toll-Free 1-888-313-2665

Visit us on the Internet at www.arcadiapublishing.com

*In memory of Anne Marie Nadeau*

# Contents

# Acknowledgments

The Spindle City Historic Society's Arcadia Committee had assistance and cooperation from many individuals who loaned us their cherished postcards and memories. We are indebted to them for their generosity; without it, this book would have been impossible. We thank Eleanor Ablett, Tom Bessette, Paul Dunleavy, Dennis Holzman, Ed Kingsley, Bernie Ouimet, Mike Pender, Tor Shekerjian, and Stanley Smithrick for their contributions. We also thank those who have donated postcards over the years to the Spindle City Historic Society, which now reside in our permanent collection. Unless otherwise noted, all images are from the Spindle City Historic Society's collection. We are also thankful to the City of Cohoes for providing us with a home to conduct programs and display our collections.

The Spindle City Historic Society hopes this book, through its historical images, will strengthen the knowledge about and appreciation for the history of Cohoes. If there have been oversights, or if readers can supplement the information in captions accompanying the postcards, we kindly ask you to inform us. Please contact the Spindle City Historic Society at P.O. Box 375, Cohoes, NY 12047, or through our website at www.spindlecity.net. We will post corrections, as well as supplemental information about the postcards in this volume, on our website. Your help is always appreciated and vital to extending our knowledge of Cohoes history.

The Spindle City Historic Society's Arcadia Committee includes Daniele Cherniak, Paul D. Dunleavy, June Cherniak, Walter Cherniak, Tor Shekerjian, Walter Lipka, Donna Riley, Bernie Ouimet, Donna Vaughn, Linda C. Christopher, and Dennis Rivage.

# Introduction

Cohoes has long held an attraction for visitors, with reports from European travelers at the Cohoes Falls dating back to the 17th century. The falls would long be a destination for writers and romantics, daredevils and diplomats. The nearby mills, drawing power from the Mohawk River and an innovative power canal system, would draw others as well. They included mill workers, many of them immigrants from Quebec or places across Europe, and industrialists and engineers studying the manufacturing innovations at the Harmony Mills. Cohoes was a crossroads for travelers because of its thriving industries, natural wonders, and location along major transportation networks—the Hudson and Mohawk Rivers, the Erie and Champlain Canals, railroads, and highways. Those arriving in Cohoes came from all walks of life and many places, from Europeans on the grand tour of the United States to locals taking the trolley to town from Northside or Troy.

In our first book, *Cohoes*, we trace the history of Cohoes through historic photographs covering various aspects of life in the community. Transportation is explored, whether by water, rail, or road. The industries of Cohoes, including world-renowned Simmons Axe and Harmony Mills, are featured. The industrial base of Cohoes spurred the growth of the city and the creation of a diverse group of local businesses. The influx of immigrants led to the development of distinctive neighborhoods with places of worship and educational institutions. The establishment of Cohoes as a village and later as a city necessitated the creation of public service agencies. Although the early immigrants often endured six-day workweeks, they also found time for leisure activities, ranging from skating on the canal to fishing on the river or picnicking by the falls.

Our second book, *Cohoes Revisited*, follows the history of Cohoes from the height of its industrial power in the late 19th century, through two world wars, the Great Depression, and other societal and technological changes of the 20th century. The story is told chronologically through photographs and through the eyes of an observer, Helen Dickey, who recounts experiences of life in Cohoes over the years in letters to her sister Adelaide. While the letters themselves are re-creations, Helen and Adelaide Dickey were real people. These letters reflect circumstances and occurrences of the time periods.

This book uses historic postcards of Cohoes to take readers on a tour of the sites visited by earlier travelers to the city. We intersperse the postcards with a small selection of trade cards and billheads from the 19th and early 20th centuries. These add another dimension to the stories that made Cohoes a vibrant place.

The earliest postcards can be traced to Germany in the 1860s. The US Post Office Department issued its first postcard in 1873. These early cards were mostly used for advertisements and notices. Picture postcards only became common around the turn of the 20th century. The first picture postcards had an undivided back. As no message could be placed on the same side as the address by law, messages were written on the front.

By the turn of the 20th century, postcards with photographic images appeared. In 1907, divided back postcards were produced, with half the back for a message and half for the address and stamp. Most postcards of this period were lithographs and were printed in Germany. These were replaced by linen postcards, with textures based on how they were produced. Linen postcards went out of fashion when color chrome (or photochrome) postcards were produced just before 1940. These are the cards still used today when we want to say "Wish you were here!"

We follow the pathways of earlier travelers, and chapters cover specific sections of Cohoes. Our tour starts along the Erie Canal, with views of flights of locks and canal boats, mules and "hoggees," stables and warehouses, and the surrounding landscape, seen back then at the pace of a few miles an hour. The canals and rivers were a common way for travelers to arrive in Cohoes, and the first commercial developments in what is now Cohoes were along the waterways. The original business district of Cohoes was at "Juncta," the junction of the original Erie and Champlain Canals. The canals provided employment for many during their construction, and later, people were hired to crew or captain canal boats, tend and maintain the locks, and keep the shops, stables, and saloons that sprang up nearby.

Next, we take our tourists northwest to the Harmony Mills district, where the mills rose up along the Erie Canal and on the banks of the mighty Mohawk River. The area developed into a model industrial complex from the mid- to late 19th century, with neighborhoods of sturdy company-built houses that were home to thousands of mill workers. Mill workers came from Ireland, England, and other places in Europe and from the province of Quebec. The mill district area drew worldwide interest in the late 1860s after workers uncovered the bones of an ancient mastodon while excavating for the foundation of Harmony Mill No. 3. The remains and replica of the mastodon remain tourist attractions to this day and are an iconic symbol for Cohoesiers. The mills themselves and the waterpower system that drove their machinery also drew worldwide attention, as engineers and industrialists visited Cohoes to marvel at the scale of production and technological innovations. Just beyond the mills stands the Cohoes Falls, the largest waterfall east of Niagara Falls, a site that has sacred significance, natural beauty, and utilitarian function as a source of power for the city's industrial growth.

Next, we head south toward downtown, the heart of the city's commercial and civic life, with magnificent structures, movie houses, an 1874 music hall, an opera house, and a traditional small-city Main Street with businesses and shops. Downtown Cohoes reflects the city's manufacturing prosperity and the imprint of its prominent philanthropists and industrialists, with buildings designed by noted architects and crafted by master stonemasons.

The book's tour continues east into the island section of the city, split from the rest of Cohoes by branches of the Mohawk River near its confluence with the Hudson River. Destinations include the Van Schaick Mansion, dating from the early 18th century, to the famous replica of Henry Hudson's ship the *Half Moon*. The mansion saw prominent visitors including George Washington, Gov. George Clinton, and the generals who planned the Battle of Saratoga, a turning point of the American Revolution. In the 1920s, visitors flocked to the replica of Henry Hudson's ship the *Half Moon*, which was given to Cohoes following its appearance in the Hudson-Fulton Tricentennial Celebration in 1909.

Our tour continues to the hill section, replete with parks, historic neighborhoods, churches, schools, and the city hospital. The postcard tour also features stories of some famous and infamous people who frequented Cohoes or made the city their home. These personalities include Pres. Chester Arthur, canal engineer Canvass White, manufacturing innovators Robert and David John Johnston and Daniel Simmons, prominent industrialist and philanthropist Horace B. Silliman, vaudeville performers Eva Tanguay and Adelaide Dickey, daredevil Bobby Leach, baseball Hall of Famer George Stacey Davis, and political boss "Big Mike" Smith, a friend of Franklin Delano Roosevelt.

Thanks to people in Cohoes who are postcard collectors, we were able to assemble this book for you!

# *One*

# The Canals

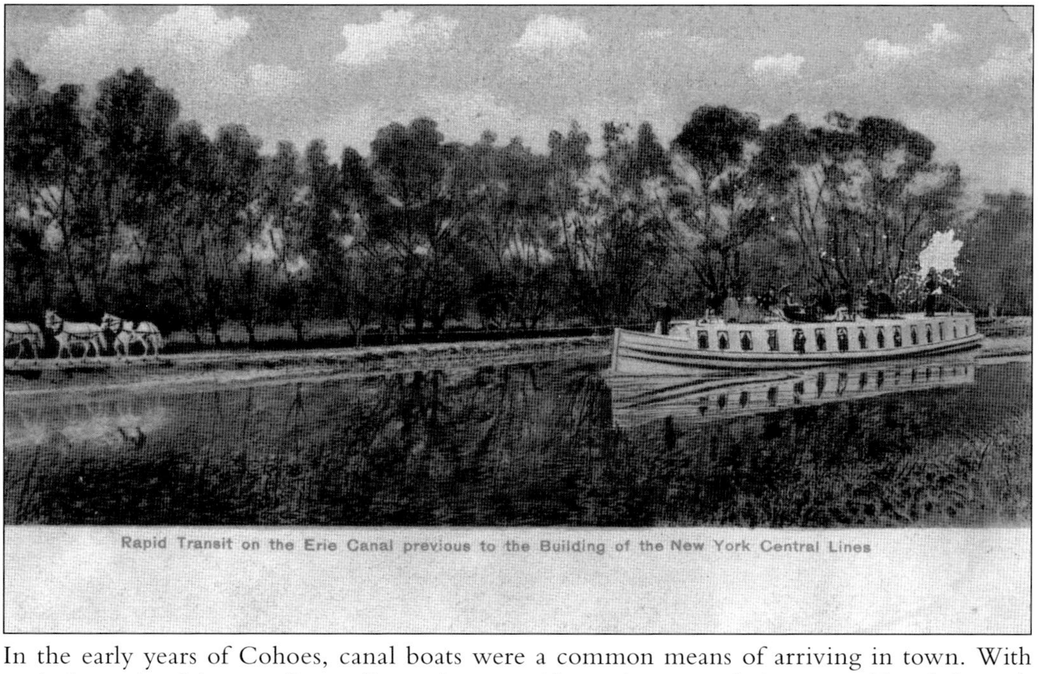


In the early years of Cohoes, canal boats were a common means of arriving in town. With typical speeds of three to four miles an hour, rapid transit was a relative term. Travel through Cohoes, with its many locks, could be even slower. In summer, canal boat interiors were horrid, driving passengers to the deck. At low-clearance bridges, cries of "low bridge, everybody down" warned these passengers to duck to avoid injury.

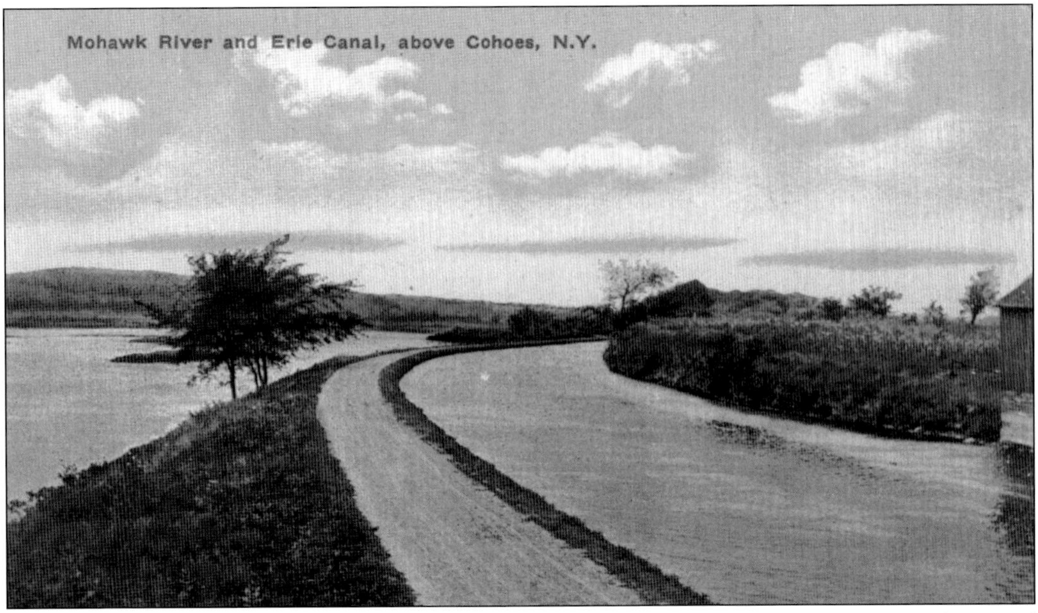


This view shows the enlarged Erie Canal just outside Cohoes. To the north, the canal crossed the Mohawk River on an aqueduct at Halfmoon, near the Route 9 bridge today. As canal travelers approached Cohoes, they faced "the Sixteens," a series of 16 locks through Cohoes into Maplewood that was a stretch of canal notorious for long travel times due to extended waits at locks and the slowness of "locking through."

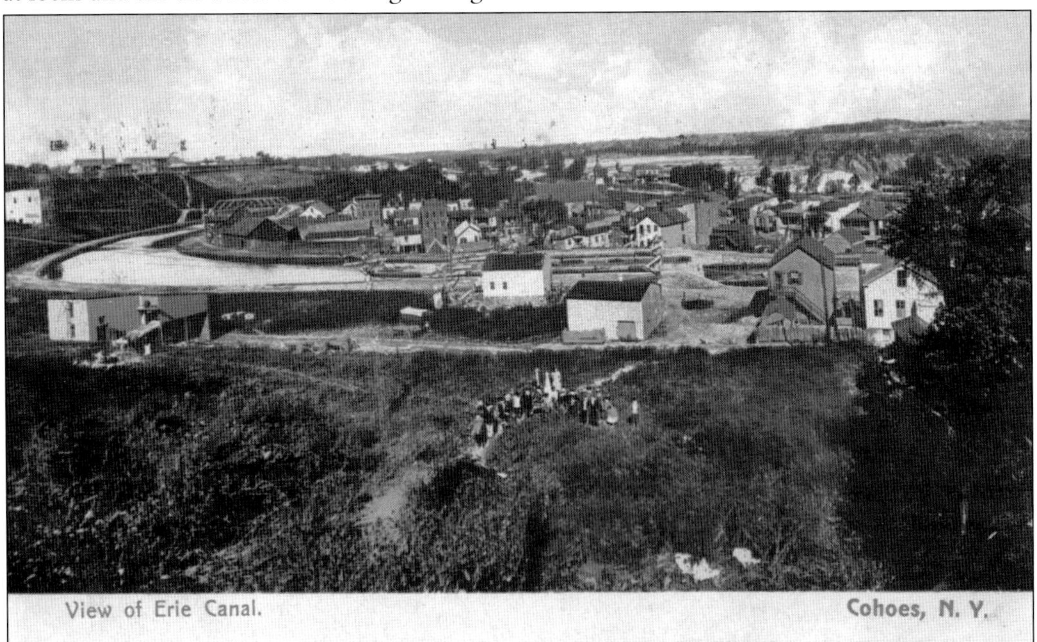


The enlarged Erie Canal, with Lock No. 17, cuts across this view of the orchard section of Cohoes. The Cohoes Falls are on the upper right, and St. Patrick's Church is toward the center. A brickyard is on the hill on the left side of the image, along with a small bridge crossing the canal. This neighborhood also had an icehouse for storage of ice cut from the Mohawk River.

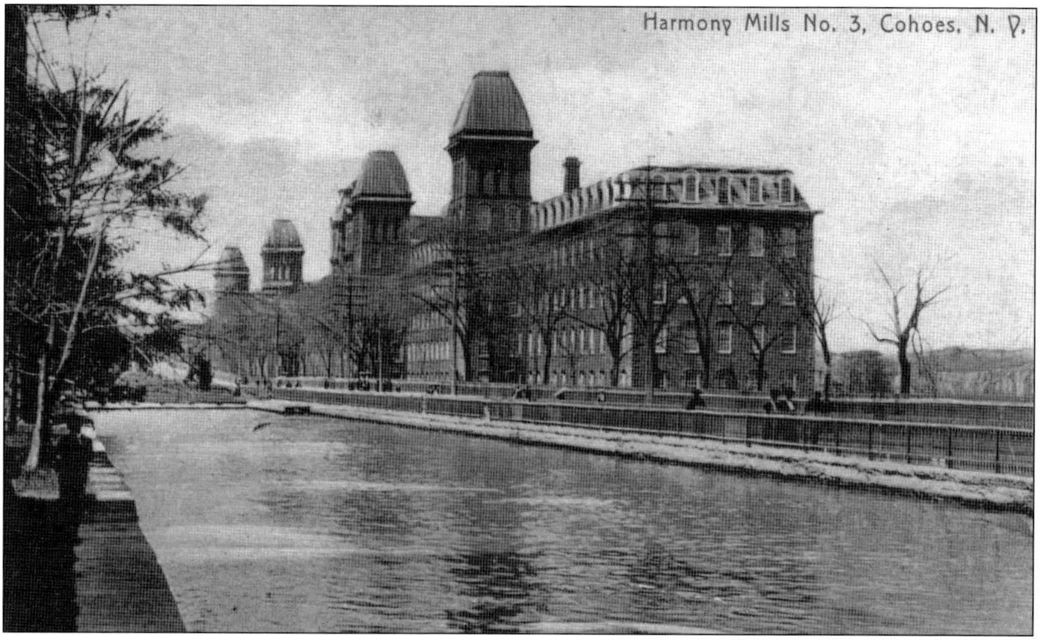


Both power canals and transportation canals were important to Cohoes. The canal in this image was once a section of the original Erie Canal. When the canal was enlarged and realigned in the late 1830s, New York State transferred sections of the original canal to the Cohoes Company in exchange for land for the new canal. The old canal sections were converted into power canals for Cohoes industries.

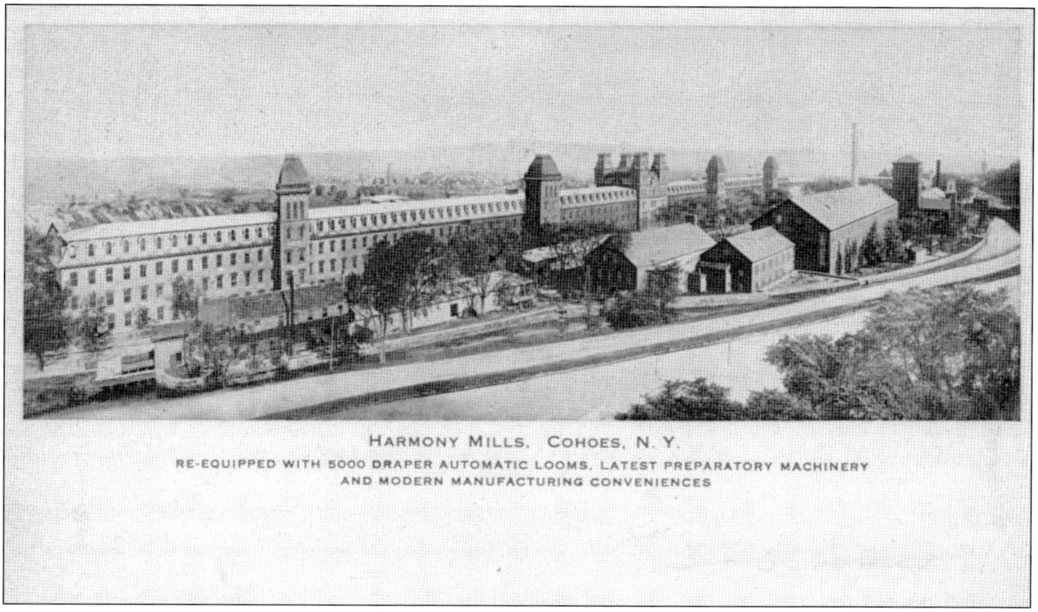


This view of the Harmony Mills complex and the Erie Canal illustrates the close connection between the development of the canals and the rise of manufacturing in Cohoes. Industrial development grew rapidly with the ease of shipping that the Erie Canal provided for bringing raw materials into and finished products out of Cohoes. The original 1837 section of the Harmony Mills complex was designed to directly face the enlarged Erie Canal.

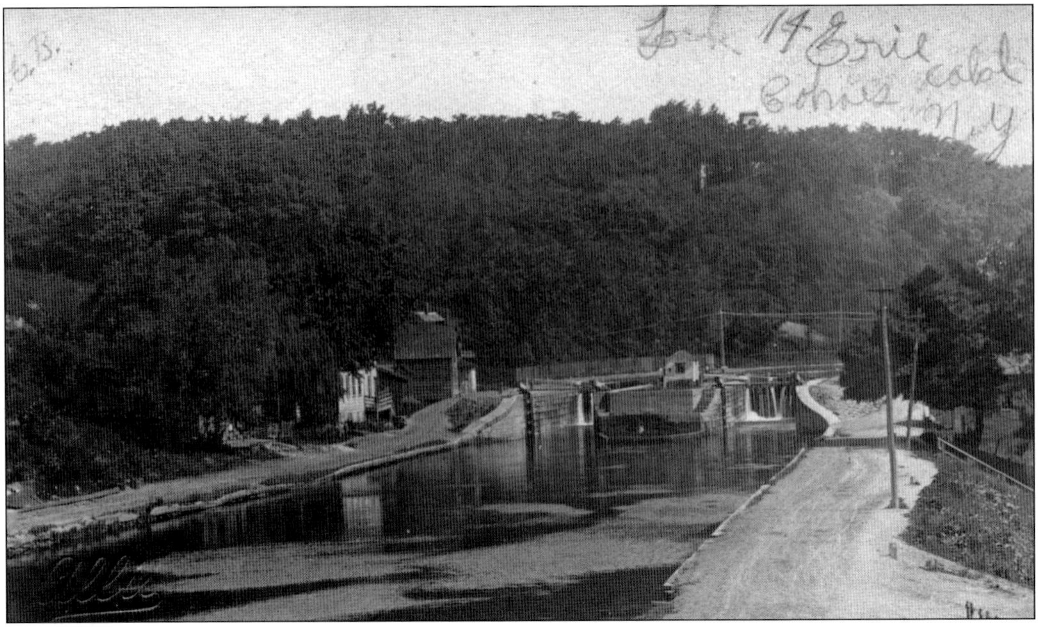

The postcards show two views of Lock No. 14 of the enlarged Erie Canal, constructed in the late 1830s to early 1840s. The steep rise in elevation that carried boats around the Cohoes Falls gave Cohoes the largest concentration of locks in any community along the canal. In the image above, the wing (curved) walls and gates of the lock can be clearly seen. The postcard below shows St. Agnes Church on the hillside. This modified canal was larger (70 feet wide) and deeper (7 feet deep) than the original canal, which was 40 feet wide and 4 feet deep. It had double-chamber locks, which allowed simultaneous boat travel in both directions. The enlargement of the canal also permitted the use of larger boats that could carry more than eight times the cargo of boats used on the original canal. Remnants of Lock No. 14 can be found at the end of Standish Street.

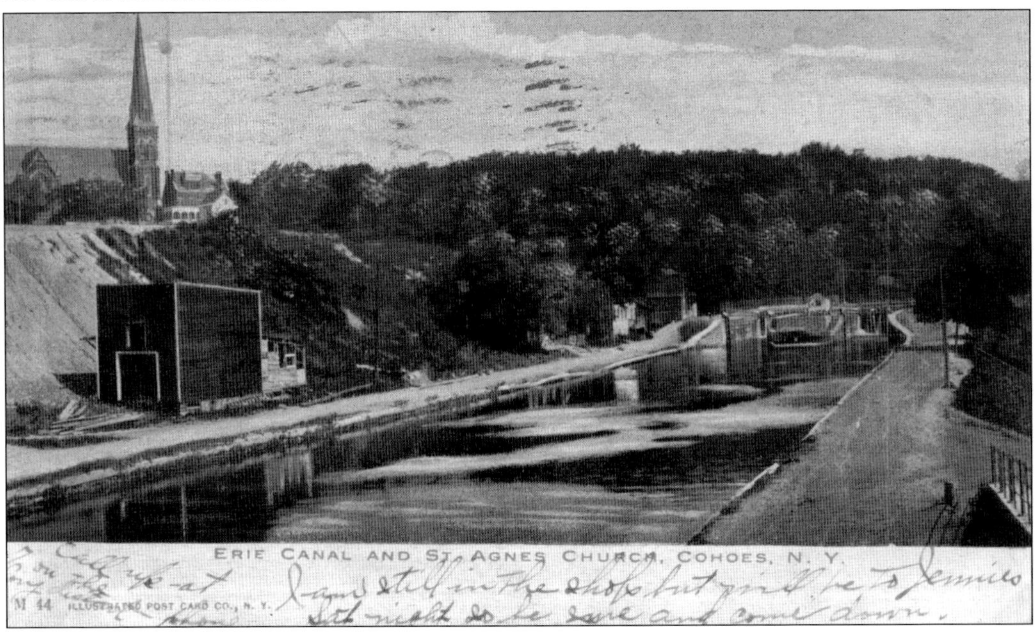

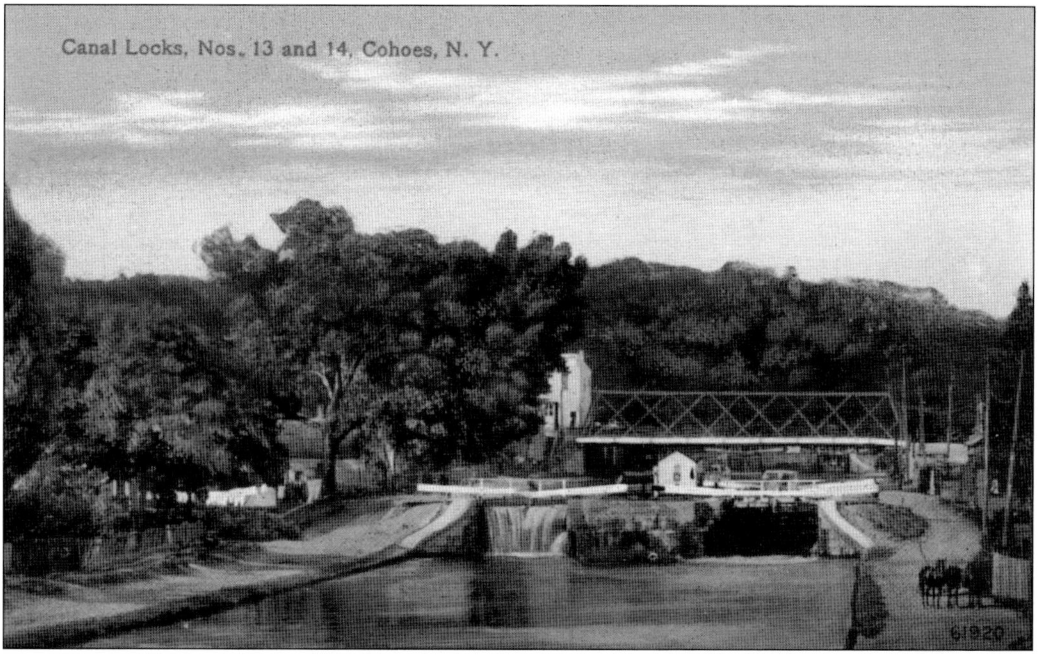


This is a view looking north along the Erie Canal; the closest lock in the postcard is Lock No. 13, now underneath Bedford Street. The lock tender's station is between the lock chambers. The bridge crossing the canal was at High Street. Before Cohoes became a manufacturing center, it was a canal town. Businesses first developed in Cohoes at "Juncta," the junction of the original Erie and Champlain Canals. This site is alongside Route 787.

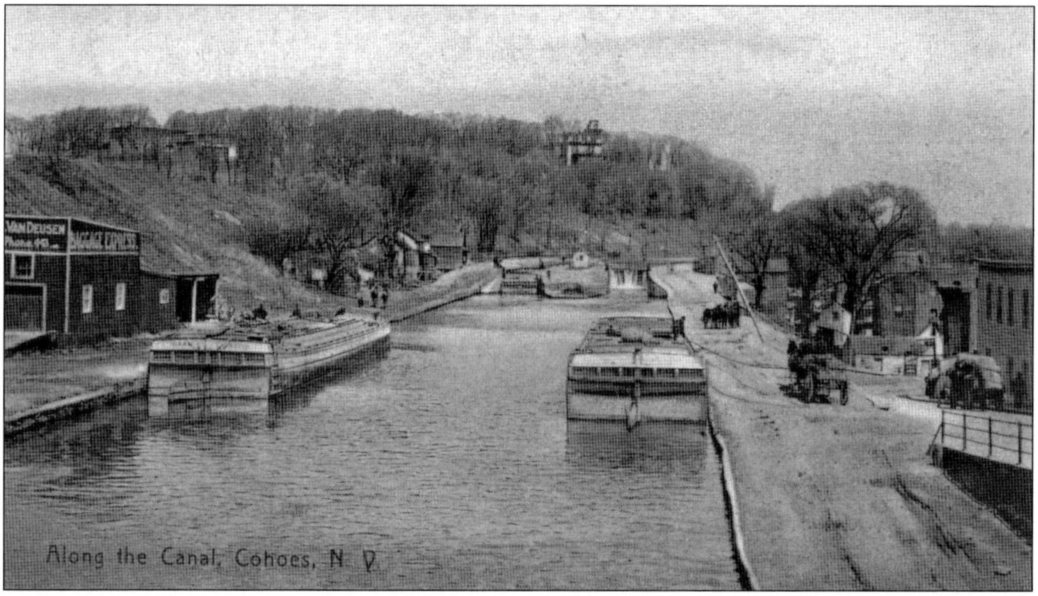


This postcard of Lock No. 14 is north of Lock No. 13 past the High Street Bridge. On the hillside is Longview, the residence of David J. Johnston, superintendent of the Harmony Mills. Note the canal boats and their mules along the towpath. Some canal workers were boys employed as drivers, or "hoggees," walking along the towpath with the mules to keep them moving at three to four miles per hour.

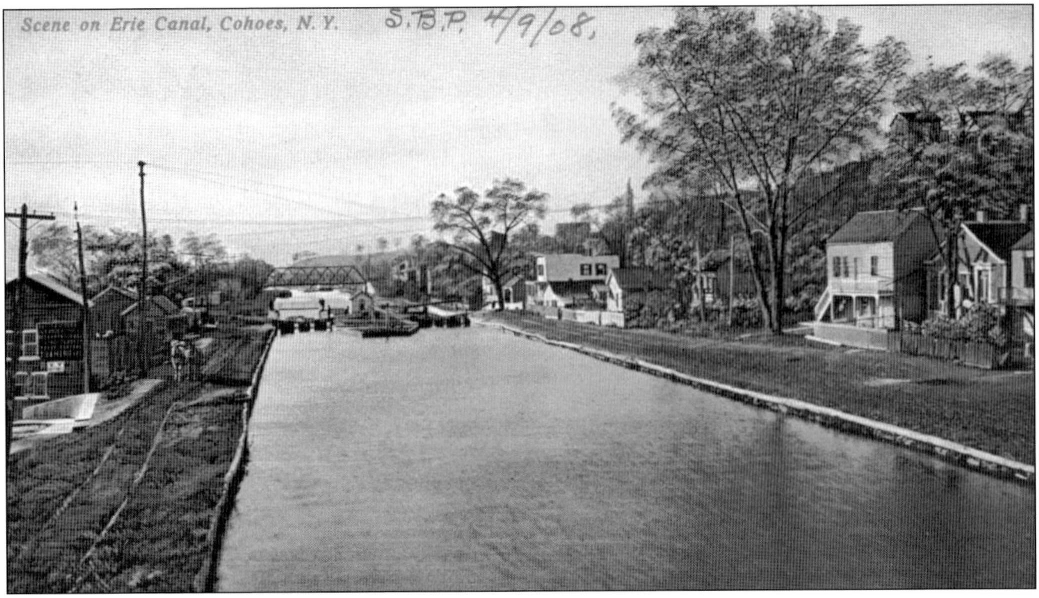


This pair of color (above) and black-and-white photograph (below) postcards captures the same scene, a view looking south on the canal. They show Lock No. 14, not Lock No. 13 as printed on the postcard below. The distant bridge is the High Street Bridge. A pair of mules can be seen heading toward the camera along the canal. The area around the canal was a lively and dangerous place, with stables, shops, and warehouses. Competition among boatmen for precedence in locking through often led to altercations, as did drinking at the numerous saloons near the canal. Some lock tenders were unscrupulous, demanding payment for passage through the locks and threatening travelers if they did not receive it. Drowning in the canal was not unusual. "Canallers" or their passengers fell from boats, and local residents sometimes slipped into the water while crossing the canal.

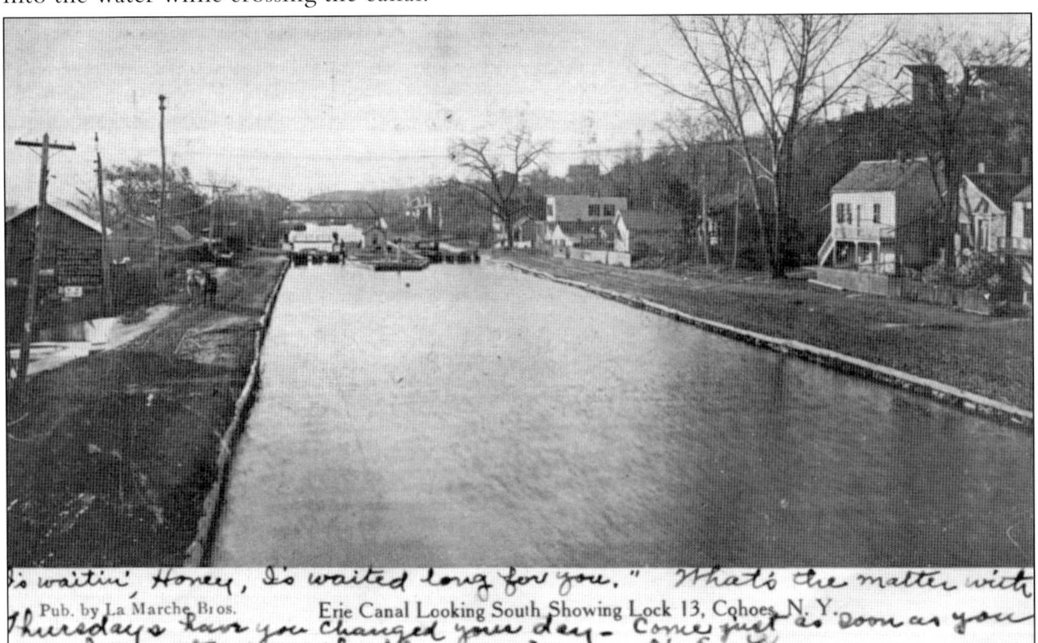

# *Two*

# THE MILL DISTRICT

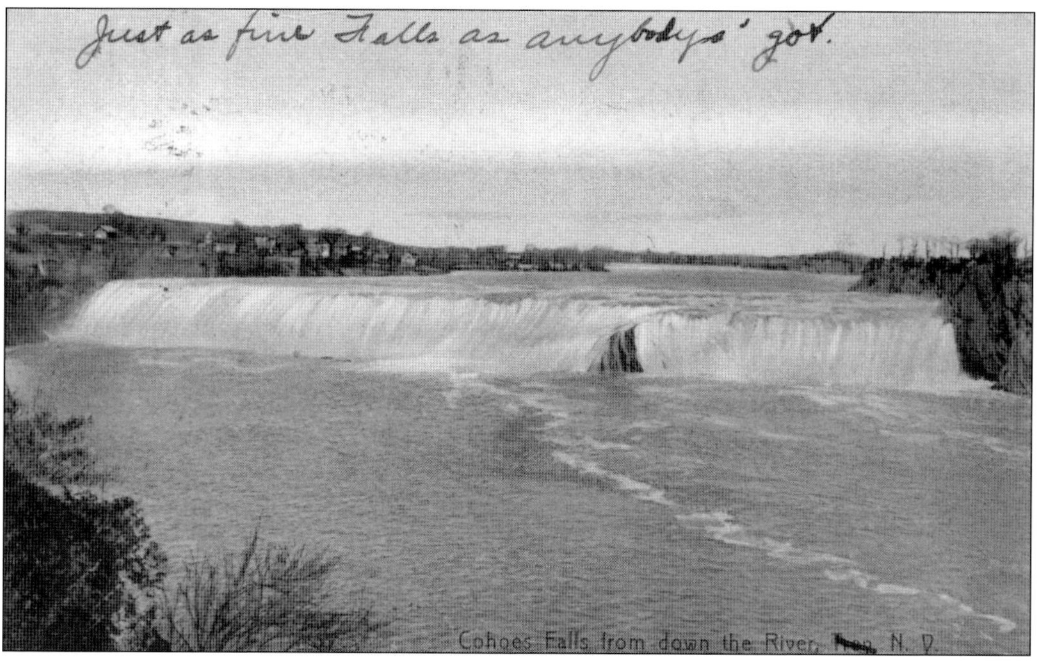


"Just as fine Falls as anybodys' got." So goes the postcard writer's apt description of the largest waterfall east of Niagara, with a shale outcropping near the center of the falls that creates their distinctive beauty. The Cohoes Falls were a sacred site for Native Americans, a longtime tourist destination, and the source of the waterpower that drove the machinery that made Cohoes an industrial power in the 19th century.

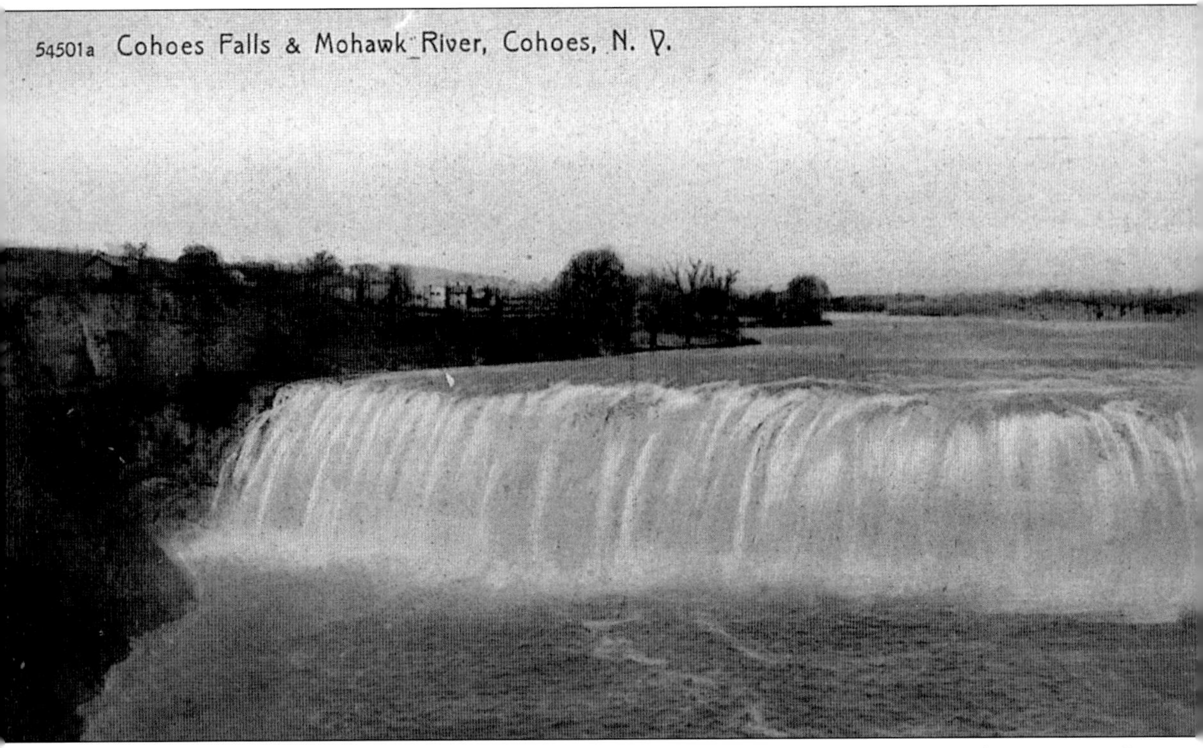


The formation of the Cohoes Falls began about 20,000 years ago when ice age glaciers started receding northward, leaving behind vast lakes from the melted glacial ice. One of these lakes was Lake Albany, which covered parts of present-day Cohoes. As the glacial waters of Lake Albany slowly subsided, a river many times larger than the present Mohawk River began pouring into the Hudson Valley from the west, flowing at a level at least 80 feet higher than its present bed.

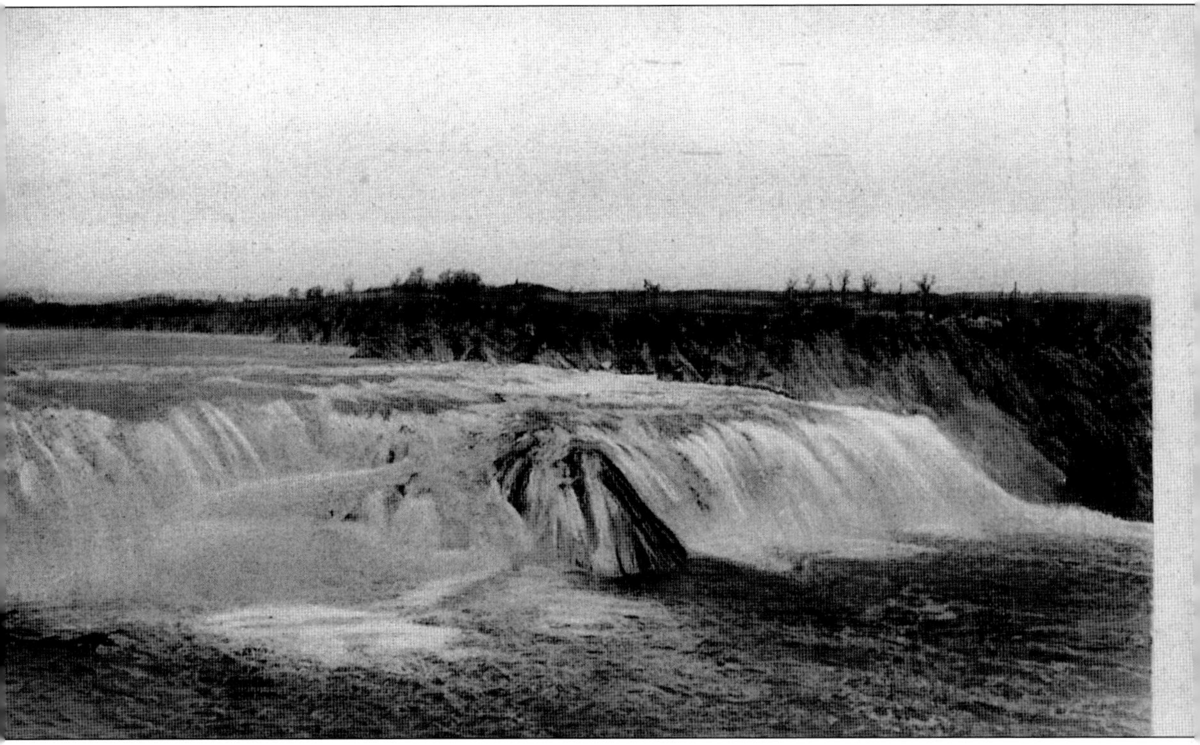

The postglacial Mohawk River formed a great waterfall at Cohoes where it descended from the west rim of the ancient preglacial river gorge. This waterfall carved huge potholes into the bedrock, and the remains of a mastodon were caught in and later discovered in two of these potholes. Cohoes Falls has receded over time to its present location about 2,000 feet upstream from its original site.

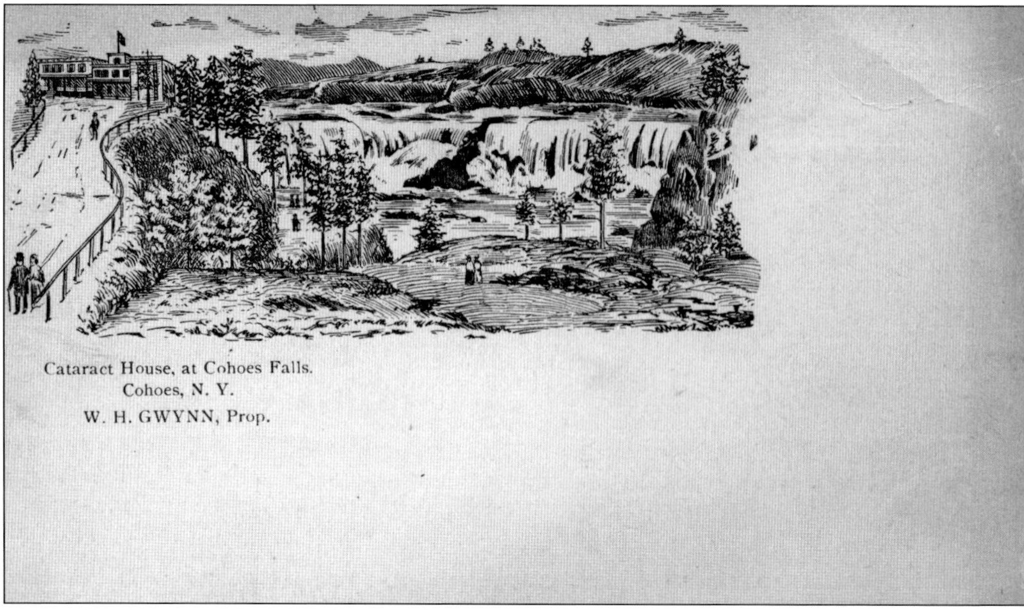


Until 1867, John Partridge operated the Cataract House, built in 1860. Shortly thereafter, a New York City firm decided to restore the hotel. Col. William H. Gwynn was manager. Its sizeable fireplace was large enough to roast an entire ox. Each room had a great bed and straight-backed chairs covered with Russian leather or velvet. The floors were patterned or had small rugs. Breakfast consisted of steak, fish, eggs, and cakes. The day's last meal was similar, with the addition of cold ham and chicken. Patrons paid $1.50 to $2 per day. Brandy and Hollands (gin) and some other spirits were free, while others cost extra. Cataract House closed around 1910. In June 1912, at 1:15 a.m., a fire alarm sounded; the hotel was ablaze. A swing bridge, the hotel's only access, hampered the firemen's efforts, resulting in a total loss. Cataract House was never rebuilt.

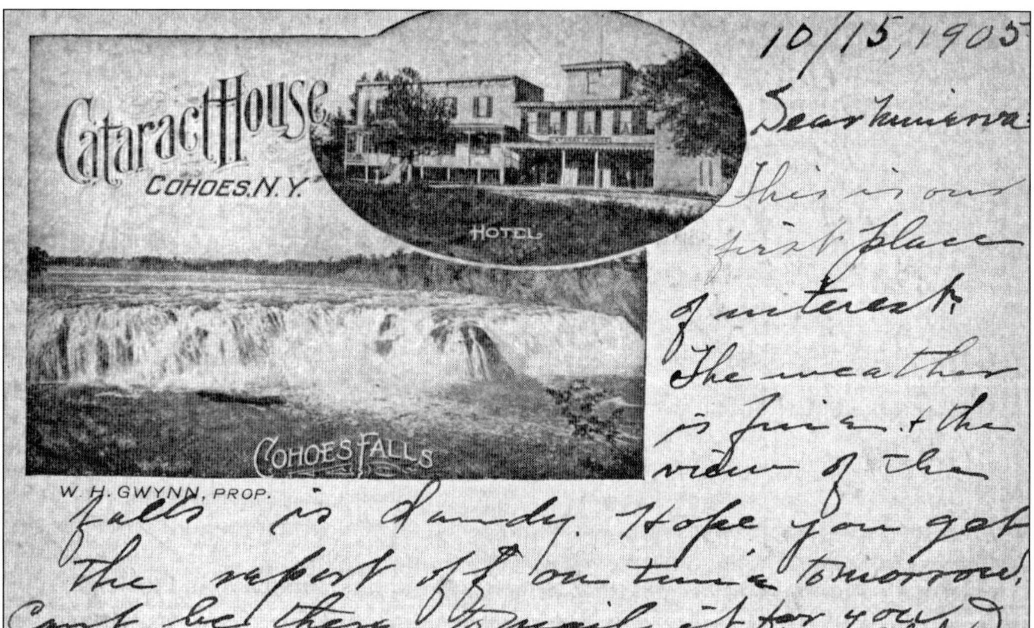

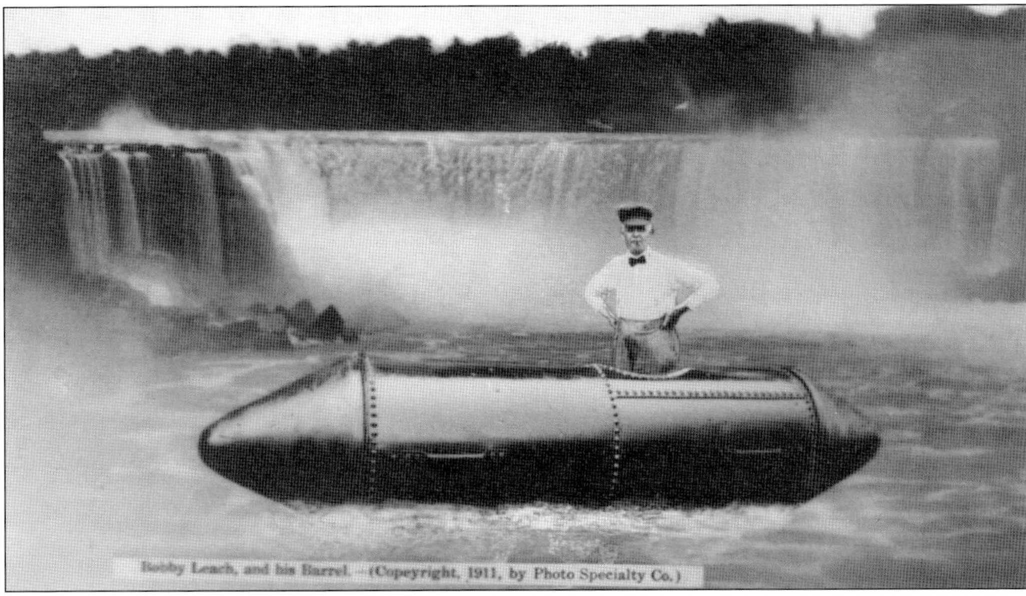


On April 15, 1899, a British-born tavern-keeper and daredevil named Bobby Leach went over the Cohoes Falls in a barrel, a feat witnessed by a crowd numbered at 10,000. He survived the plunge, suffering only a few lacerations. He repeated the performance the following Saturday, financing his exploits by passing a hat among spectators. Leach was a colorful character, a hard-drinking pool shark, consummate storyteller, and a performer in the Barnum & Bailey Circus. Twelve years after his appearance in Cohoes, he successfully went over Niagara Falls in his barrel, the second person ever to do so. He profited from his renown by touring the United States, Canada, and England with his barrel, recounting his experiences in vaudeville shows and lecture halls. Ironically, Leach met his end while on tour in New Zealand, when he slipped on an orange peel and succumbed to complications from the fall.

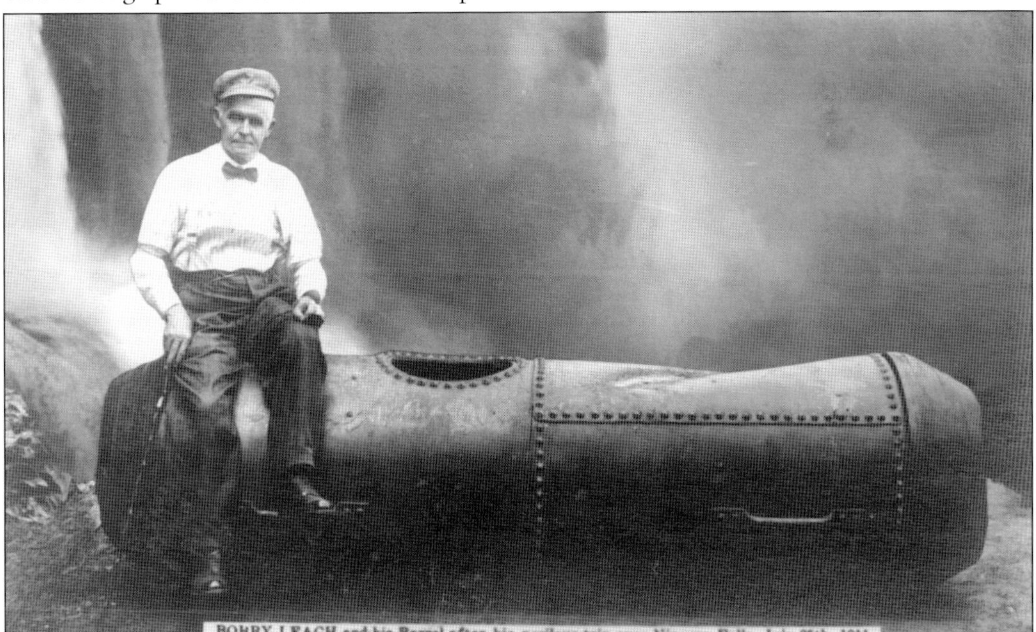

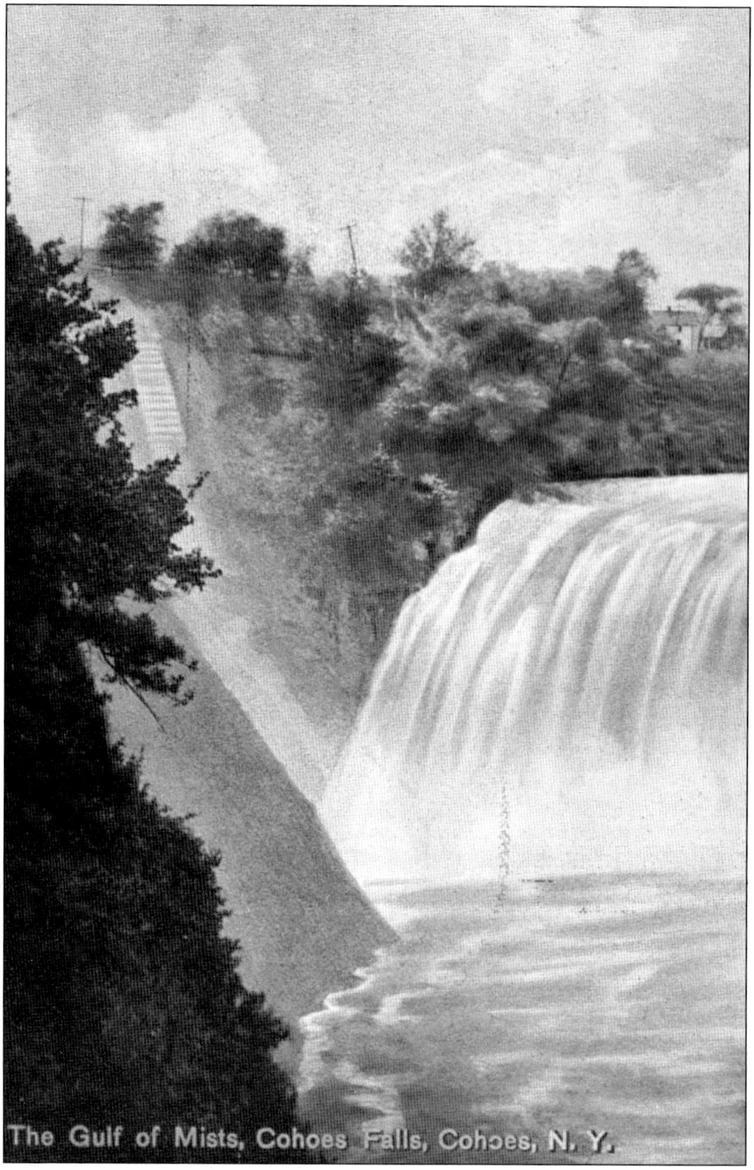


The Cohoes Falls played a significant role in the formation of the Haudenosaunee (Iroquois) League, originally composed of the Mohawk, Oneida, Onondaga, Cayuga, and Seneca Nations. These warring nations were united by the Peacemaker, a Huron Indian named Deganawida. Deganawida developed the idea of the Great Law of Peace, a message of peace through the power of unity, reason, and law. To spread these ideas, he journeyed eastward to the lands of the warring Iroquois nations and invited Ayonhwathah (Hiawatha) to assist. The Peacemaker traveled to the Cohoes Falls in Mohawk country and climbed a tree over the gorge. The Mohawks felled the tree, but the next morning they found the Peacemaker sitting by a fire. His survival of the turbulent waters convinced the Mohawks of his power. They accepted his message and became founders of the confederacy, leading the way for the other nations. In the mid-18th century, Benjamin Franklin met with the Haudenosaunee at the Cohoes Falls, where he learned of their system of law, which would be an inspiration for those drafting the Constitution of the United States.

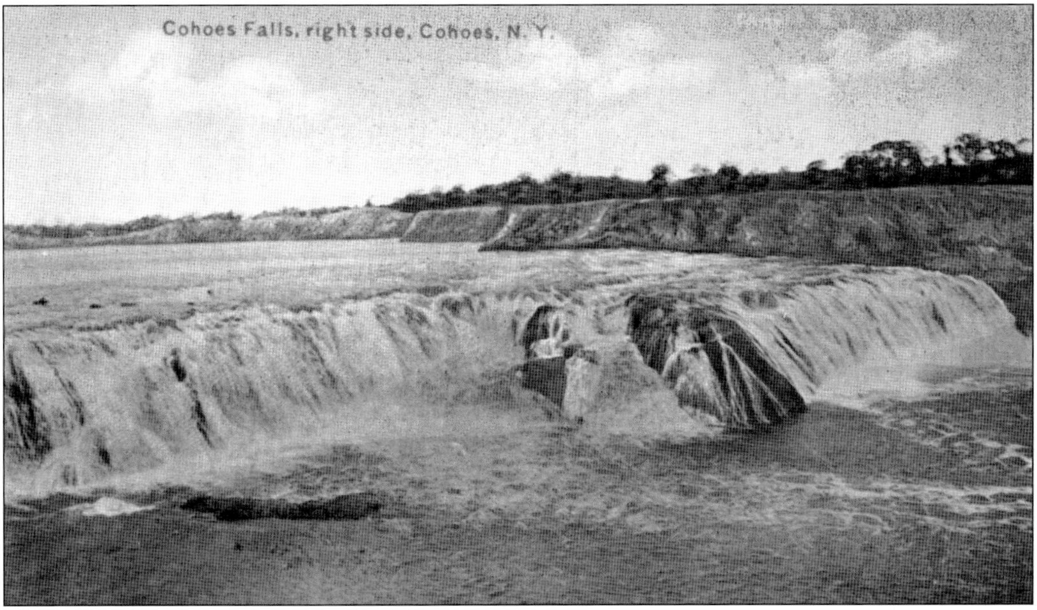


The size and beauty of the falls have long attracted appreciative visitors. Henry Hudson and his crew were the first Europeans known to see the falls. Many people from abroad, among them the novelist Charles Dickens, found a journey to the falls a must during their visits to America. Thomas Moore, the Irish poet, penned a poem about the falls, "Lines Written at the Cohos, or Falls of the Mohawk River," in 1804 following a tour of the United States and Canada that included a stop at the falls. Another visitor to the falls was Col. Henry Knox. On January 5, 1776, during the winter he was directing the transfer of cannon from Fort Ticonderoga and Crown Point to the Dorchester Heights in Massachusetts to break the British siege of Boston, Knox traveled alone on horseback from Albany through the snow to visit the falls and recorded his impressions in his diary.

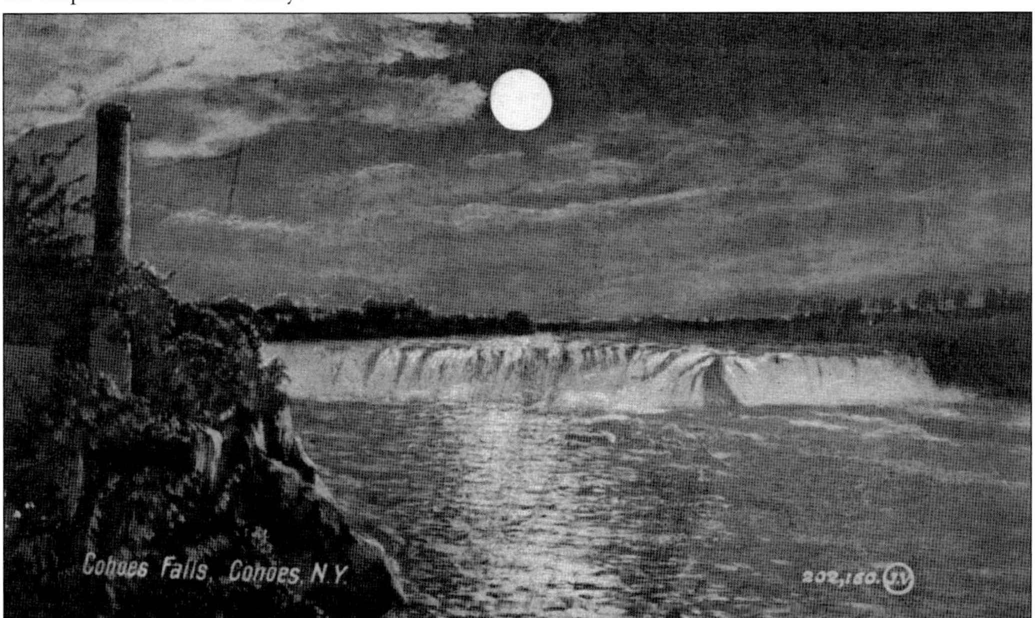

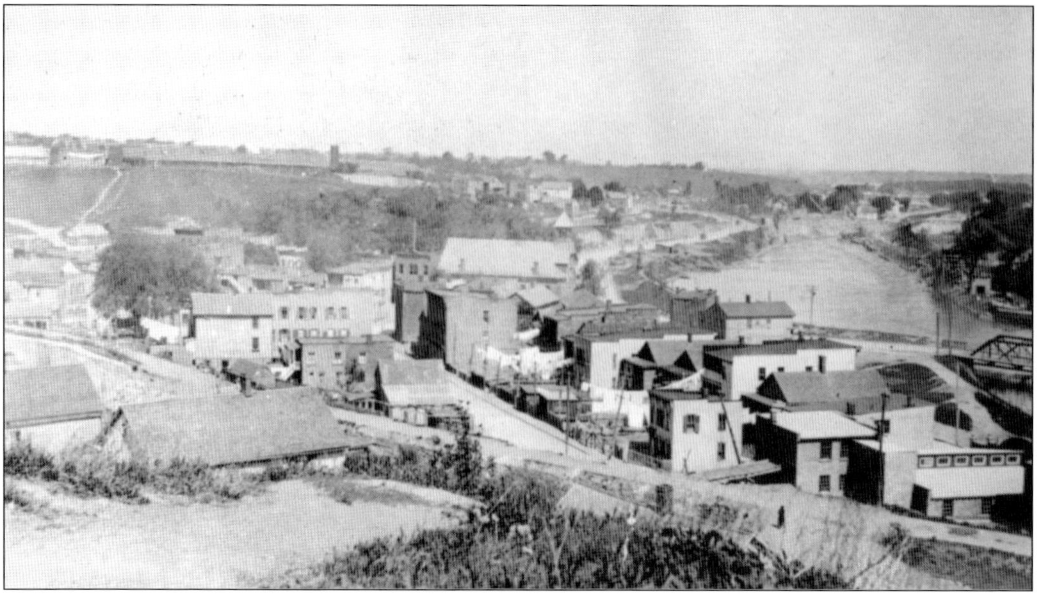

These two postcard views of the Orchard neighborhood show similar vantage points in different time periods. In both, St. Patrick's Church is visible. The parish was founded in 1886, and the church was built in 1895. The parish originally served residents of the Orchard neighborhood, who were primarily workers in the Harmony Mills. This neighborhood of Cohoes was built on the site of the Lansing family's fruit orchard. The image below dates from the early 1900s when the enlarged Erie Canal was still active. The lock in the image is Lock No. 17. In the above image, from the 1920s, the canal is no longer in use, but its alignment can be seen; the New York State Barge Canal, routed through Waterford, replaced the canal. A bridge spans the power canal, which was the route of the original Erie Canal. The falls and Mohawk River are in the upper sections of both images.

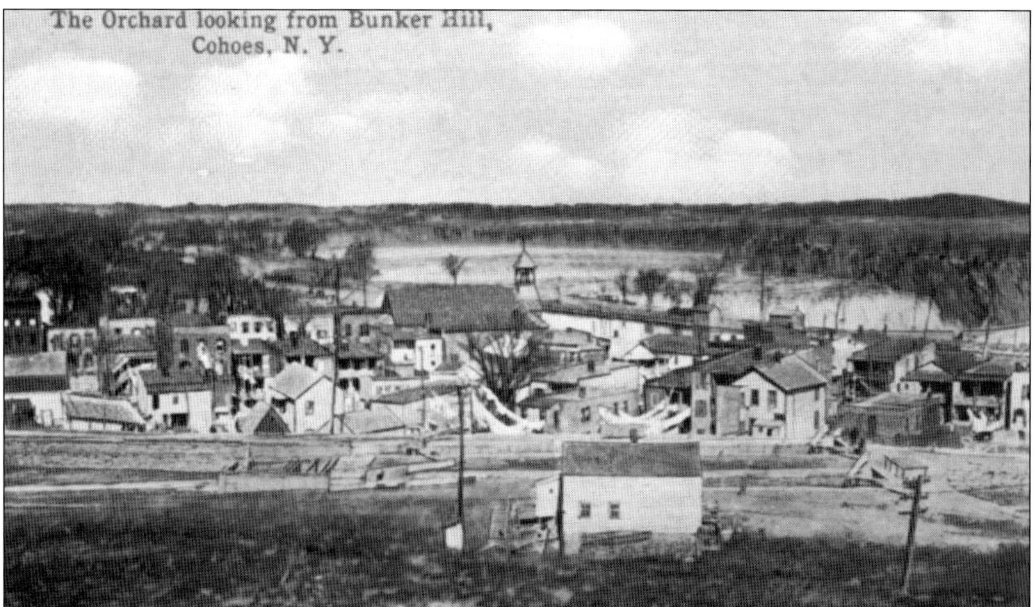

The Cohoes Company, established in 1826, was first to utilize the waterpower of the Cohoes Falls. The company sold power to Cohoes industries. The first dam was built by the company above the falls in 1831, and an innovative series of power canals, designed by Erie Canal engineer Canvass White, brought waterpower to factory buildings. In 1887, the Cohoes Company contracted with the City of Cohoes to supply arc lights on the city's streets. The company built and maintained the city's first electric light plant, powered by water from its own canals. In 1911, the company constructed a hydroelectric plant just north of School Street to generate electricity from the falls. This plant is shown in the postcard at right. General Electric supplied the generators and the other power equipment for the plant. By 1923, the plant supplied power to all Cohoes industries, and parts of Troy and Albany as well.

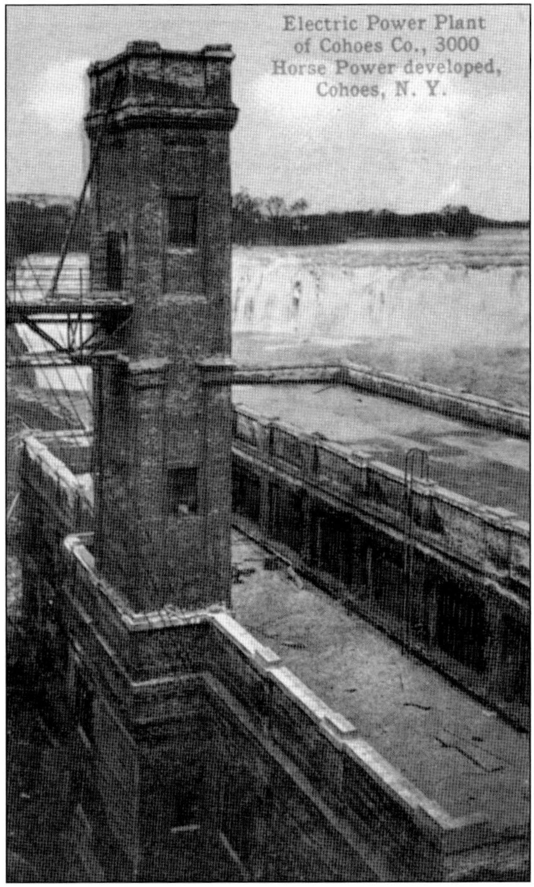


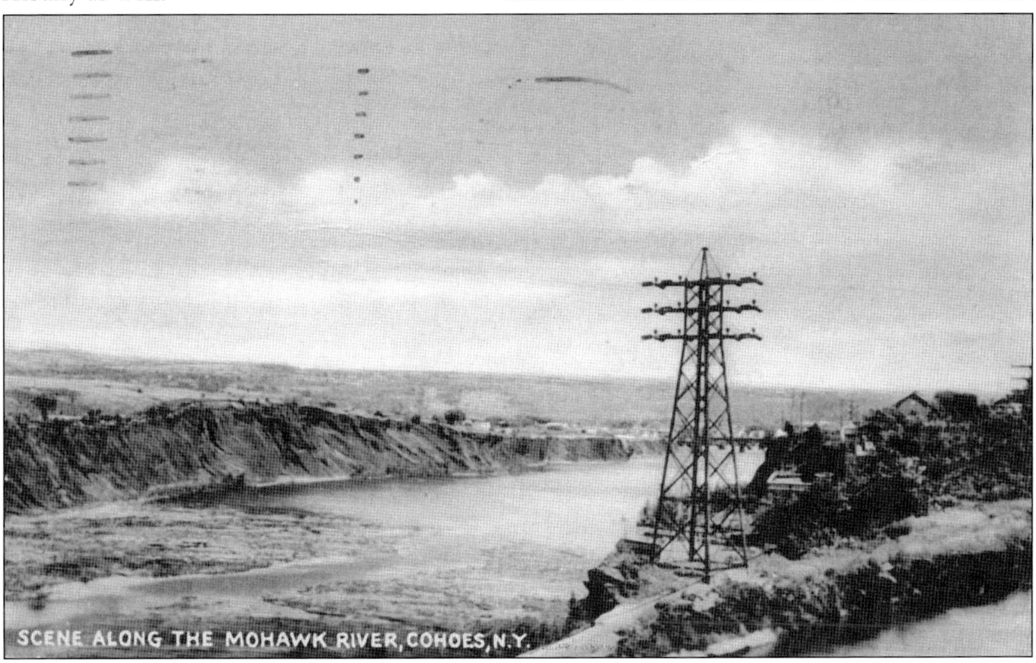

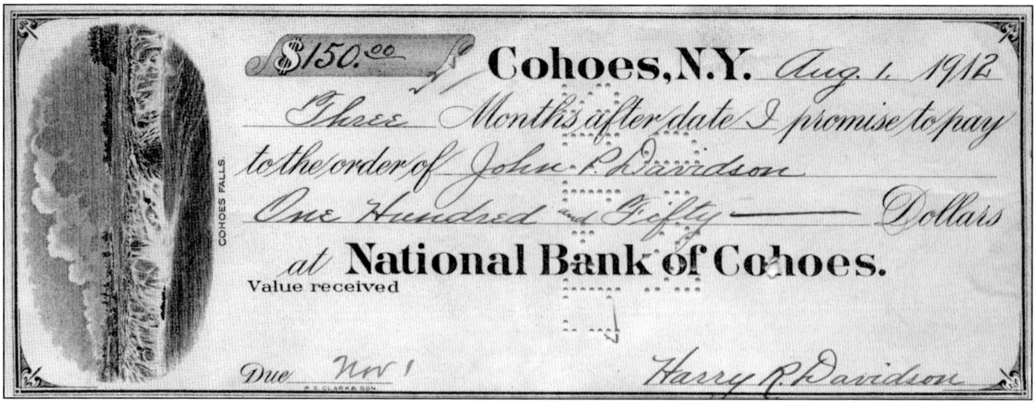
$150.00 Cohoes, N.Y. Aug. 1, 1912

Three Months after date I promise to pay

to the order of John P. Davidson

One Hundred and Fifty Dollars

at National Bank of Cohoes.

Value received

Due Nov 1 Harry P. Davidson

COHOES FALLS

The Cohoes Falls, second only to Niagara Falls in New York State, is used as a symbolic emblem for the City of Cohoes. It is found on the city's logo and on the uniform patches for both the police and fire departments. It has been the subject of paintings, pen and ink drawings, and lithographs. For the tourist trade, it has been applied on porcelain, pottery, and sterling spoons (often produced by local jewelers). Many Cohoes merchants and city organizations include the majestic falls in their publications. The National Bank proudly uses it on this IOU. When the falls are flowing in the spring, the roar can be heard at great distances. The mist is carried by the wind, and rainbows can be seen through the mist on sunny days. When it is drier, many have walked across the rock formations and even picnicked on the larger ledges.

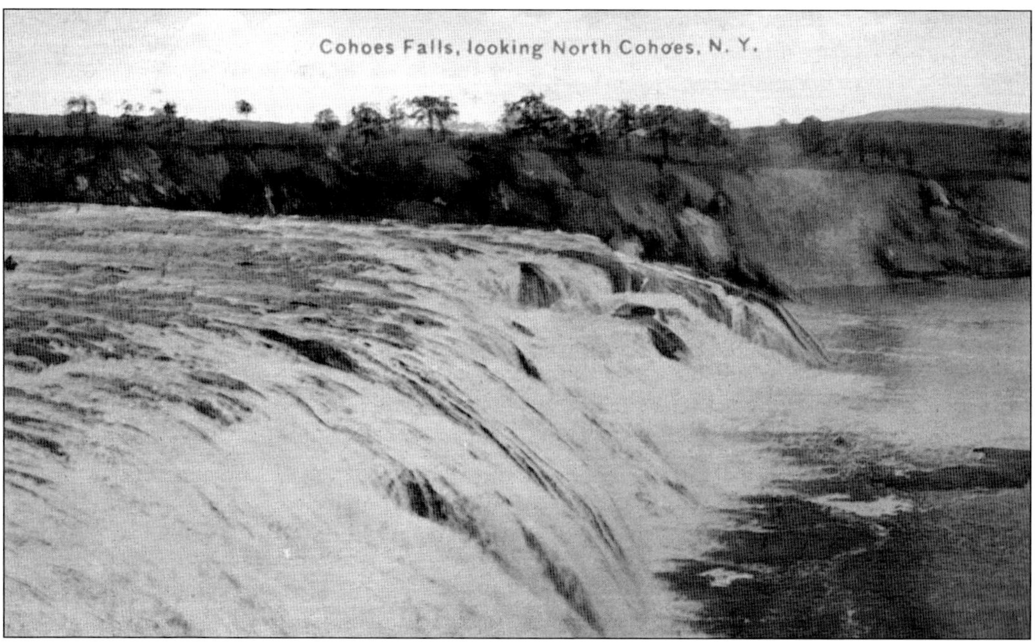

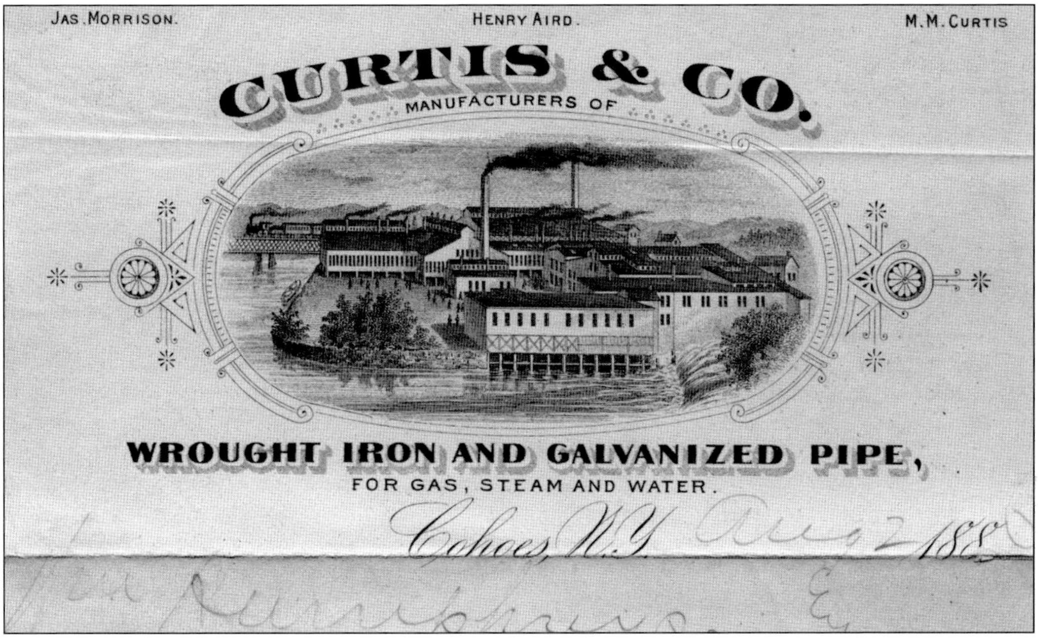


Curtis and Co. made wrought-iron and galvanized pipe and boiler tubes. In 1883, the company was located on Courtland Street, near the rolling mill. Proprietors were James Morrison, Mary Curtis, and Henry Aird, later joined by John Don. By 1891, the company moved to Pine Street near the railroad station and, by 1894, became the Cohoes Tube Works under proprietor Henry Aird. The firm moved to Troy in 1900.

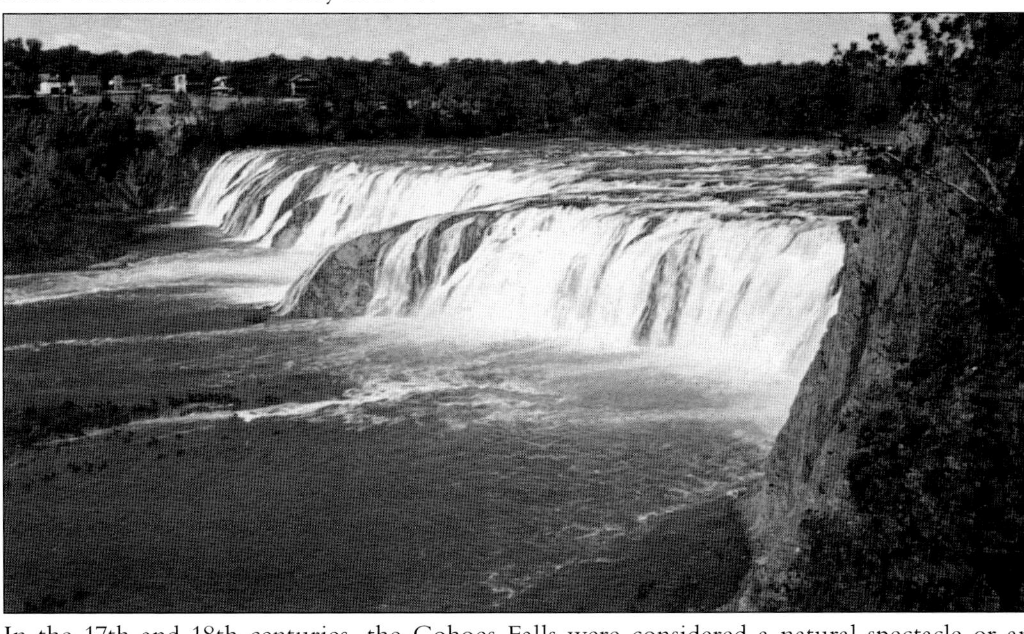

In the 17th and 18th centuries, the Cohoes Falls were considered a natural spectacle or an obstacle to be surmounted on water journeys. Later, they were a source of power for industrial machinery. The falls are now used for hydroelectric power. When water is diverted for power, the falls dry and reveal the shale formations beneath. During periods of snowmelt or heavy rain, the falls are a torrent.

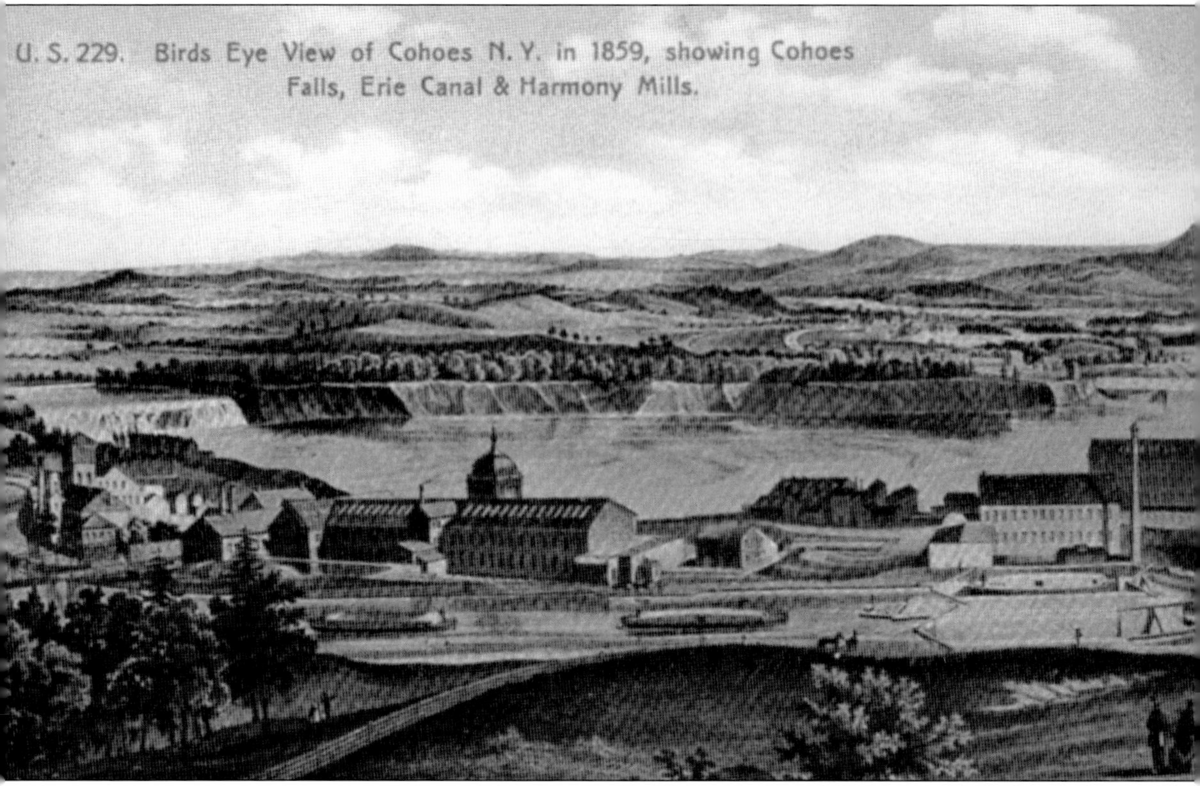


This postcard view of the Harmony Mills in 1859 shows the enlarged Erie Canal, with several canal boats traveling along it, in the foreground. Lock No. 15 of the canal is near the center of the image, and Lock No. 16 is on the left. Harmony Mill No. 1 is on the far left, directly behind Lock No. 16, with Mill No. 2 to the right. The bridge crossing the canal between Mills Nos. 1 and 2 is where Vliet Street is today. This image also shows one of the power canals for the

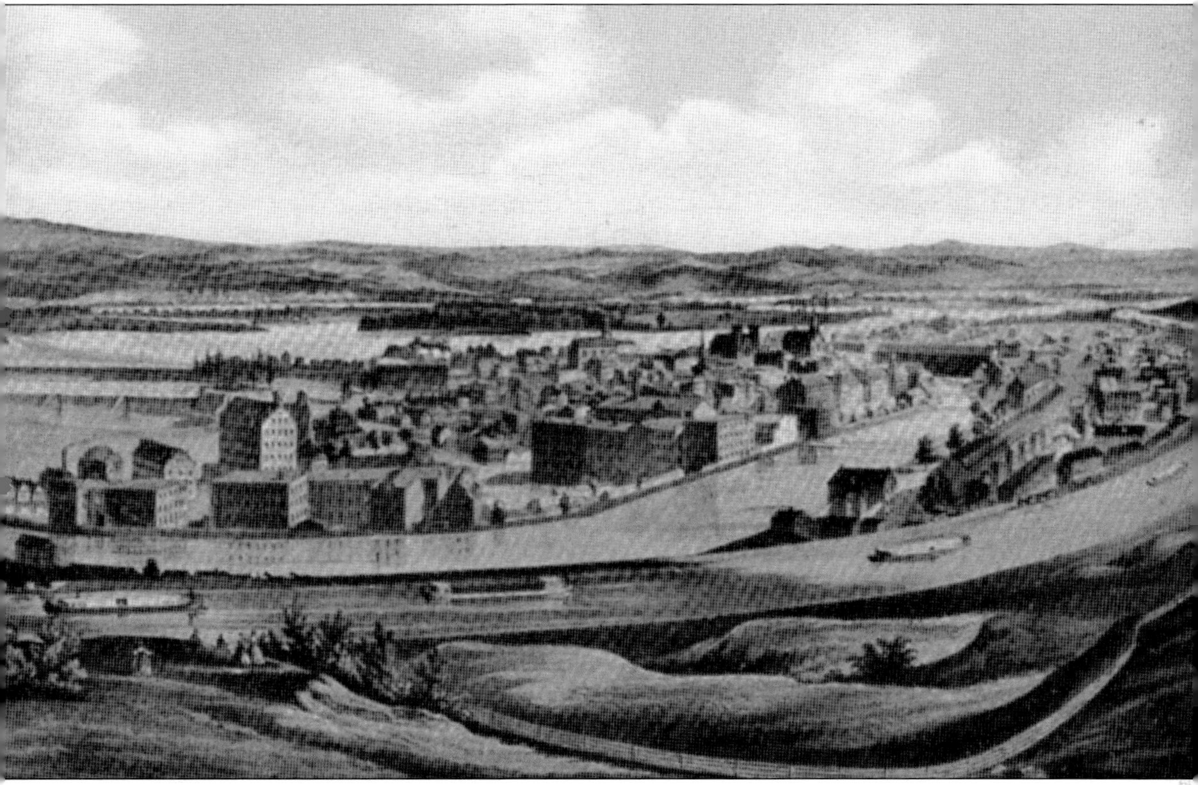

mills, located between the Erie Canal and the Mohawk River. Note that Harmony Mill No. 3 had not yet been constructed at this time. The Cohoes Falls are in the upper left of the image. The bridge between Cohoes and Waterford can be seen downriver from the falls. The span at that time was a covered toll bridge.

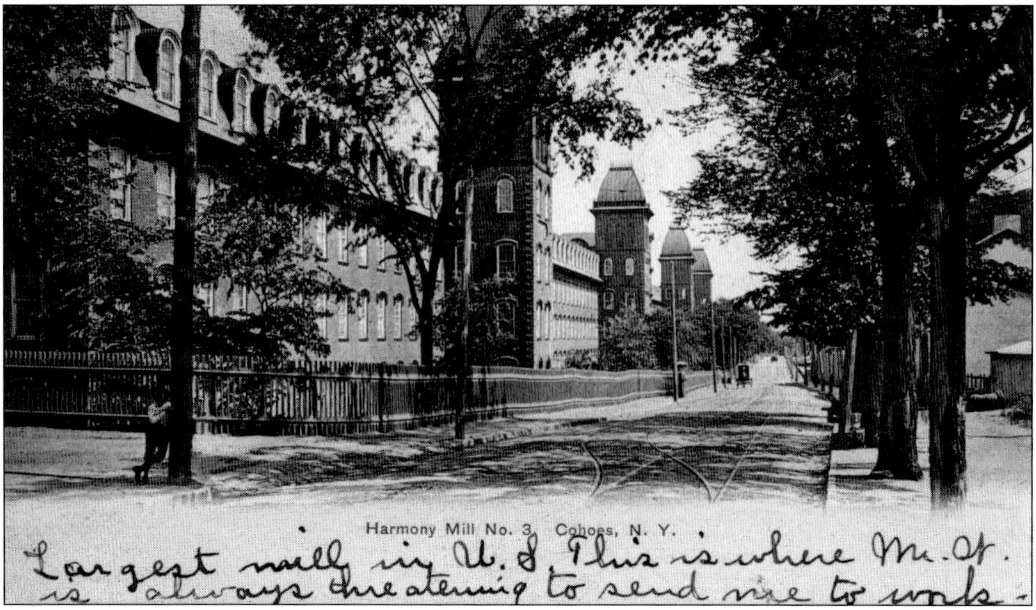


On this postcard of Harmony Mill No. 3, the sender writes, "Largest mill in the U.S. This is where Mr. W. is always threatening to send me to work." This was not always an idle threat; mill workers included children as young as nine. In many cases, their labor was necessary for a family's survival, and few children in 19th-century mill worker families remained in school beyond the age of 12.

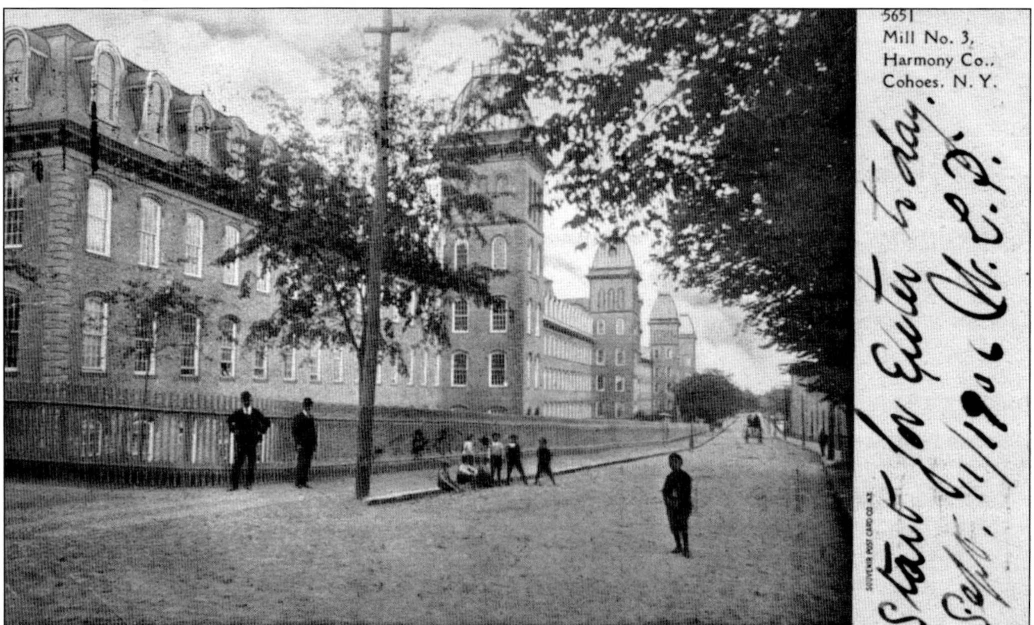


Frank writes of Harmony Mill No. 3, "Here is the 'big' boy." Stretching 1,185 feet long and five stories tall, it truly was a wonder of its day, attracting interest from cotton manufacturers worldwide. The mill contained 130,000 spindles and 2,700 looms, making it America's largest complete cotton mill. The northern half was constructed in 1866. It was extended to the south in 1872, and a central tower was added.

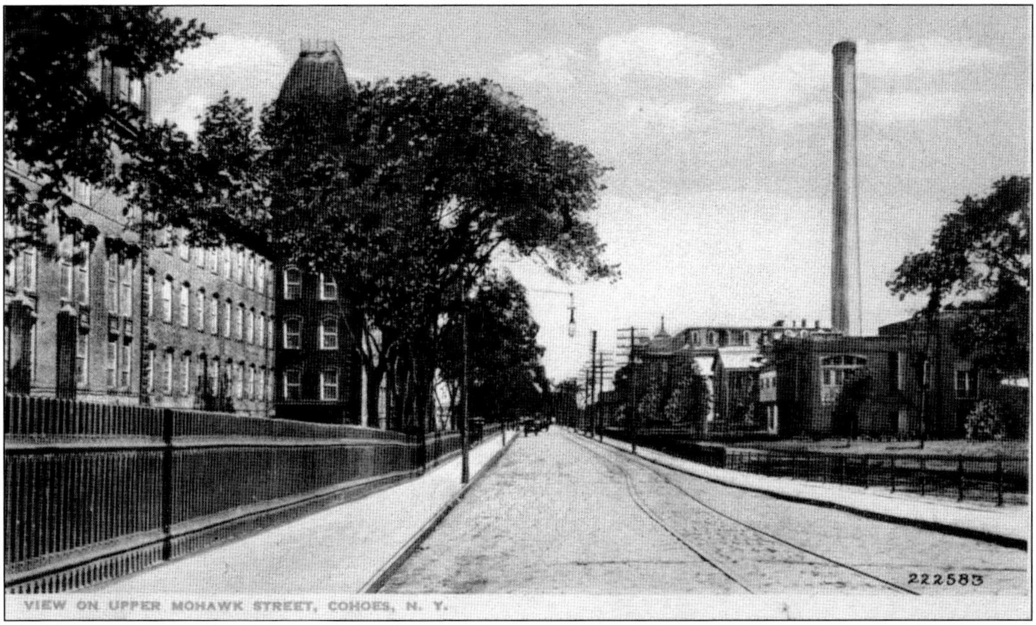


This view of North Mohawk Street shows Harmony Mills Nos. 3 and 2 and the boiler house (with smokestack). Next to the boiler house is the Harmony Mills Office and Sunday school, built in 1853. The company's offices were located on the ground floor. A meeting hall that could seat 800 was upstairs, along with a small library for company employees. The Harmony Mill Union Sabbath School also used this space.

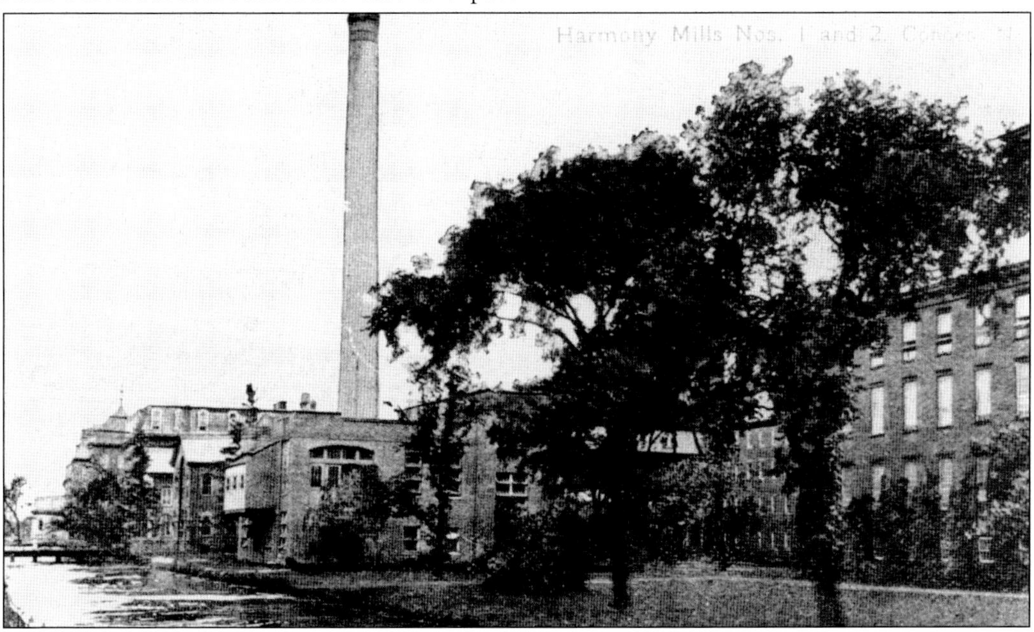


This postcard shows the boiler house with Harmony Mill No. 1 on the right. The original section of Harmony Mill No. 1 was built in 1837. The four-story building contained a wheelhouse, flumes, waterwheels, and a driving pulley. In 1853, the new owners of Harmony Mills, Thomas Garner and Alfred Wild, built another structure to the north of the original building, connecting them with an arched entranceway and massive tower.

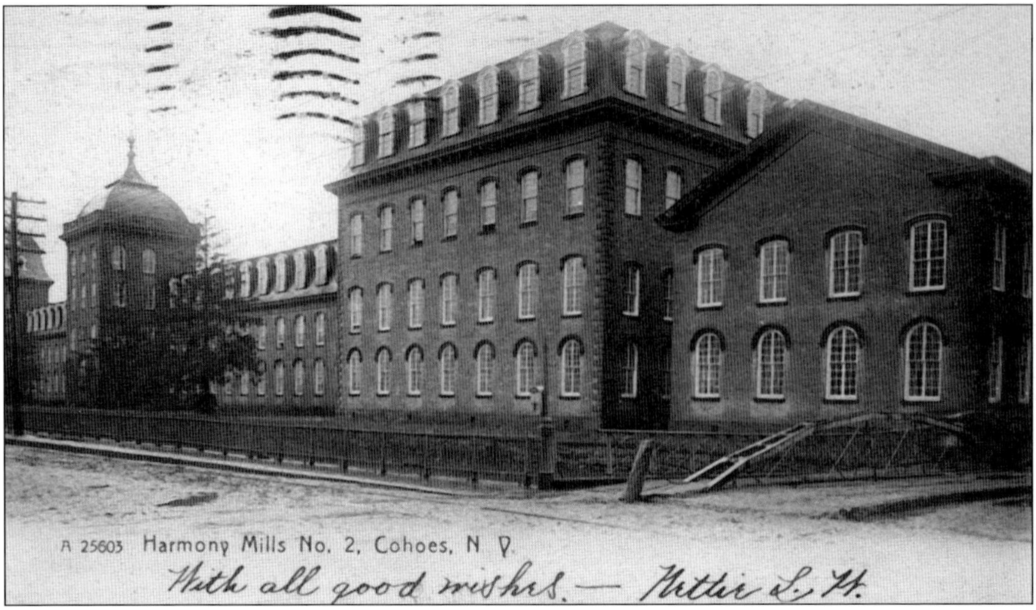


The northern end of Harmony Mill No. 2 was completed in 1857 and the southern section in 1866. The foundation stones for the mill were lock stones taken from a lock on the original Erie Canal, which ran along the eastern side of the mill. The bridge shown crosses the power canal at the base of Vliet Street. Mill No. 2 had underground tunnels as part of the power canal system.

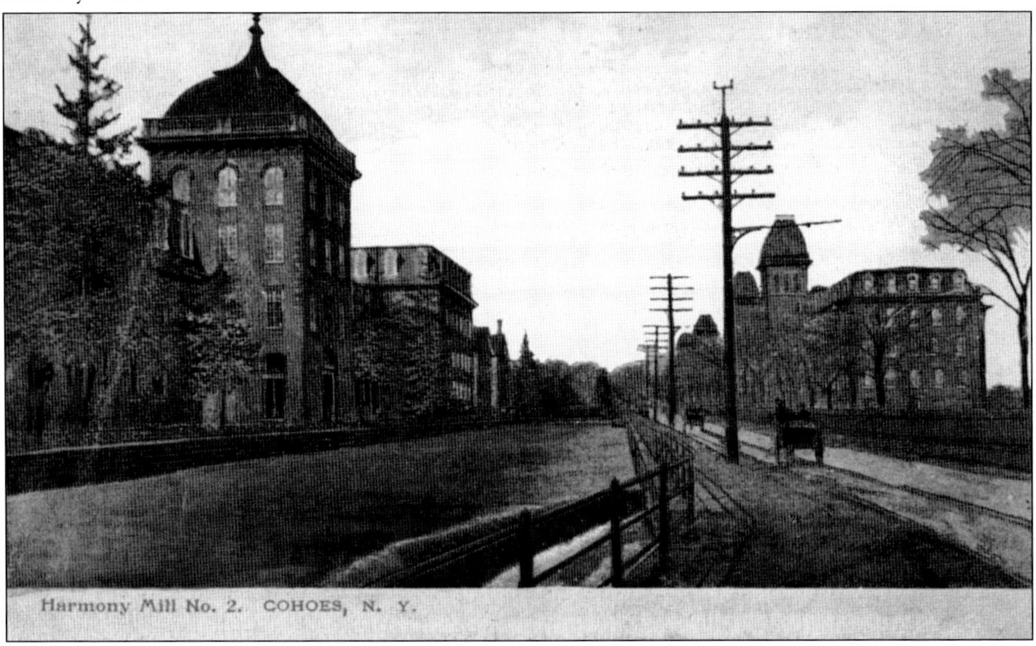


Here, in a view looking northward, are Harmony Mills Nos. 2 and 3 and the power canal serving Mill No. 2. The canal was once a section of the original Erie Canal, which was traded by New York State to the Cohoes Company for land to the west when the Erie Canal was enlarged and realigned. It was then incorporated into the company's extensive power canal system. This area is now Power Canal Park.

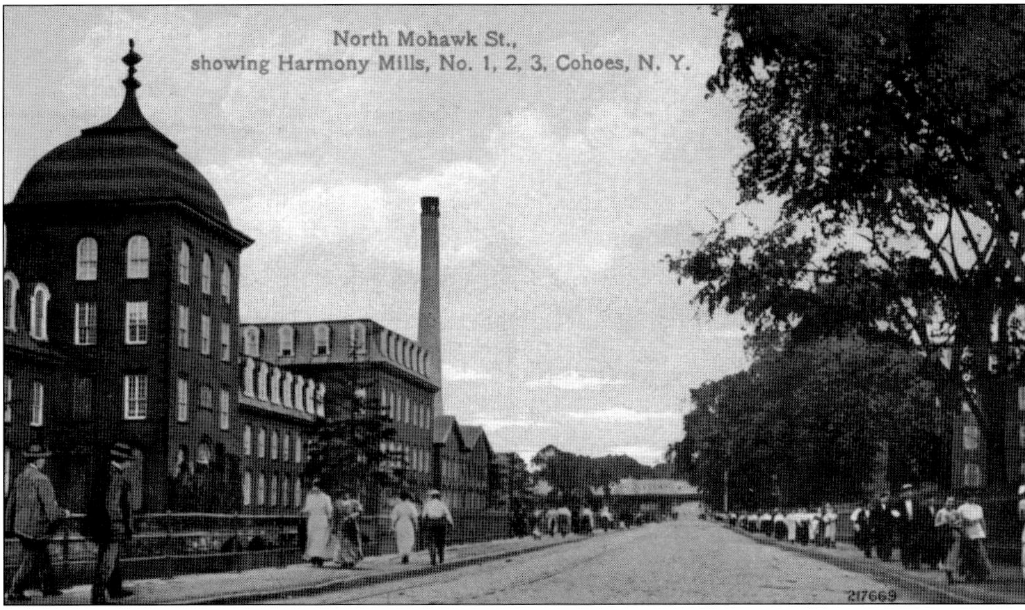


This view up North Mohawk Street shows workers near the Harmony Mills. The mills relied on a large group of workers in its operation, mainly Irish or French Canadian immigrants. In 1869, some 3,100 people were employed there, with two-thirds of them women. In 1860, more than half of the employees were Irish immigrants. By 1880, due to an extensive recruitment program in Quebec, more than one-third of the workers were French Canadians.

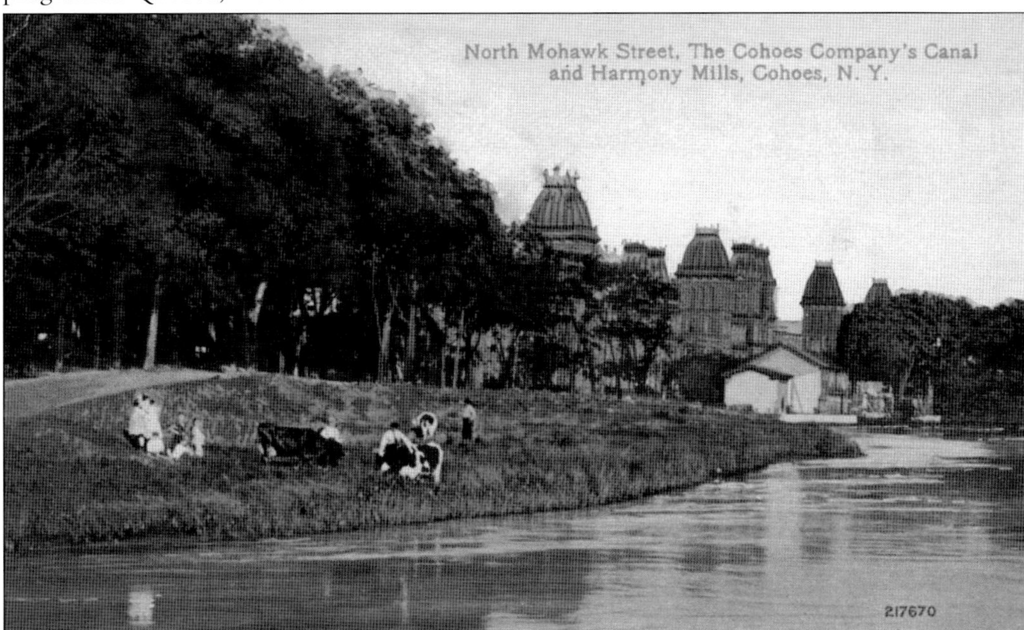


The Cohoes Company's power canal system was the first and greatest in the region. The original channels were dug in 1834. They evolved into a series of roughly parallel, connected canals that brought water to successive levels and returned it to the Mohawk River. With this system, the same water could be used six different times to power industries in the mill district and downtown.

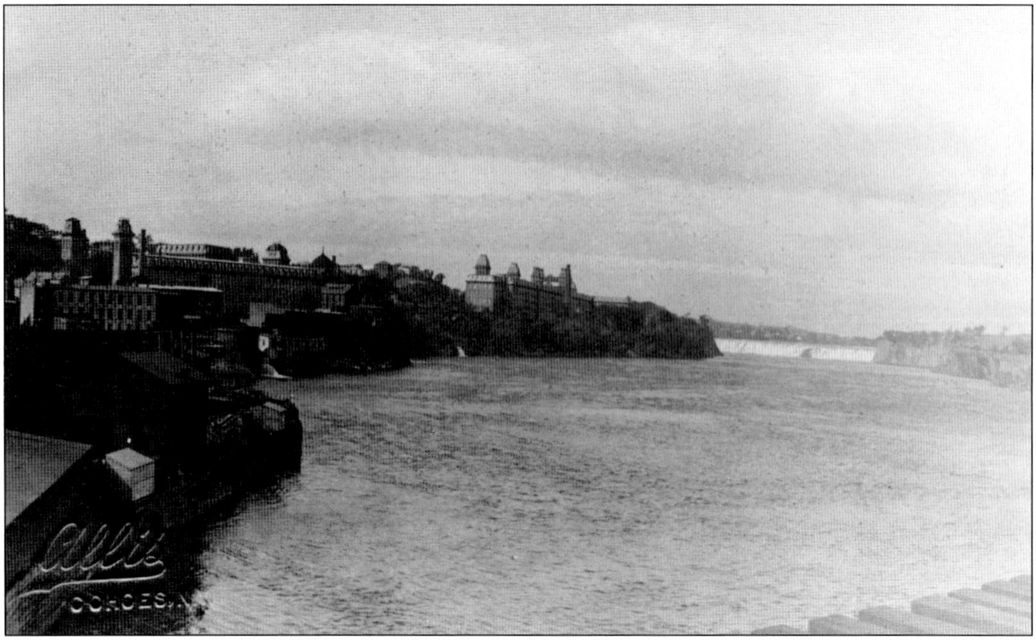


The Harmony Mill district is a complete neighborhood in itself. It contains almost a quarter of the total area of Cohoes, spread over a hilltop at the northern edge of town and extending to the Mohawk River. At its peak, the district contained five large textile mill buildings, a picker house, a storehouse, a pump house, a company office building, and a full range of housing for various economic levels of mill workers. In the late 1860s, the Harmony Mills Company transformed farmland on Harmony Hill above the mills into a thriving village of 6,000 people. Altogether, the company eventually owned 800 tenement houses, five large boardinghouses, and a company store in this area. The company maintained its own police force and repair crews, provided street paving, garbage pickup, and sanitary improvements, and contributed to the construction of schools and churches of all faiths in Cohoes.

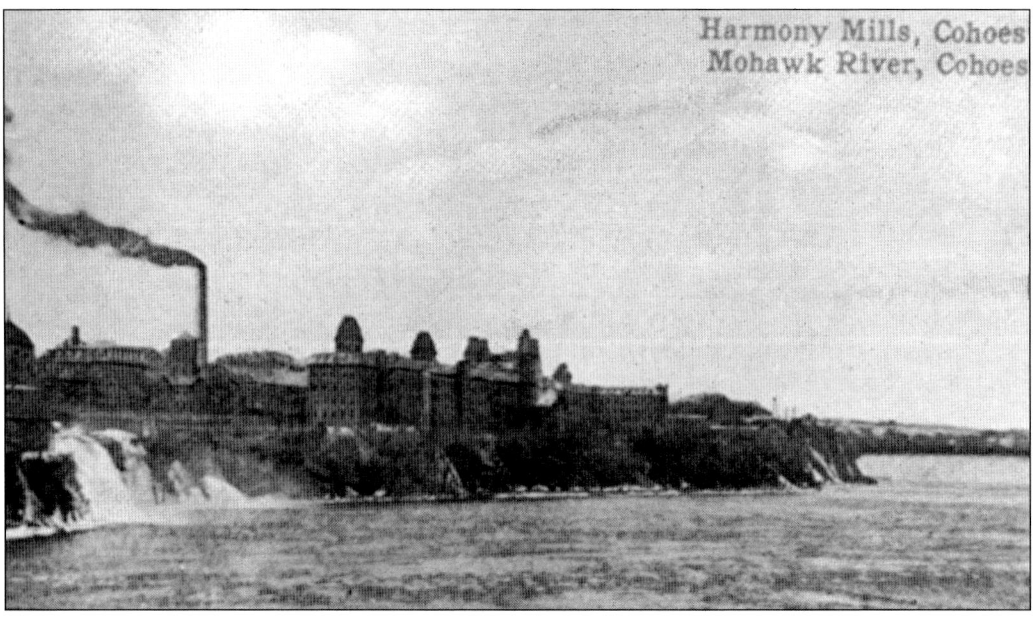

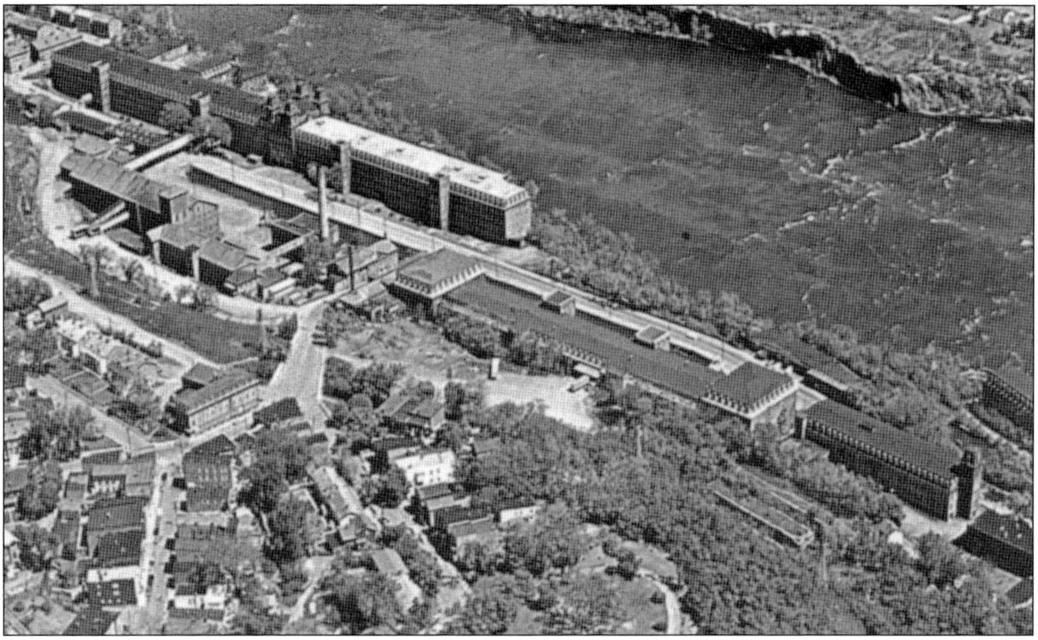

This aerial view shows the Harmony Mills, which became the Cohoes Industrial Terminal Corporation in 1967. The postcard advertises 1,000,000 square feet of industrial space in the complex of mill buildings and ancillary structures. In the lower left of the postcard is a section of the Harmony Hill neighborhood, with brick row housing originally built for mill workers. The larger building near this housing was once a boardinghouse for workers.

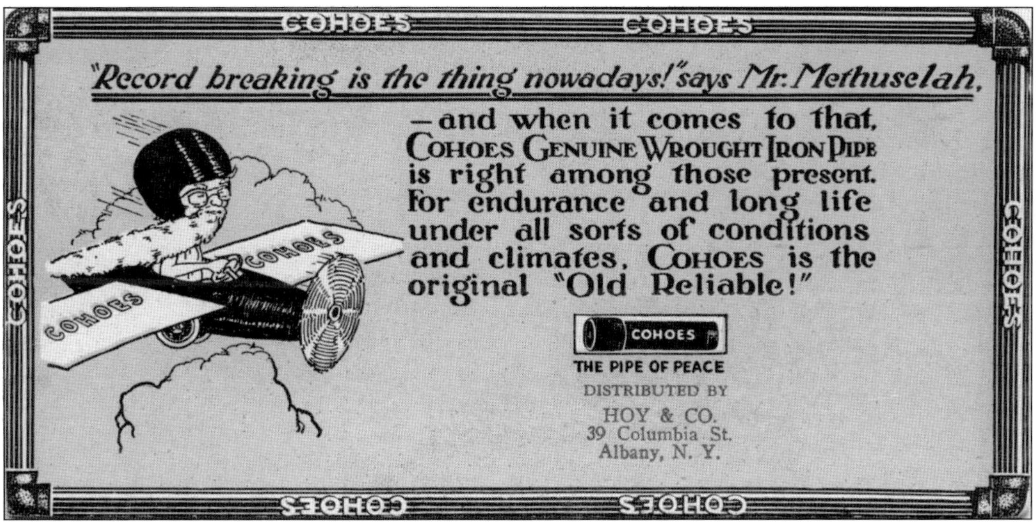


This advertising ink blotter highlights the durability of Cohoes genuine wrought-iron pipe. The manufacturer, the Cohoes Rolling Mill Co., located on Courtland and Canvass Streets, was established in 1858 and incorporated in 1901. The company manufactured steel and conduit pipes for steam and gas distribution. It also made steel used in handles and poles for local axe, pick, and mattocks manufacturing and building materials for trestles and bridges.

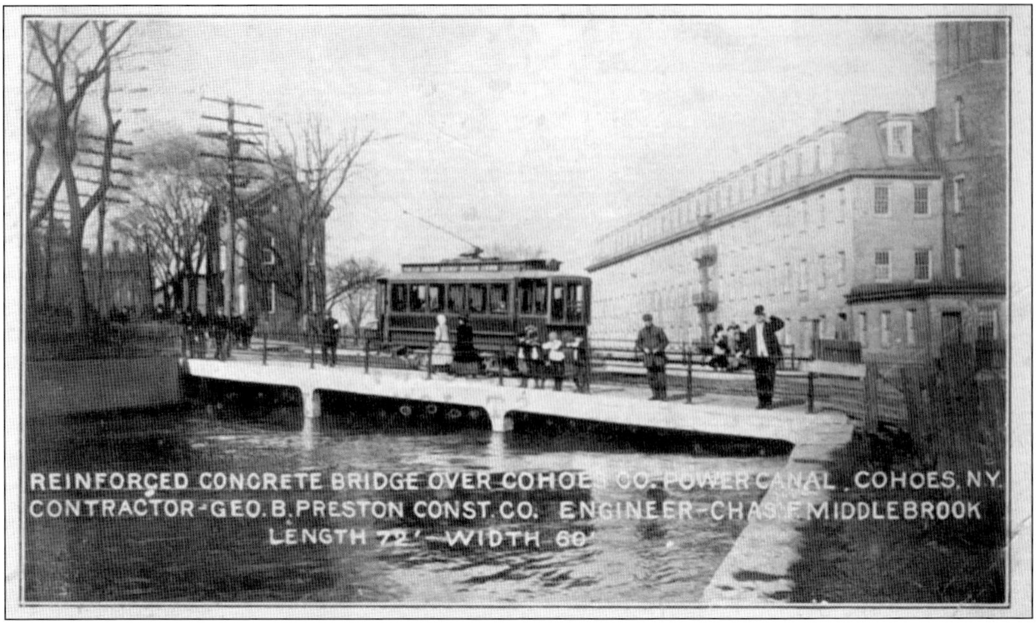


William M. Chadwick built the Strong Mill in 1846. The three-story brick building housed 2,700 spindles, supplying yarn for 80 looms. The mill consumed nearly 300 bales of cotton per year and employed 69 people. A fire on July 8, 1854, destroyed much of the mill, but it was rebuilt within a year. It was purchased by the Harmony Company in 1865 and underwent extensive alterations, including an enlargement and remodeling of the roof in the Italianate style, with a mansard and imposing tower to complement the other structures in the Harmony Mills complex. The mill was referred to as Harmony Mill No. 5. The postcard above shows a bridge spanning one of the city's power canals. The offices of the Cohoes Power and Light Co. are to the left of the trolley, with the Strong Mill to the right.

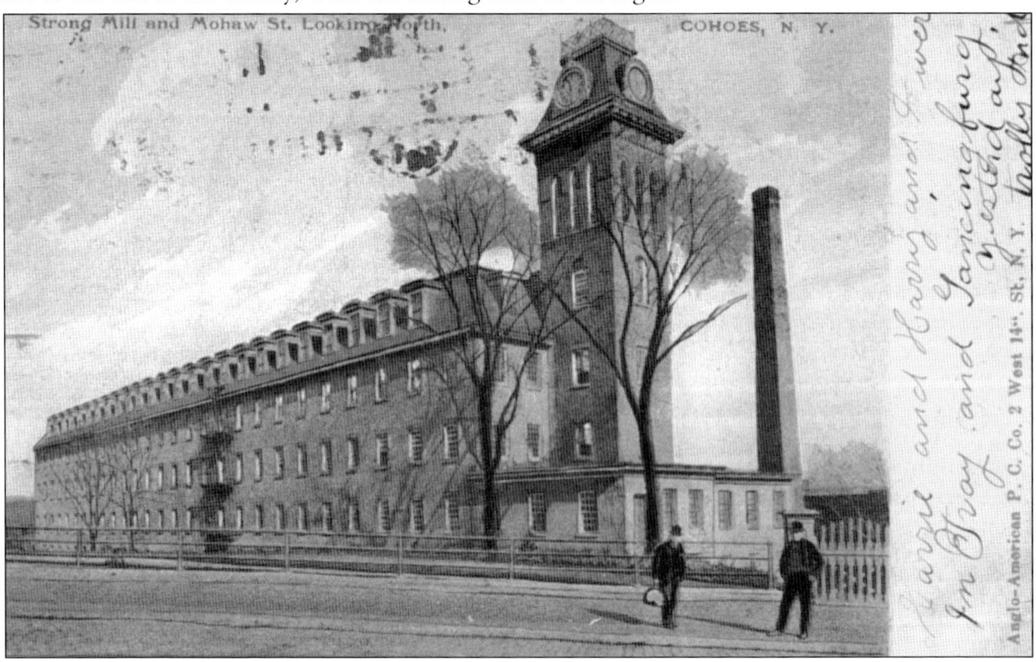

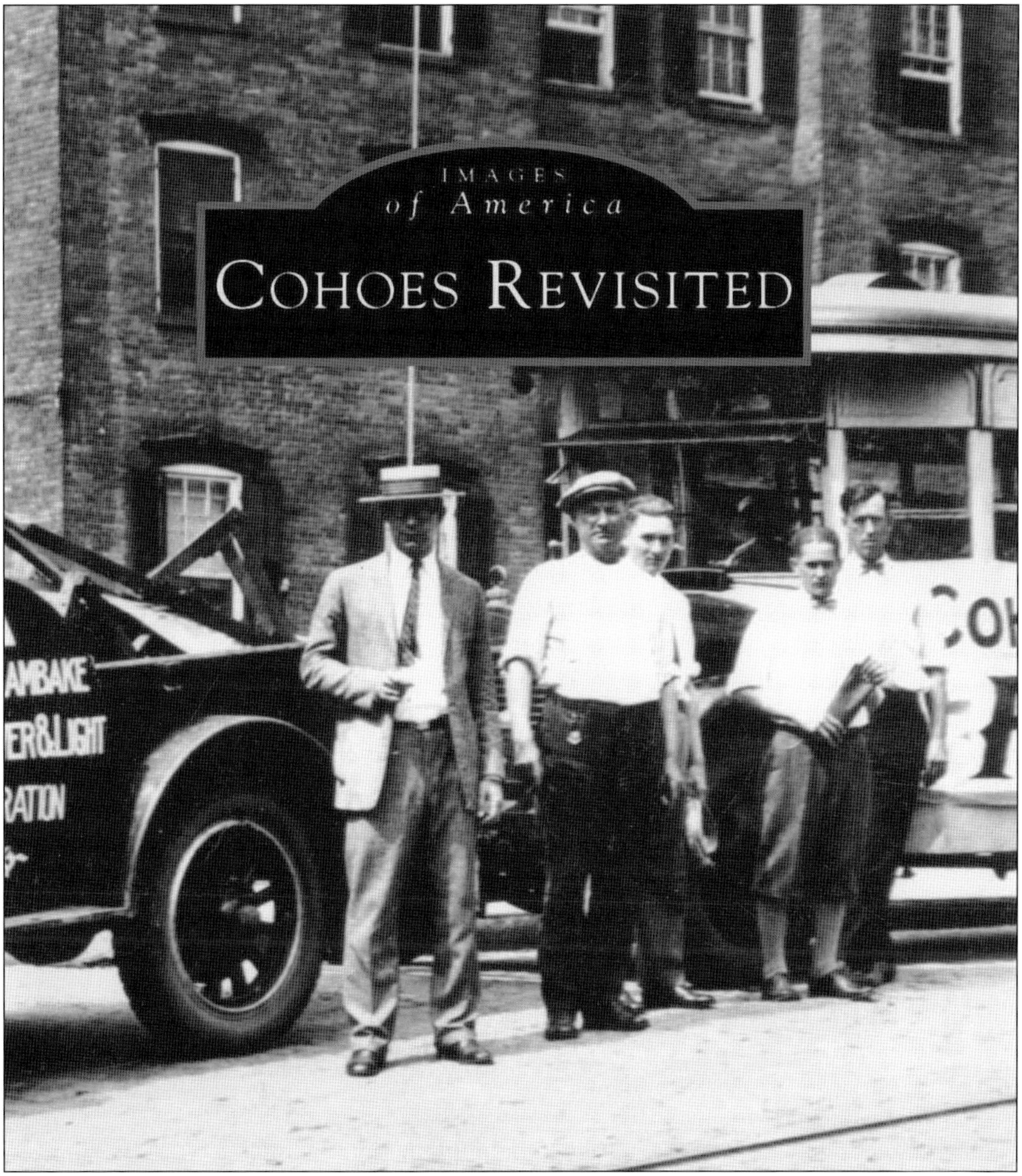


*Cohoes Revisited* continues the pictorial history begun in Spindle City Historic Society's first book, *Cohoes*. It offered a view of the city and its residents from the 19th century forward, honoring the rich heritage of Cohoes. Cohoes was transformed from a farming village to a center of commerce by the construction of the Erie Canal. The Cohoes Falls was the motive force that made Cohoes an industrial hub during the 19th and early 20th centuries. Massive mill buildings, including one of the largest cotton mills in the world, were erected along the riverfront and a network of power canals. To the mills came workers, a diverse group of immigrants who gave Cohoes its distinctive character. This book traces the history of Cohoes from the height of its industrial power in the late 19th century, through two world wars, the Great Depression, and the societal and technological changes of the 20th century. The story is told through photographs and through the eyes of an observer who recounts experiences of Cohoes over the years in letters to her sister.

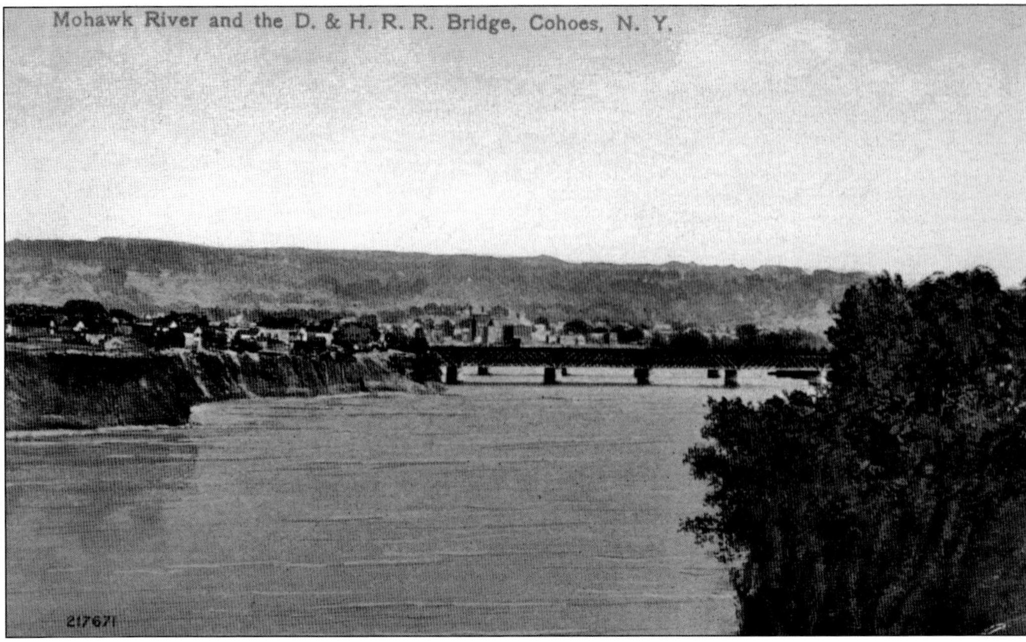


The railroad tracks in these postcards were once owned by the Delaware & Hudson (D&H) Railroad. The line was originally the Albany Northern Railroad, built north from Albany, through West Troy (Watervliet), Cohoes, Waterford, Schaghticoke, Buskirk, and Eagle Bridge. It was opened in April 1853. The line was later taken over by the Rensselaer & Saratoga Railroad, which extended the route north from Waterford to Mechanicville. The railroad retains this route to the present day. In 1870, the Delaware & Hudson, seeking markets for its coal, acquired the line, eventually extending it to Montreal. By the early winter of 1875, it was possible to travel by train from New York City to Montreal in approximately one day. The growth of the railroad line meant expanded markets for manufacturers in Cohoes and easier travel to Cohoes for immigrants embarking from New York City and Canada.

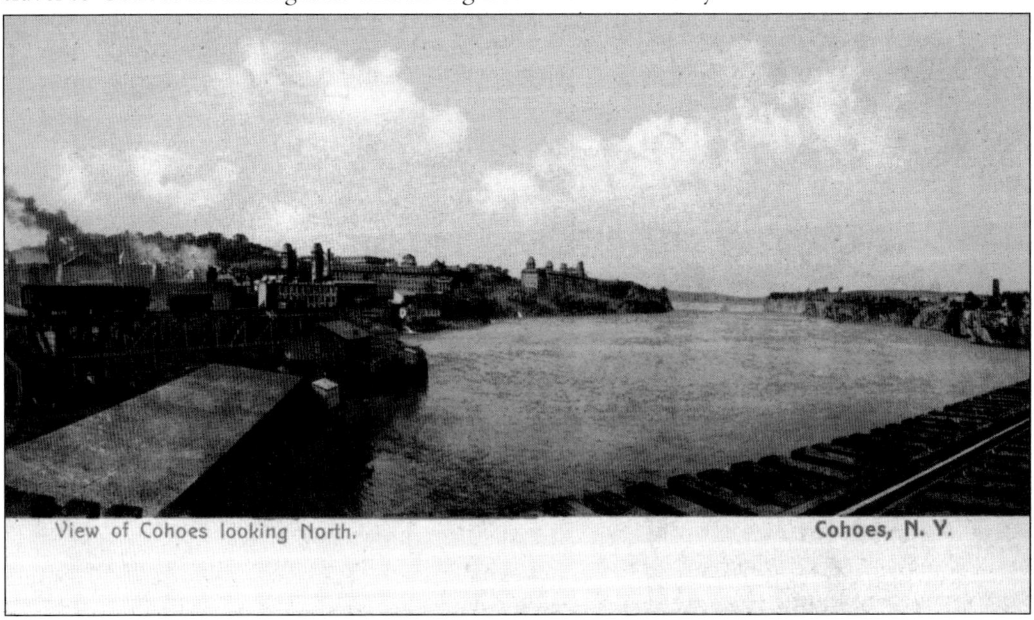

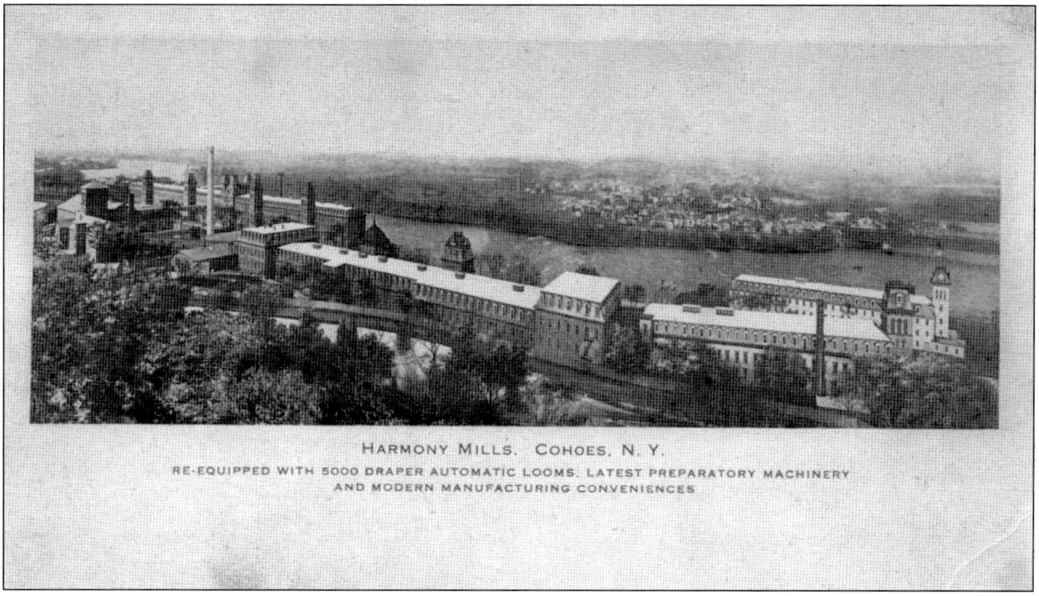


These panoramic views of the Harmony Mills complex show its massive scale. In the postcard above, with a view looking east, are, from left to right, Mills Nos. 1, 3, 2, 4 (Jute Mill), and 5 (Strong Mill). The postcard below, with a view looking west, shows Harmony Mill No. 3 extending along the riverbank. The cards state that the mills were "Re-equipped with 5000 Draper automatic looms. Latest preparatory machinery and modern manufacturing conveniences." The Harmony Mills had a long history of innovation. Beginning in 1850, under the leadership of Robert Johnston, a protégé of Samuel Slater, and his son David Johnston, the Harmony Mills constantly improved the technology of cotton cloth manufacturing processes. In publications from the 1870s, the eminent British textile engineer Evan Leigh recognizes Mill No. 3 as one of the best examples of technological achievements in cotton mill design in America.

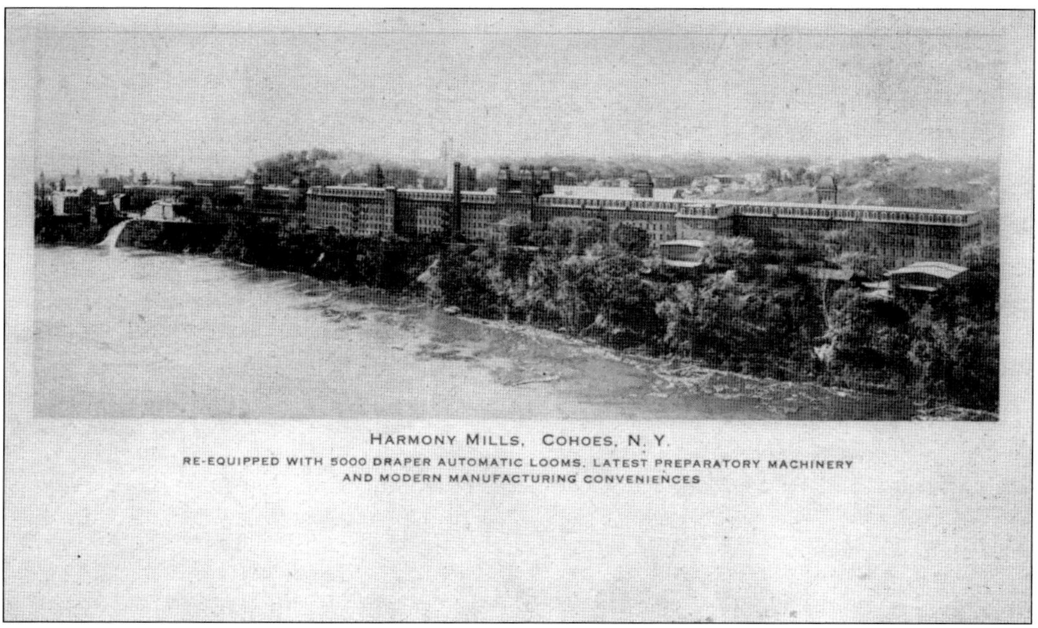

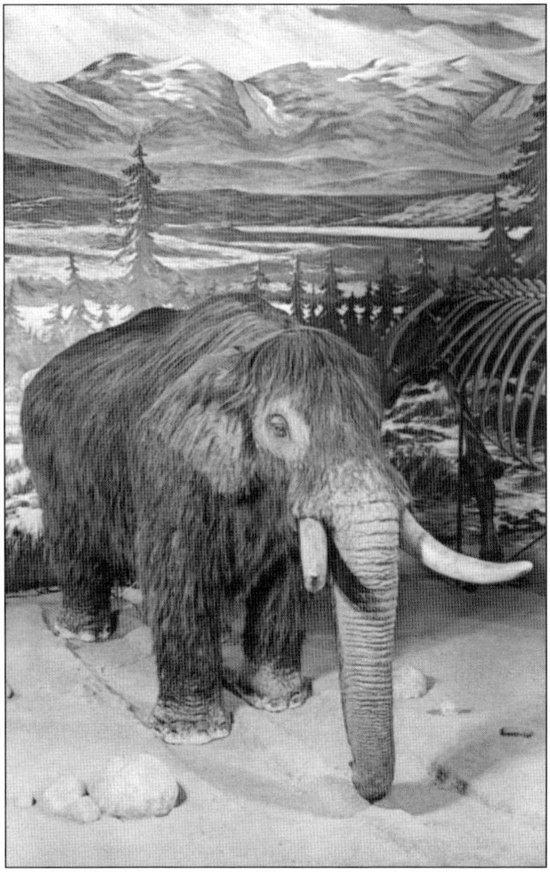

The Cohoes Mastodon was discovered in September 1866 during excavations for the foundation of Harmony Mill No. 3. The mastodon's skeleton was first displayed in the offices of the Harmony Mills Company, and later exhibited at the Troy County Fair and other places. In 1867, the State of New York purchased the mastodon bones for $2,000. The almost-complete skeleton was assembled and displayed at the State Cabinet of Natural History on State Street in Albany; it was later on exhibit in the museum in the State Education Building, alongside a furry replica, as shown in these postcards. The Cohoes Mastodon was a young male who lived about 11,000 years ago and stood about eight feet, five inches tall, with tusks four feet, six inches long. Today, the conserved and reassembled Cohoes Mastodon stands in the New York State Museum. The furry replica resides in the Cohoes Library.

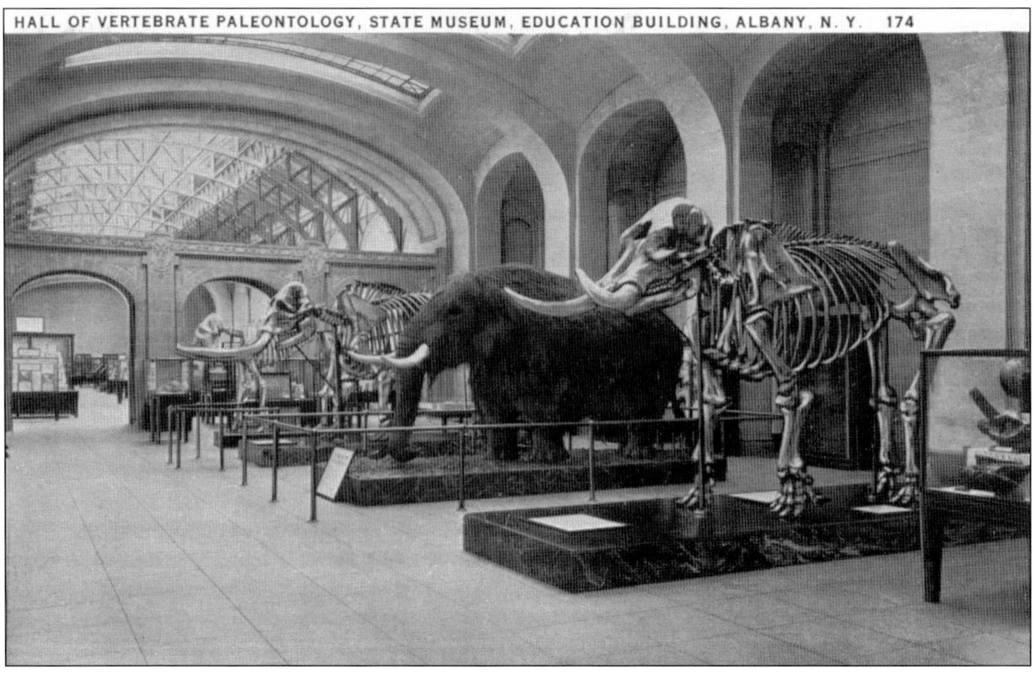

This vertical Boyden turbine was manufactured by the Holyoke Machine Company. It was among the largest in the United States at the time of its installation in 1873. Several Boyden turbines converted waterpower, transmitted through a network of power canals, to mechanical energy to operate a belt-driven system that ran machinery in Harmony Mill No. 3. The two largest turbines, each producing 800 horsepower, were located in the lower level of the south end of the mill, with their shafts running vertically. Gearing transferred the power from these shafts to a horizontal shaft that drove 12-foot-diameter pulleys to spin two-foot-wide leather belts throughout the building. The American Society of Mechanical Engineers designated the turbines as National Historic Mechanical Engineering Landmarks in 1975 as "probably the largest and nearly the most powerful water turbines ever built in the United States to supply direct mechanical power to a manufacturing plant."

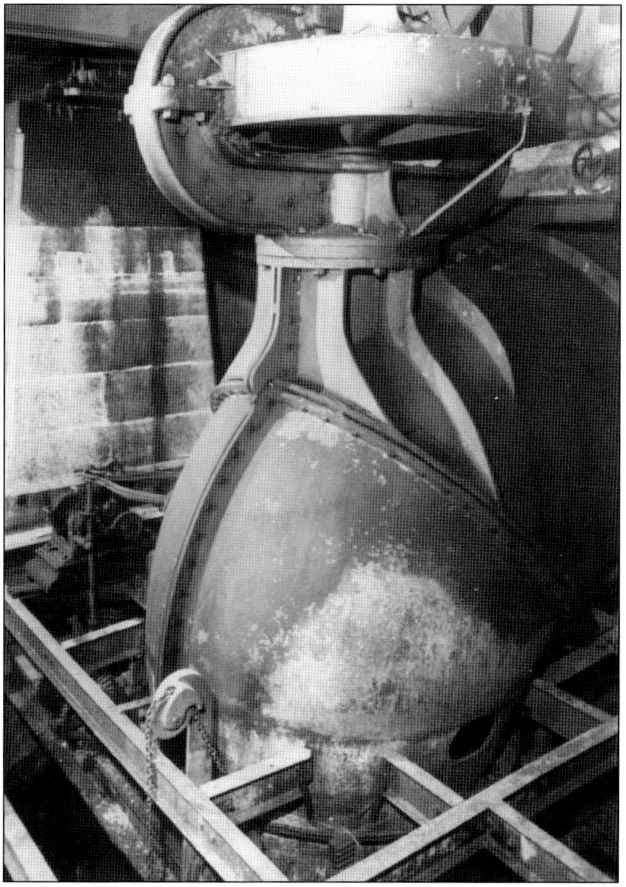

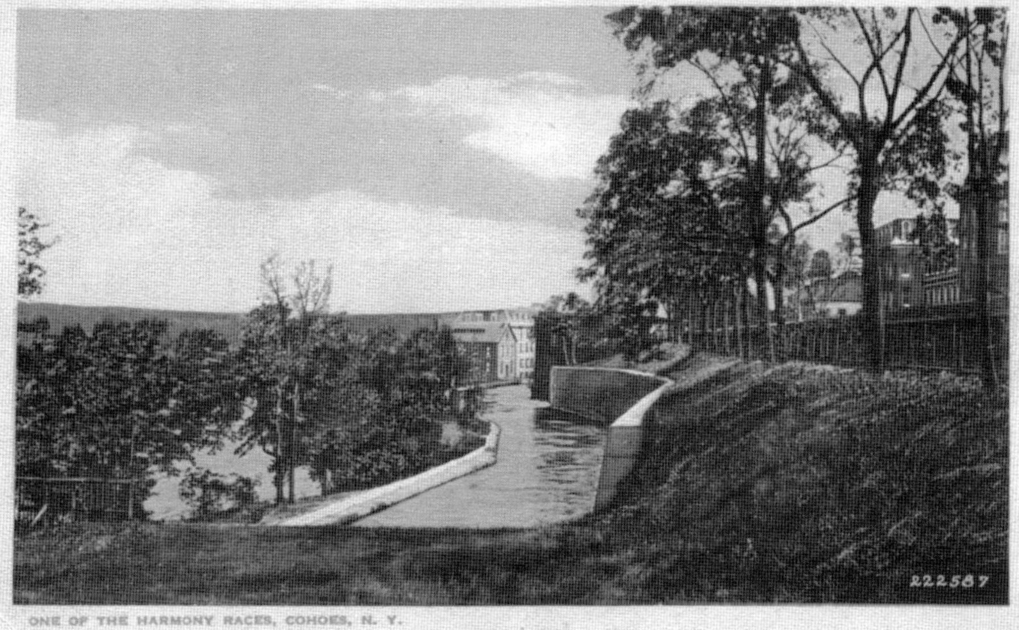


ONE OF THE HARMONY RACES, COHOES, N. Y.

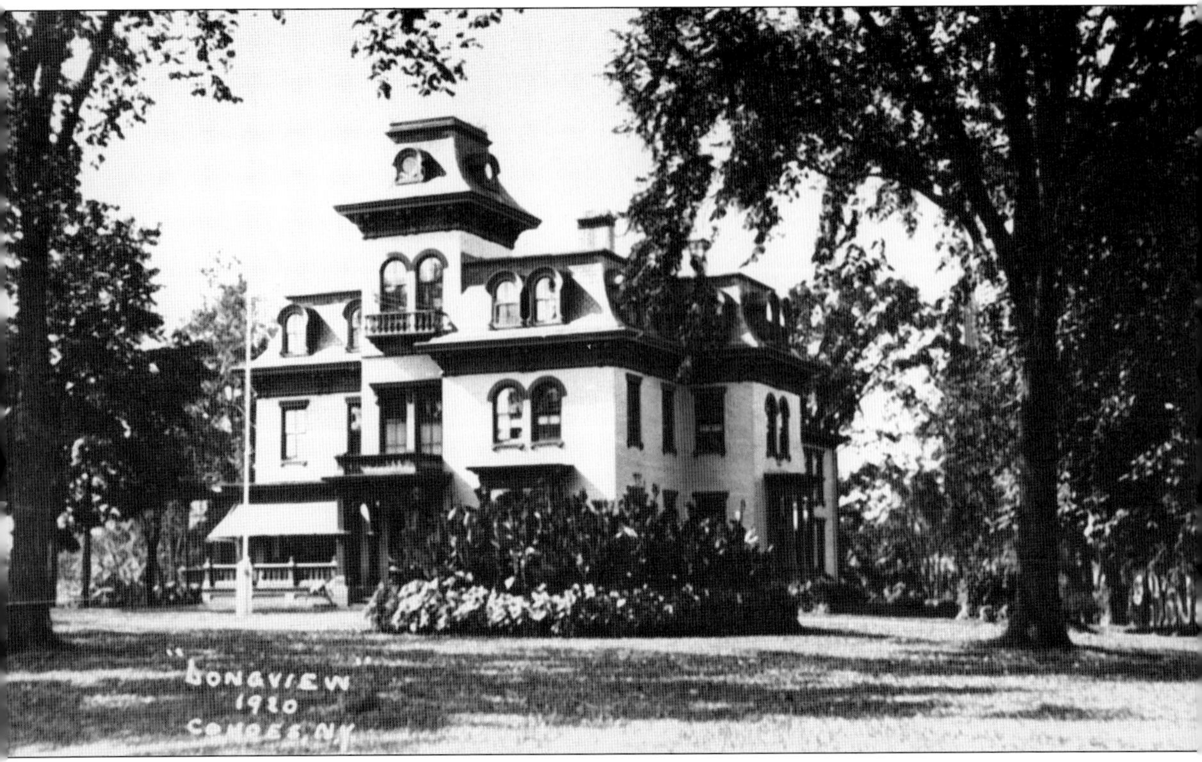


Known as Longview, this home was built for David John Johnston by the Harmony Company in 1866 when he became superintendent of the mills following his successful supervision of the design and construction of Harmony Mill No. 3. Longview is a three-story Italianate mansion with a mansard roof and hooded dormers. Perched high atop Harmony Hill, it symbolically oversees the mill complex. David and his father, Robert Johnston, developed efficient and large-scale means of textile production in the Harmony Mills and brought Cohoes to industrial prominence in the mid- to late 19th century. David Johnston also served twice as mayor of Cohoes, in 1872–1874 and 1876–1878. In 1871, a local newspaper said the following of David John Johnston: "As a civic administrator, a merchant and a philanthropist he is second to none." The house later served as the Cohoes Public Library and offices for the Cohoes Board of Education. The house of Robert Johnston, an Italianate villa built to his specifications by the Garner Company in 1856, was located at the base of Summit Street, just down the hill from Longview.

# *Three*

# DOWNTOWN

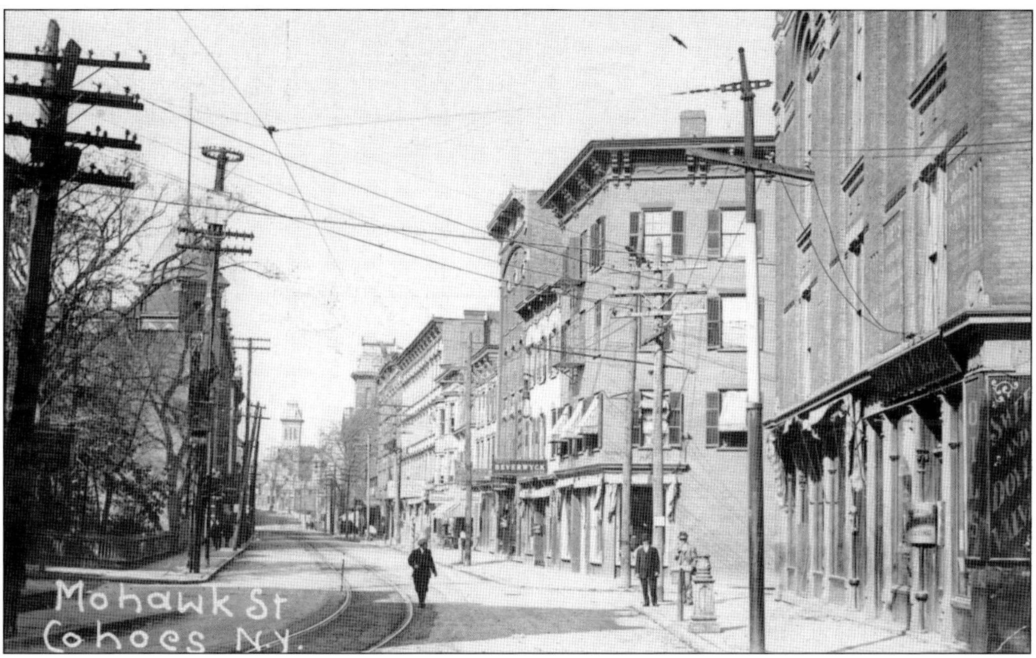


The view in this real-photo postcard takes a look north up Mohawk Street. The large building in the distance is the Strong Mill. The small Greek Revival–style buildings in front of the mill still stand today. The tall building on the left side of the street is the Harmony Hotel. Among the industries on the right side of the street are the Campbell & Clute Machine Co. and the Enterprise Paper Box Factory.

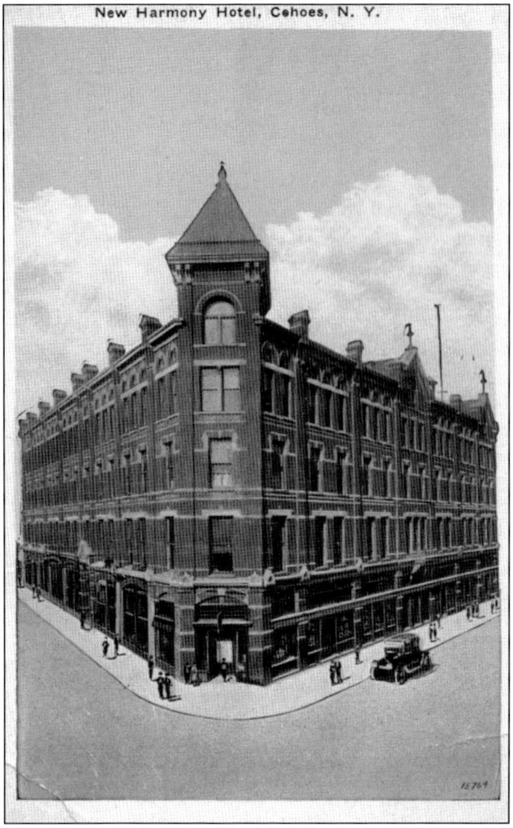


George Simmons opened the original Harmony Hotel in 1880. The New Harmony Hotel, located near the intersection of Remsen and Mohawk Streets, also had Willie's Wonder Bar on the ground floor. The hotel is probably most remembered for its association with the notorious gangster Dutch Schultz. In March 1935, Schultz shot and killed business associate Jules Martin at the hotel because he suspected Martin of stealing funds.

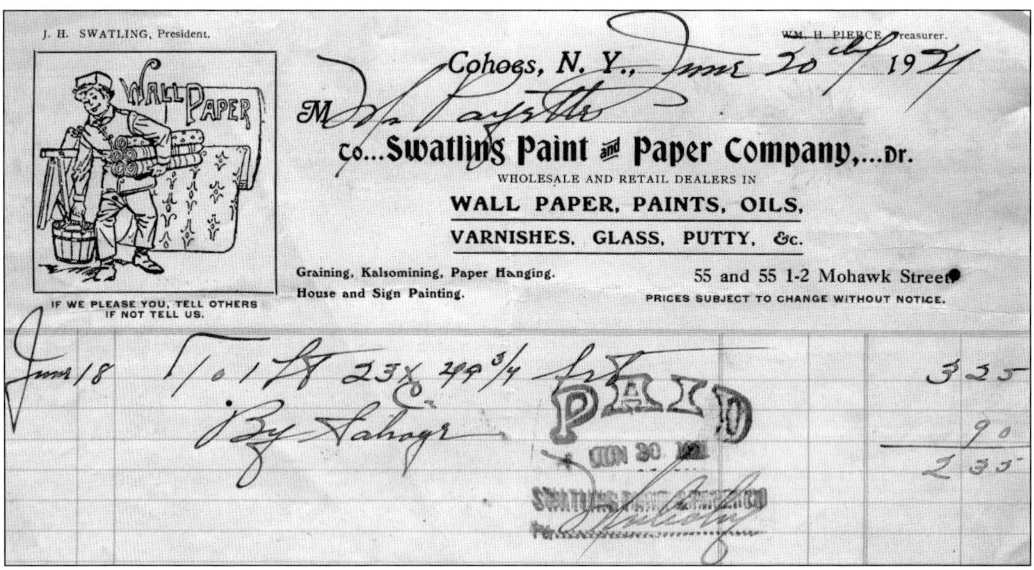
J. H. SWATLING, President.
WM. H. PIERCE, Treasurer.
Cohoes, N. Y.,
M
To... Swatling Paint and Paper Company,... Dr.
WHOLESALE AND RETAIL DEALERS IN
WALL PAPER, PAINTS, OILS,
VARNISHES, GLASS, PUTTY, &c.
Graining, Kalsomining, Paper Hanging.
House and Sign Painting.
55 and 55 1-2 Mohawk Street.
PRICES SUBJECT TO CHANGE WITHOUT NOTICE.
IF WE PLEASE YOU, TELL OTHERS
IF NOT TELL US.
PAID

Swatling Paint and Paper Company, founded in 1885, was originally located at 50 Oneida Street. James H Swatling was the owner. In the early 1900s, the business moved to 55 Mohawk Street. Clara Irene Swatling became company president in 1922. Swatling's store moved to 77 Mohawk Street in 1937, where it remained until closing in the 1990s. This building at 77 Mohawk Street was the last remnant of Cohoes's original downtown commercial district.

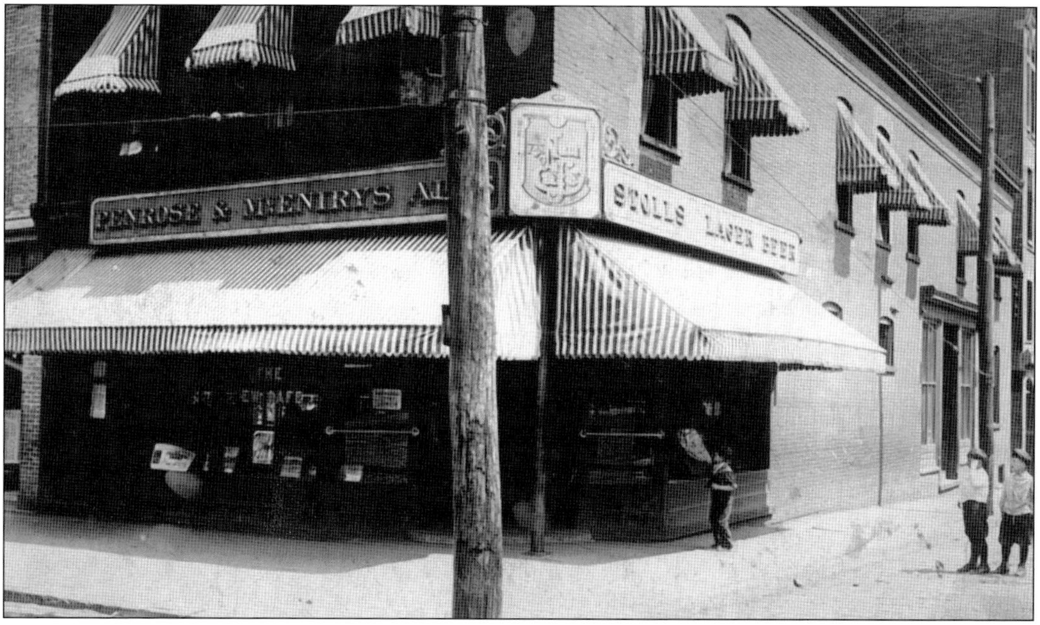


This Cohoes establishment featured Penrose & McEniry's Ale. The Penrose & McEniry brewery opened in 1892 at the corner of Lansing and Newark Streets. James Penrose was brewmaster in his father's business until its closure in 1923 during Prohibition. John Hay bottled beer for family use on St. John Street. After Prohibition was repealed, Penrose became master brewer for the Oneida Brewing Co. in Utica.

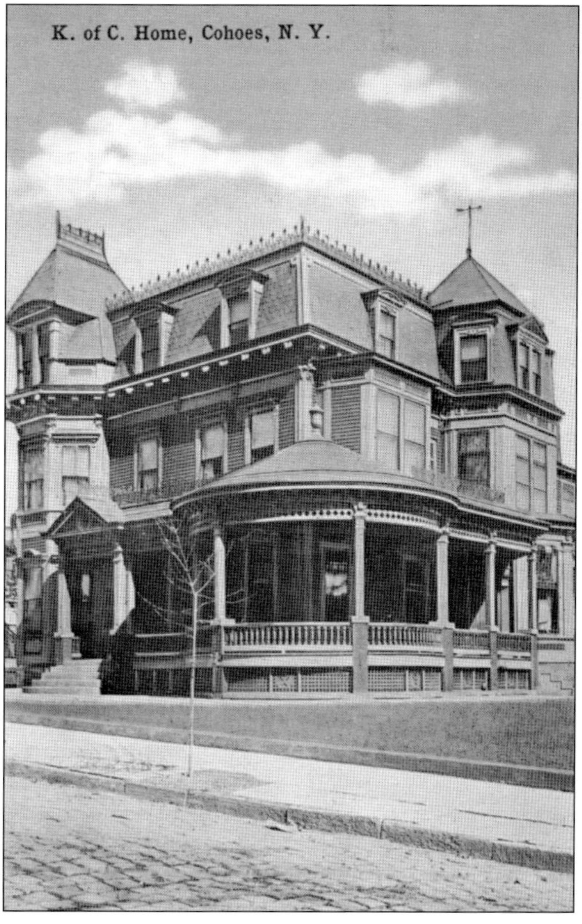


A group called the Bachelors Club started the Cohoes Knights of Columbus. The Cohoes Council received its charter on October 24, 1896. P.H. Spillane was the first grand knight. After using rented space at various locations in downtown Cohoes, the council purchased the Jacob Brooks residence, a three-story Victorian at 255 Remsen Street, in 1913. The house served as the council's home until 1970, when it was replaced.

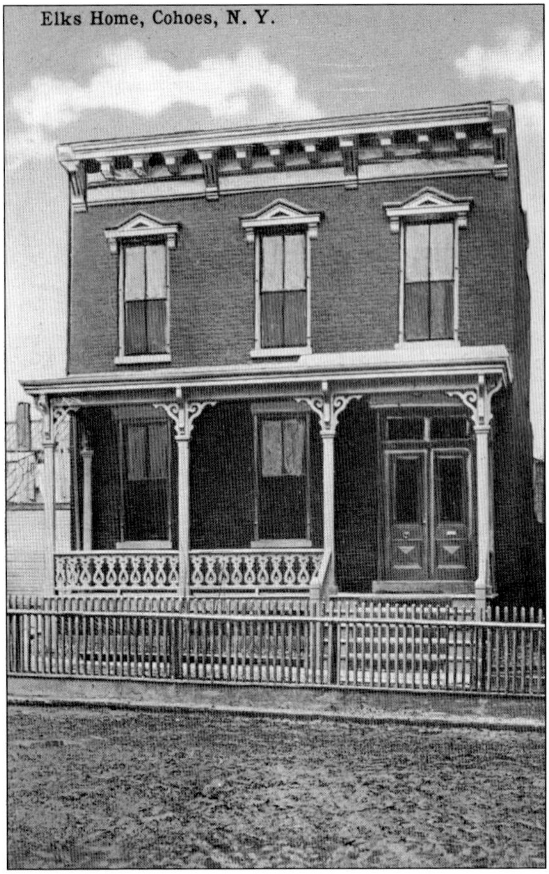


The Cohoes Lodge of Elks No. 1317 was first chartered on September 16, 1914, with 49 charter members. The group leased a building from the Harmony Company at 93 Oneida Street, where the E.T. Ruane American Legion Post is now located. By 1922, the Elks lodge had 1,000 members. To accommodate the growing membership, it constructed a new building on the corner of Oneida and Mohawk Streets, on the site of the Andrew Root residence. The cornerstone was laid on June 15, 1922. Participants in the celebration included more than 2,000 Elks from other lodges. The building was designed to exact Grand Lodge specifications. The Elks eventually sold the property to the City of Cohoes in 1977, and a new lodge was constructed on North Mohawk Street at the former location of the Strong Mill. In 1982, the lodge incorporated its membership with Waterford.

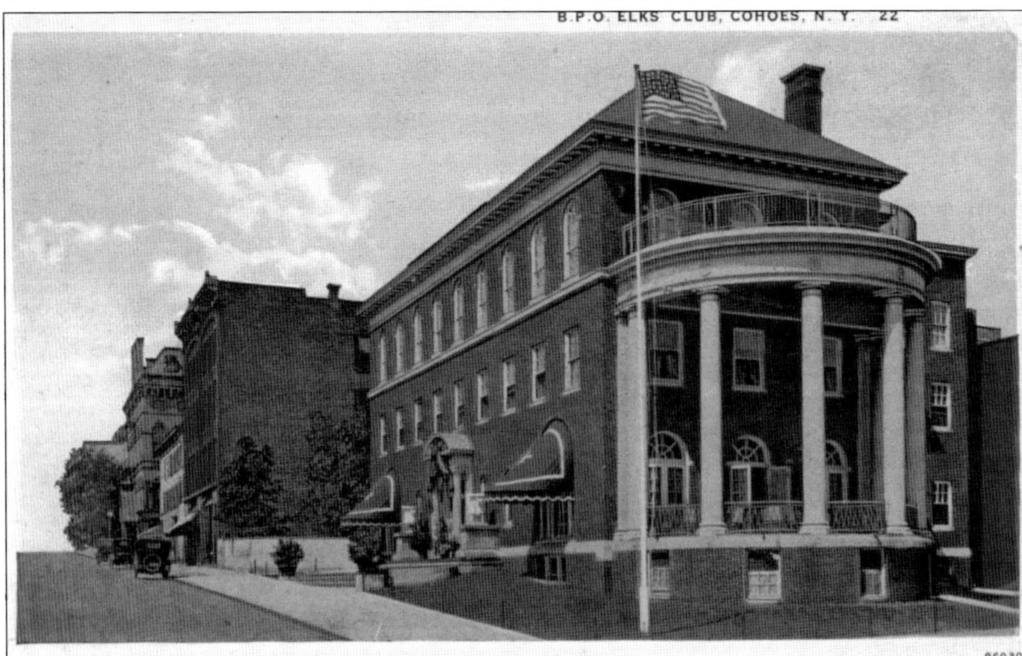

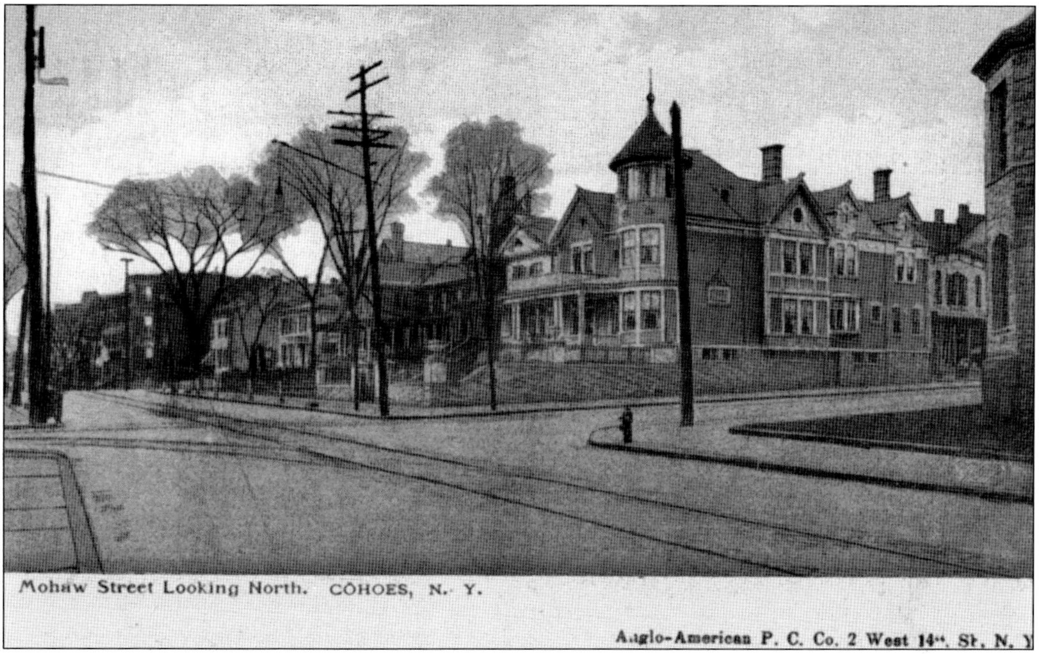


The house shown on the southwest corner of Ontario and Mohawk Streets was the home of John Van Schaick Lansing, an officer for the Bailey Manufacturing Company and Troy Manufacturing Company. He was an organizer of the Manufacturers Bank and the first board of fire commissioners in Cohoes and served as an alderman in Cohoes. Van Schaick played the organ in the Dutch Reformed church, and contributed generously to its purchase.

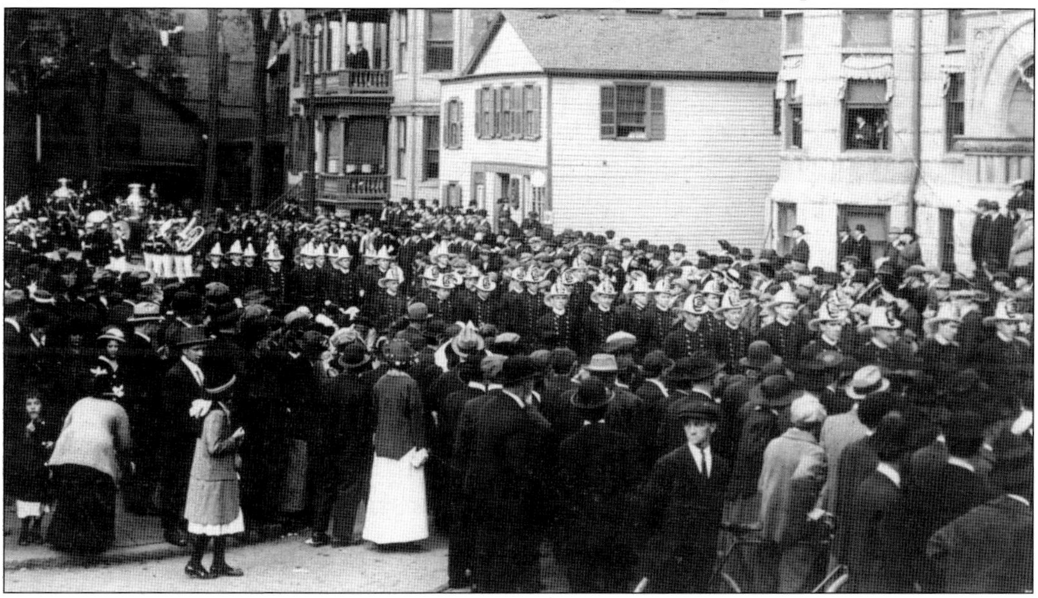

This early-20th-century real-photo postcard shows firemen on parade on Mohawk Street before an enthusiastic crowd of Cohoesiers. Note the mayor and his staff looking out from the windows at city hall, and the horse-drawn steamers in the parade. The section of Mohawk to Oneida Streets was residence to many 19th-century Cohoes notables, including David Wilkinson, Hezekiah Howe, and William Caw (Chester Arthur's brother-in-law).

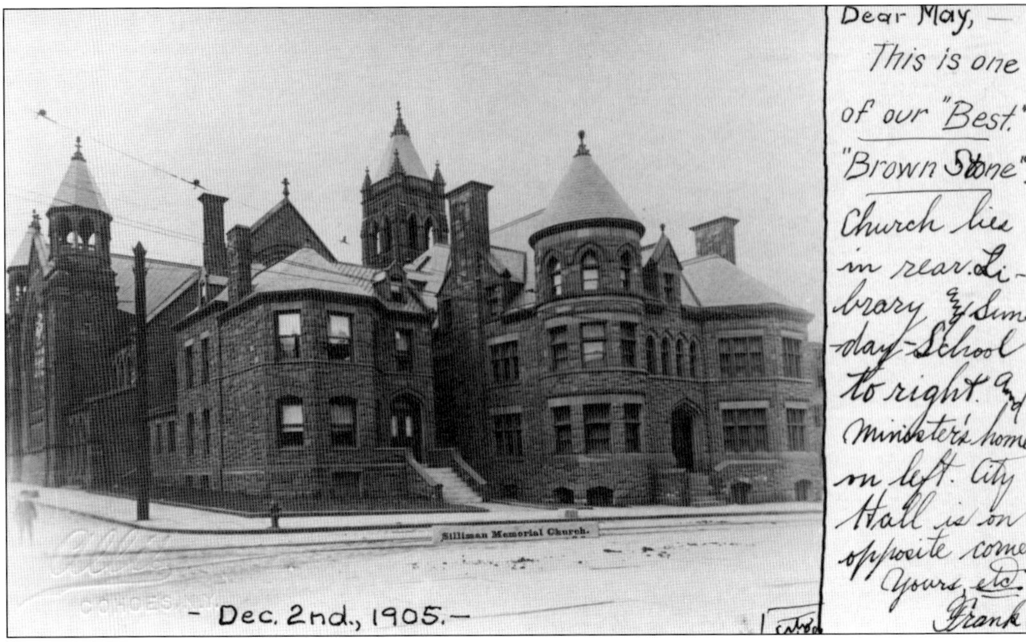


The writer in December 1905 states, "This is one of our 'Best.' 'Brown Stone.' Church lies in rear. Library and Sunday School to right. And minister's home on left." This was the Silliman Memorial Church, located on the corner of Mohawk and Ontario Streets. It was indeed one of the best. The church was built in 1896 by philanthropist Horace Silliman in memory of his parents, Levi and Clarissa, who were instrumental in organizing a Presbyterian church in Cohoes. Horace was also active in the church and the community, serving as superintendent of the Sunday school and first president of the Cohoes chapter of the YMCA. He was a leader in organizing a school district in Cohoes, involved in improvement of the community cemetery grounds, on the committee that established Cohoes Hospital, first president of the C.H. Adams Steamer Company, and trustee of the Waterworks Sinking Fund.

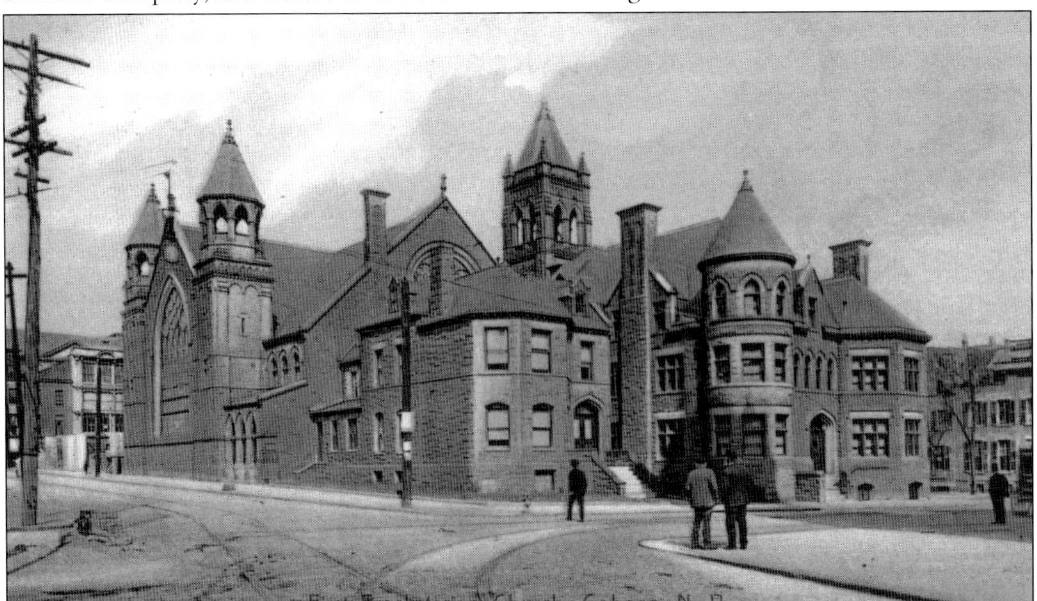

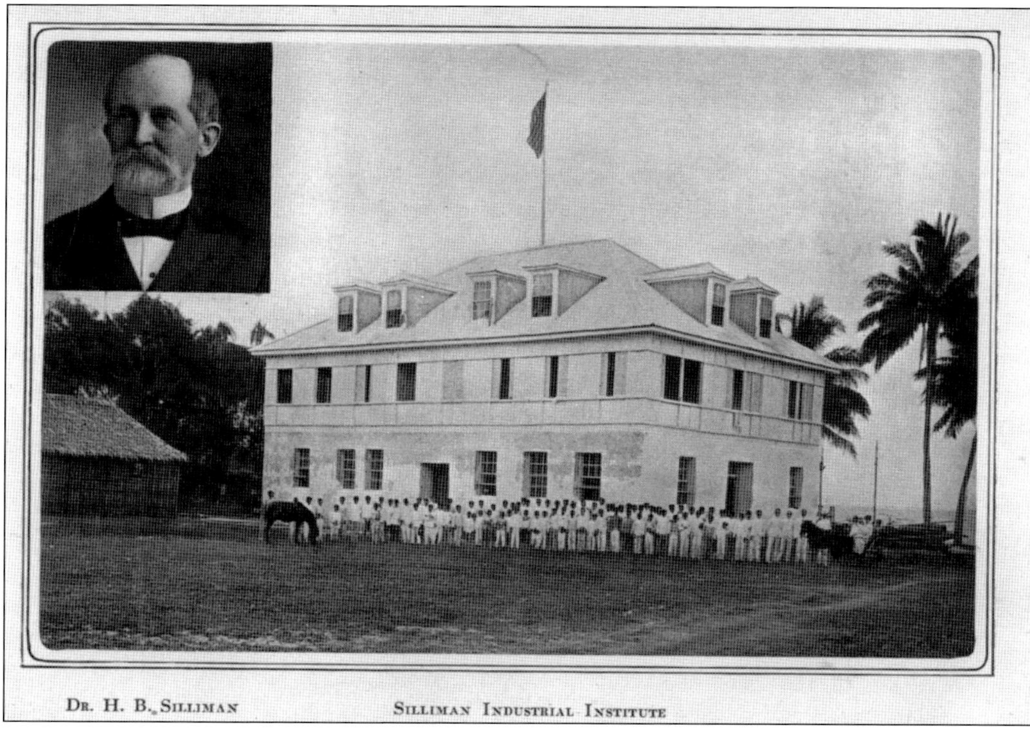


The Silliman Institute was established in 1901 in Dumaguete City in the Philippines through a donation from Horace B. Silliman. Begun as an industrial school for boys and expanded to become a college in 1910, it acquired university status in 1938. As one of the foremost institutions for higher education in the Philippines, Silliman University today comprises ten colleges, four schools, and two institutes, enrolling over 8,600 students.

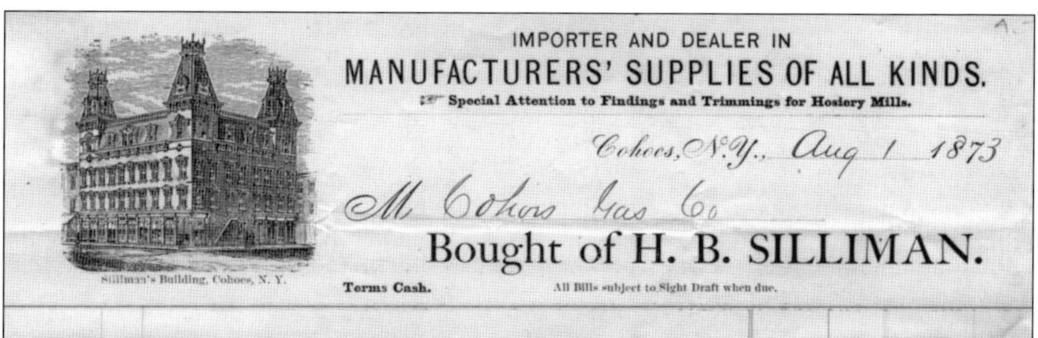


The Silliman Building was located next to the National Bank Building (music hall) on Remsen Street. Horace Silliman was a dealer and importer of manufacturers' supplies and became very successful in Cohoes, with its numerous knitting mills. Silliman was an active community leader, and used his wealth for philanthropic purposes in Cohoes, at Hamilton College, at his alma mater Union College, and as far away as the Philippines.

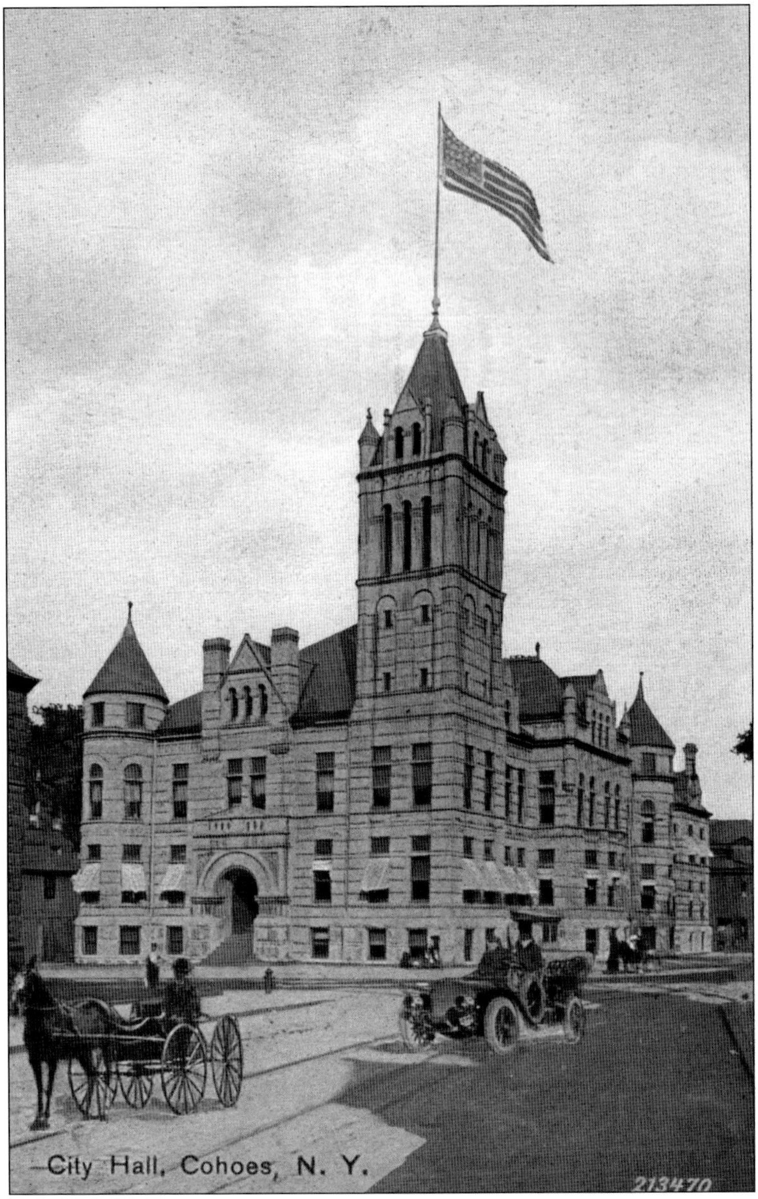


"An act to authorize the purchase of a suitable site in the city of Cohoes and to erect thereon a city hall, station house and jail and to provide means to defray the expense thereof" was introduced by M.W. Douglas in 1894. This legislation created a commission to oversee the building of city hall at a cost not to exceed $100,000. On April 17, this was signed into law. On May 8, an estate on the corner of Mohawk and Ontario Streets was selected (once the land of Peter Harmony), which then contained a merry-go-round with discordant music. Prizes for the best building design were offered. The commissioners selected a mid-century French style designed by Franklin H. Jones of Albany. On April 6, the common council chambers overflowed with citizens in opposition; they favored the design submitted by J.C. Holland and Co. of Kansas. On April 16, the people won out, and the Holland design was approved. Ground was broken on August 1, and Gov. Levi P. Morton and Mayor James H. Mitchell Sr. laid the cornerstone on September 26.

City hall's dedication took place on September 25, 1895, with ceremonies held in the city theater. Dr. H.B. Silliman gave the main address. The events included a grand parade of about 1,800 participants. The American flag for the building was provided by the women of Cohoes (who still did not have the vote but were active in civic development) and was purchased from John Campbell, bookseller (see page 59). As a fine example of Norman Gothic Revival architecture, it has a tower and turrets over the peaked roof. The blocks of limestone projected strength, power, and the endurance of civic institutions. This was the first building constructed in Cohoes with public funds. It is as sound today as on that day of dedication; and is a distinctive and impressive landmark and a credit to the persistence and civic engagement of Cohoesiers.

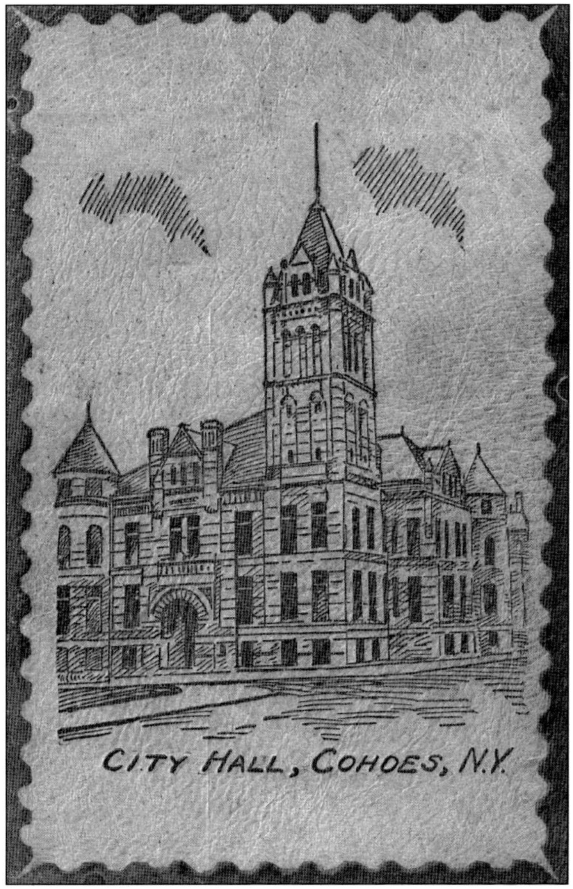


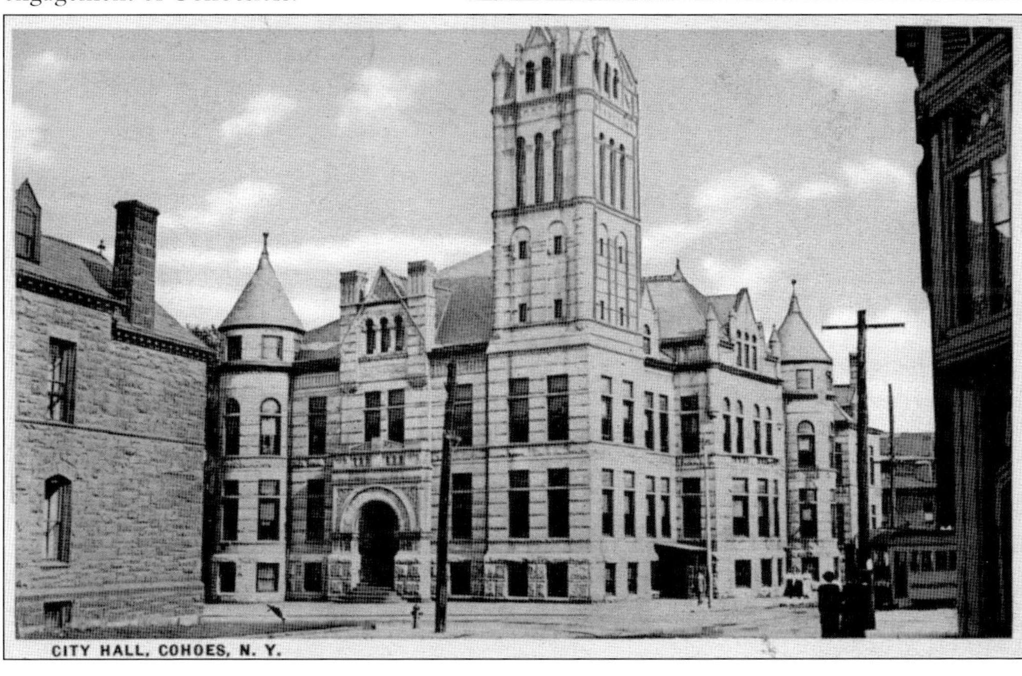

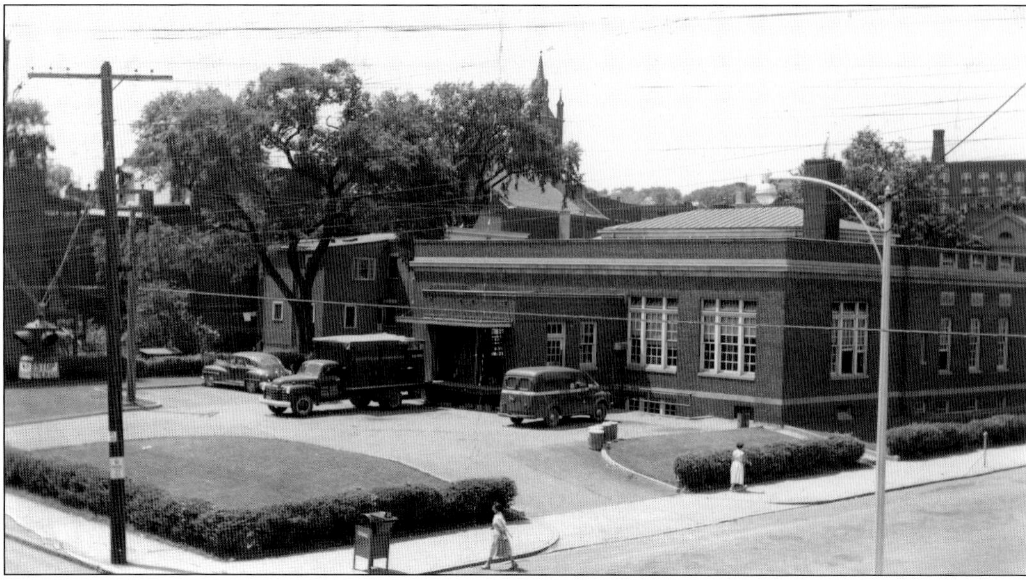

These two postcards show the front and back of the present-day Cohoes Post Office, located on the southeast corner of Mohawk and Ontario Streets. The post office was built in 1924, during the tenure of postmaster James H. McDonald, who had previously been mayor of Cohoes. The first post office in Cohoes was established on February 23, 1832, and was located in postmaster Frederio Waterman's store near the junction of the Erie and Champlain Canals. In 1833, Hezekiah Howe became postmaster and moved the post office to his store along the canal near the Jute Mill. Cohoes resident Wright Mallery, who ran a bakery, carried the mail, using his bread cart to transport the letters. The post office was in Izrahiah Chesebro's drugstore in the 1860s. At that time, local businessmen were commonly appointed postmaster and located the post office at their places of business.

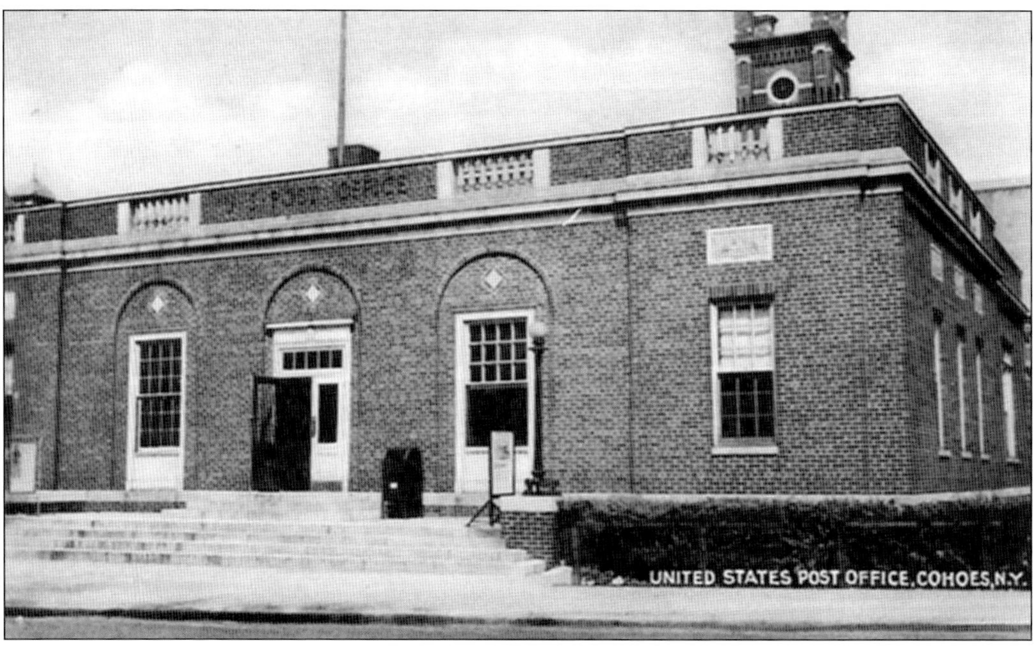

Organized in 1837 by farmers, blacksmiths, carpenters, and factory workers of Dutch, Swiss, Scots, and English ancestry, the original Dutch Reformed church was built in 1838. Prior to that time, services were held in the seaming room of the Egbert and Bailey Woolen Mill, on the corner of White and Remsen Streets. This church was replaced in 1860 with a new church, the one pictured here. Cohoes industrialists Egbert Egberts, David J. Johnston, and John V.S. Lansing donated the organ to the church. Many of the elders of the church over time were prominent citizens of Cohoes, including Dr. Henry Adams, father of Charles Adams, the first mayor of Cohoes. In 1969, the Dutch Reformed church joined with the Silliman Memorial Presbyterian Church to form the United Church of Cohoes, which stands today at 123 Mohawk Street.

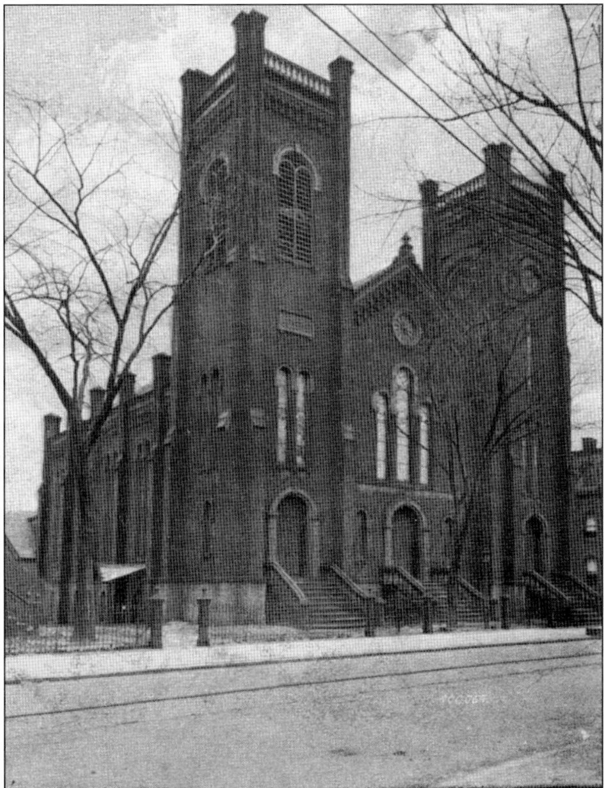

Reform Church, Cohoes, N.Y.

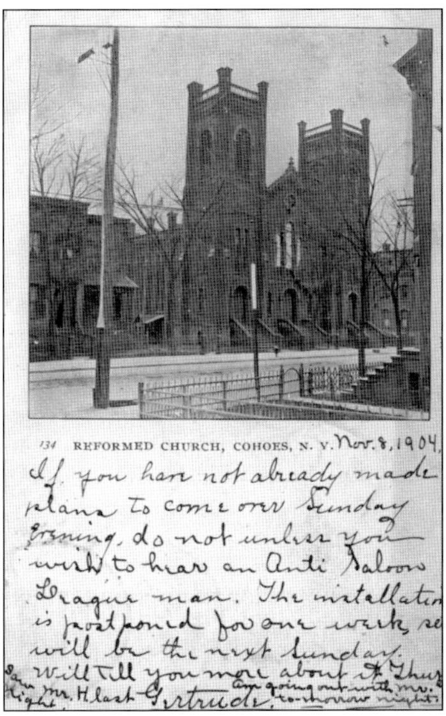

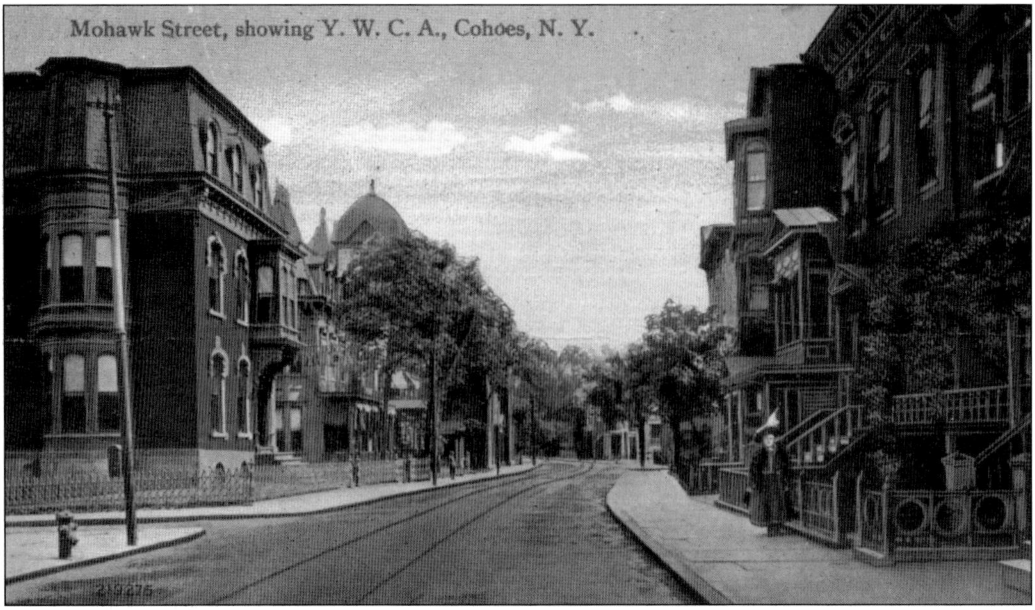


The Young Women's Christian Association (YWCA) in Cohoes was founded in 1890. The organization first had its headquarters at 53 Saratoga Street. The rooms were open during the day and evening, along with a reading room with books, newspapers, and magazines. Evening classes were offered in painting, music, and English language and writing. In 1892, the YWCA relocated to 135 Mohawk Street, an 1874 Second Empire house that was formerly the home of textile manufacturer William Moore. The YWCA provided residences for women, the use of a library, and classes in "domestic sciences." During the first decades of the 20th century, many of the young women who came from Canada to work in the mills of Cohoes stayed briefly at the YWCA. The sender of the postcard showing the YWCA's interior writes, "This is a picture of our Y.W.C.A. parlor, of which we are so proud of in Cohoes."

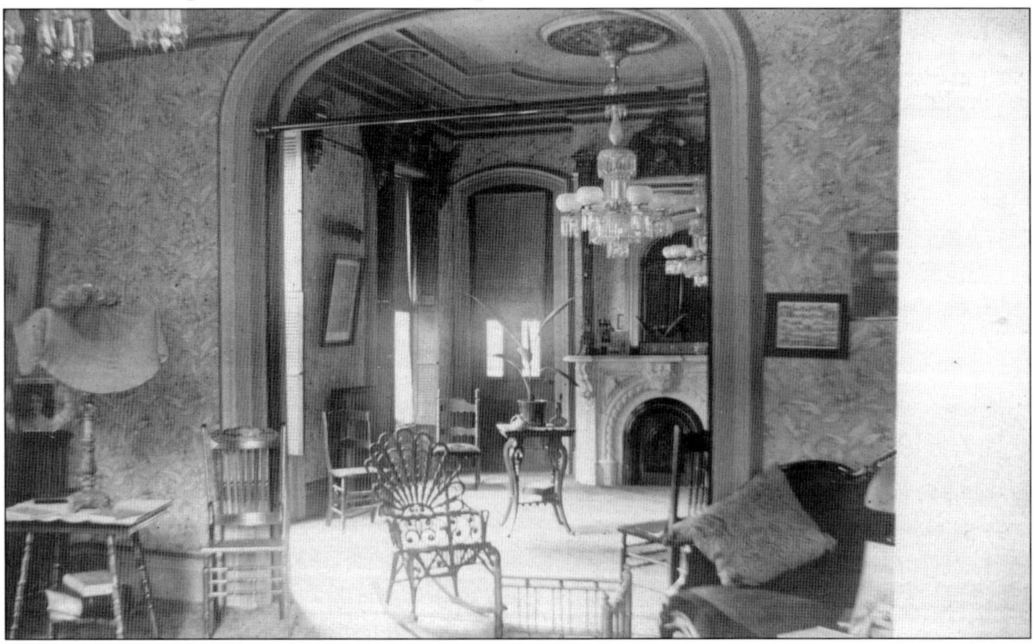

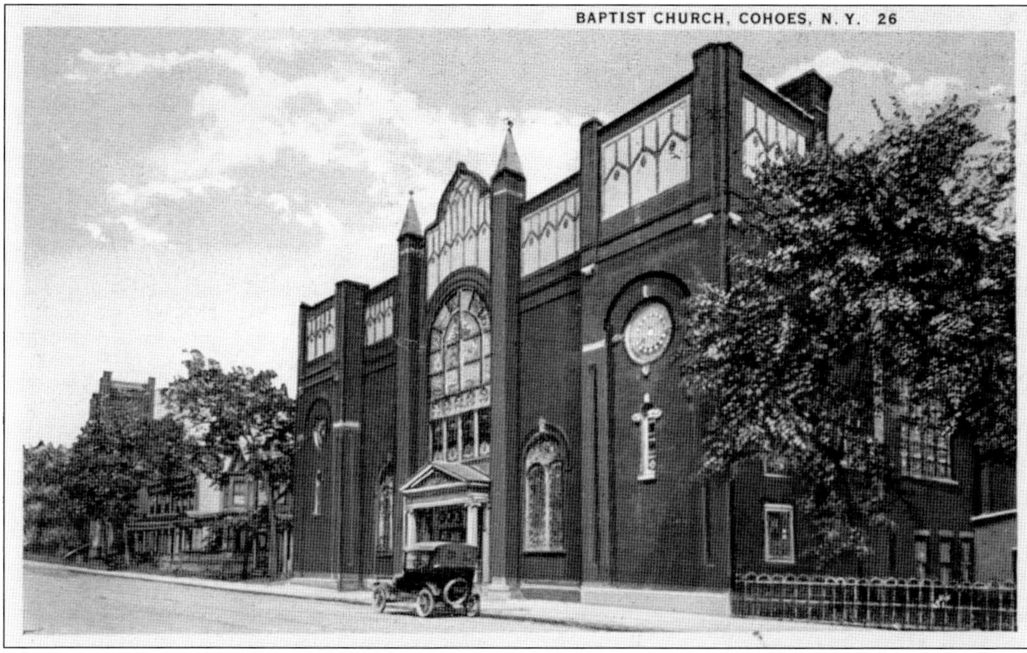


The First Baptist Church Society of Cohoes was formed on May 5, 1839. Its first pastor was Rev. John Duncan. Meetings were initially held in the dining room of the West Harmony Boardinghouse. Many church members were mill workers. The first meetinghouse was built in 1840 at the northwest corner of Remsen and Factory (now Cayuga) Streets. The land was later sold to the Harmony Mills, and a site on the southern end of Mohawk Street was acquired for a new church, which was dedicated on April 28, 1852. In 1872, the church was enlarged to a seating capacity of 600, and was renovated again in 1898 and 1911. After discovery of structural problems, the center dome of the church was removed in 1922–1923 and other renovations were made; the differences can be seen when comparing the postcards, which show the church after and before these renovations.

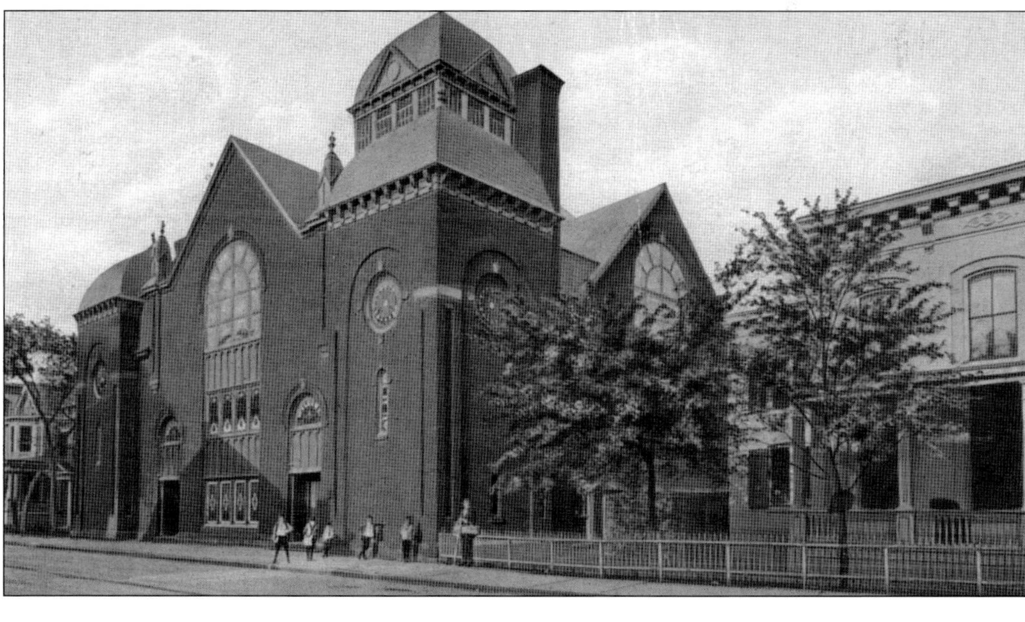

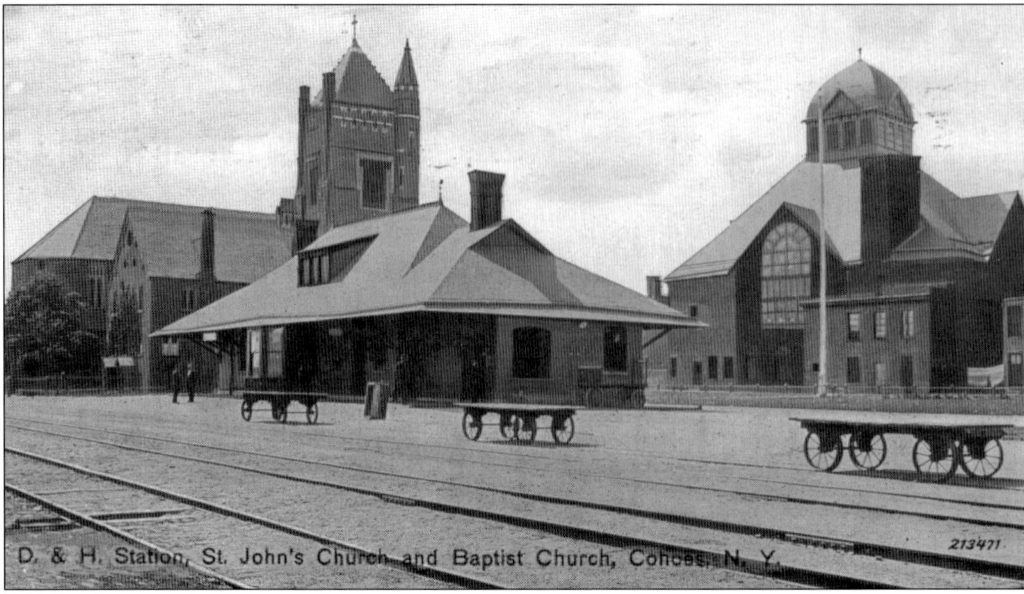


The main freight house of the D&H Railroad was located at Pine and Saratoga Streets. A D&H passenger station nearby operated in Cohoes from 1883. Most new arrivals to the city came through the passenger station from this time until the railroad abandoned most local passenger service in 1963. Several special trains also traveled through Cohoes along with routine service. Ulysses S. Grant's funeral train passed through on August 4, 1885, on the way to New York City. On September 13, 1901, Vice Pres. Theodore Roosevelt traveled through Cohoes from the Adirondacks on his way to Washington on a train the D&H had provided following the death of Pres. William McKinley. In the postcard above, the Baptist church and St. John's Episcopal Church, to the south of the station, can be seen. In the postcard below, St. Bernard's Church, to the north of the station, is in view.

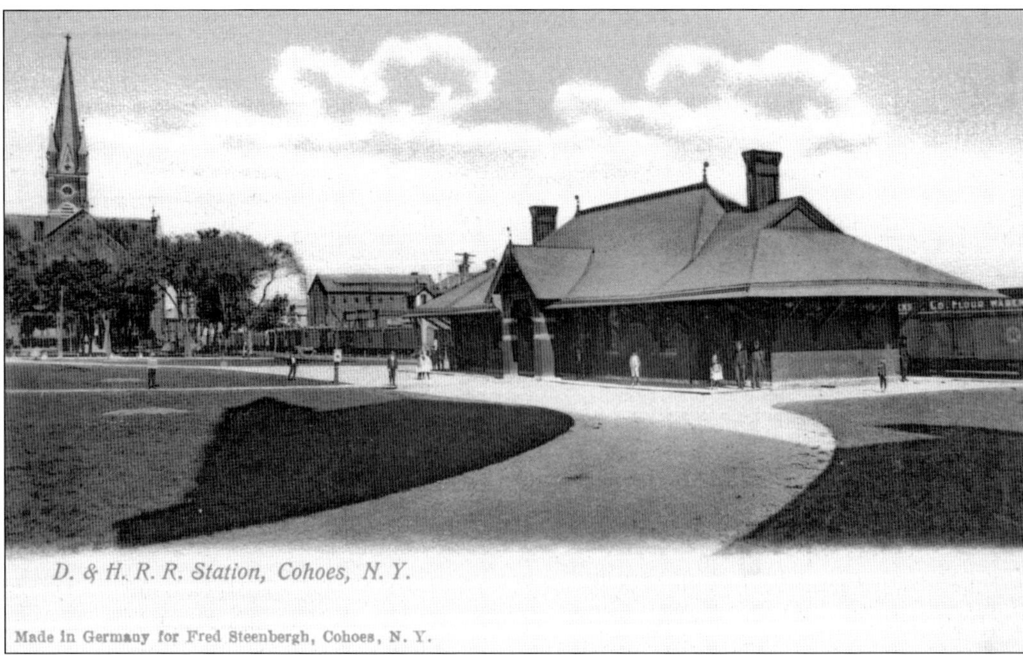

St. John's Episcopal Church was organized 17 years before Cohoes officially became a village. Among those instrumental in establishing the church was pioneering textile manufacturer David Wilkinson. The first church was built in 1831 on what was Richard Heamstreet's cow pasture, along what is now Oneida Street. The congregation grew with the development of Cohoes, and a larger church was needed. Land at Canvass and Mohawk Streets was purchased from the Cohoes Company in 1868, and a church designed by noted architect Richard Morris Upjohn was built. The church was lost to fire in 1894, and the cornerstone for a new church was set in 1896 at a ceremony with 500 in attendance. In 1971, a new St. John's Church was built on Vliet Boulevard. The 1896 church was converted to the Cohoes Public Library and is a widely recognized example of adaptive reuse.

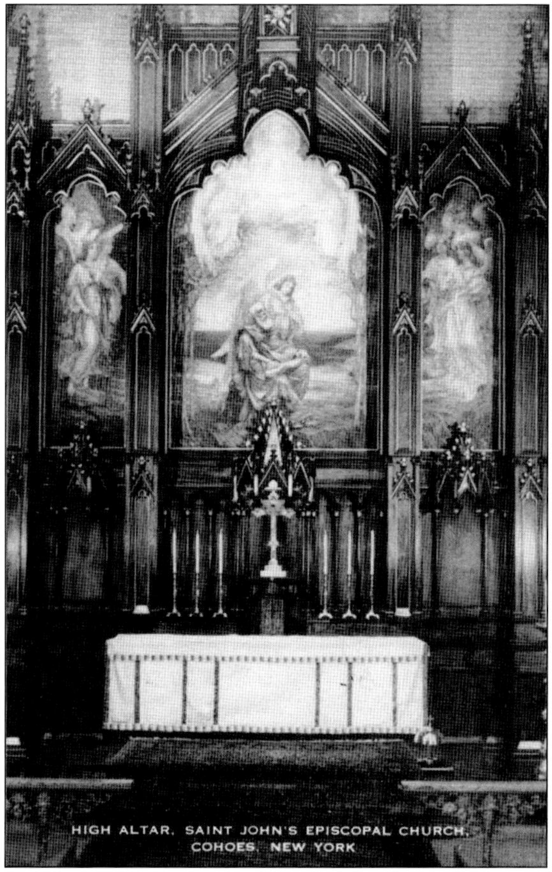


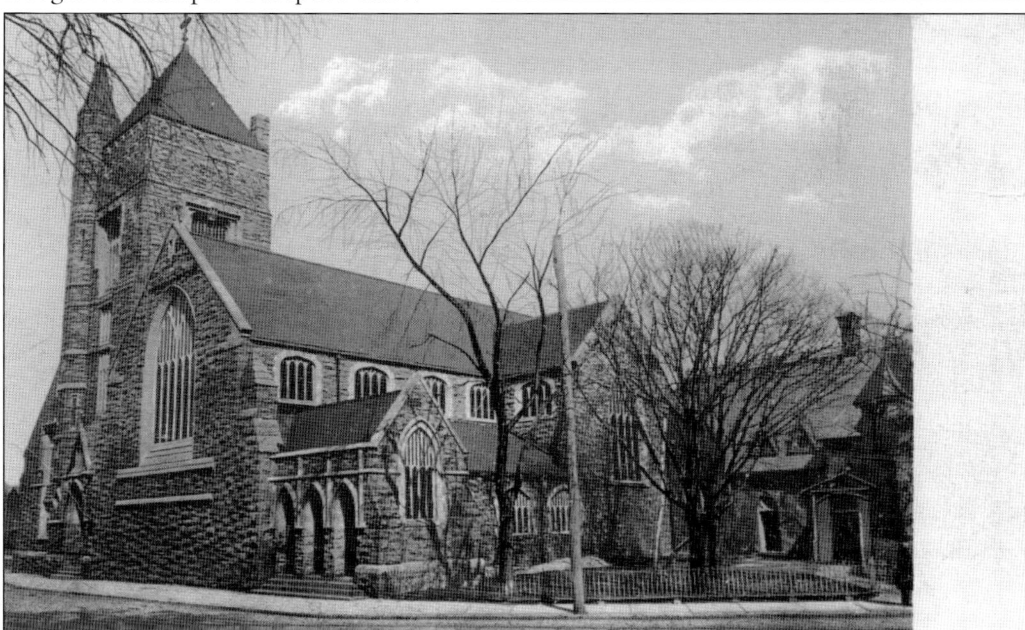

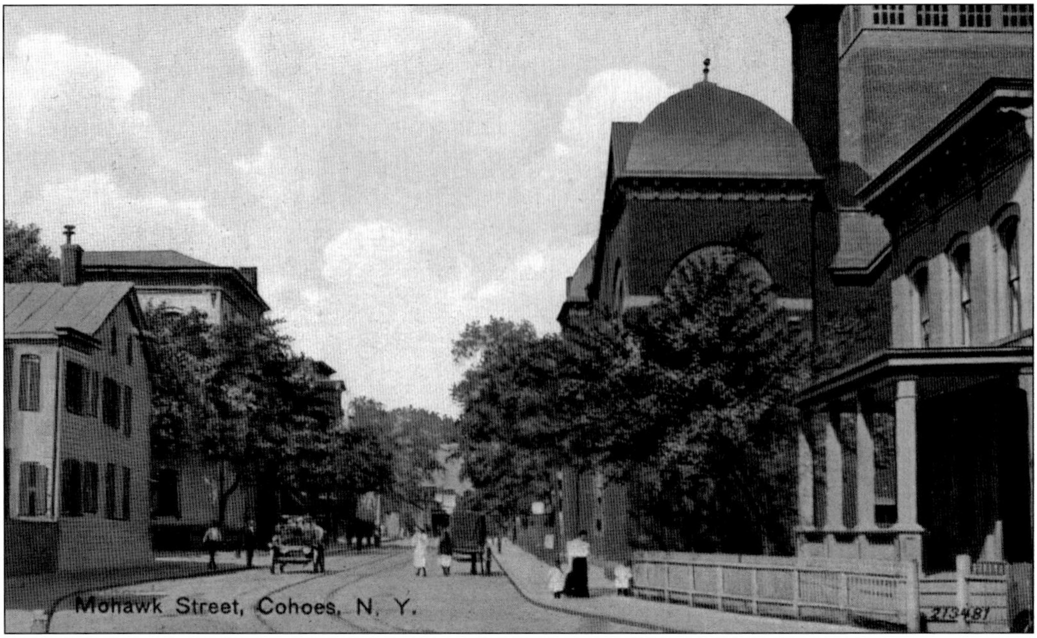


This view of the southern end of Mohawk Street shows the Baptist church on the right. The building on the left, an 1840s Federal-style house on the corner of Mohawk and White Streets, is among the few structures downtown that predate the city's industrial growth and one of the oldest houses in Cohoes. Mohawk Street was home to many of Cohoes's notable 19th-century industrialists, including axe manufacturer Daniel Simmons.

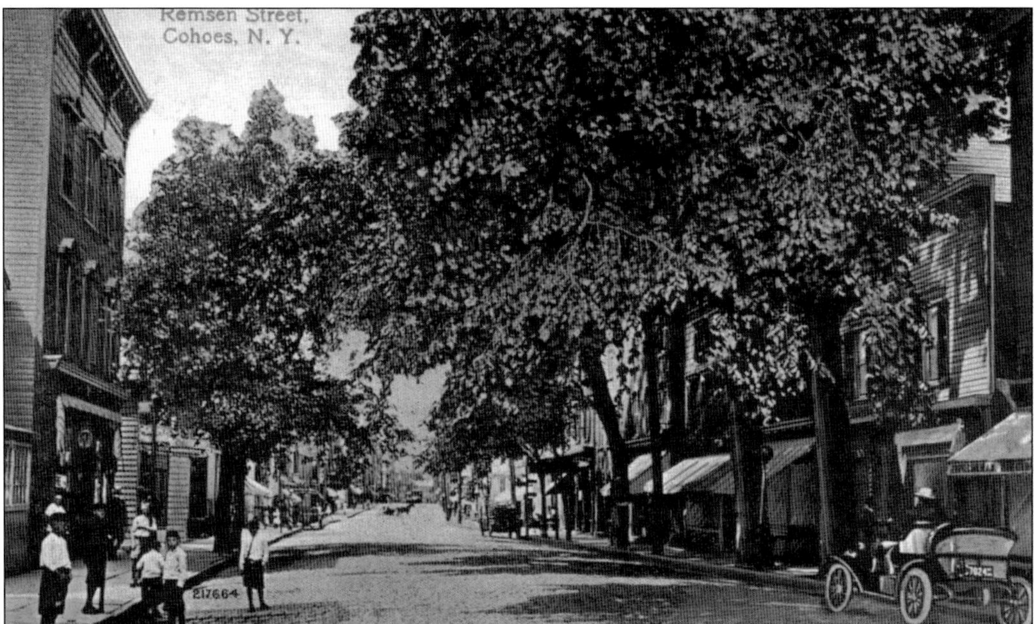


This c. 1910 view of a tree-lined Remsen Street shows the area between Howard and Columbia Streets. Among the businesses in this section were several barbershops, groceries, dressmakers, shoe repairers, a confectioner, a tailor, and a watchmaker. Note the brass-era cars parked along the street and the horse and wagon in the center of the street in the distance.

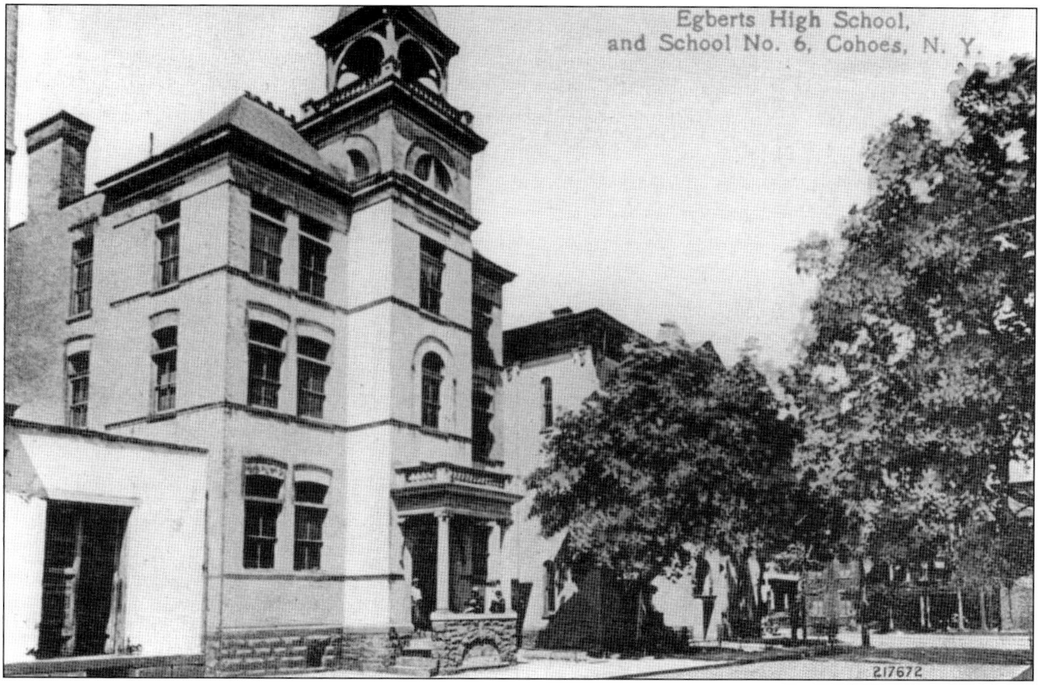


In 1863, the Egberts Institution was incorporated. The institution was endowed by industrialist and civic leader Egbert Egberts, who also presented a deed to a three-story building on White Street for use as a school. The school opened in September 1864. In 1868, the building was leased by the board of education for a high school. Evening classes were offered for students who worked at the mills during the day.

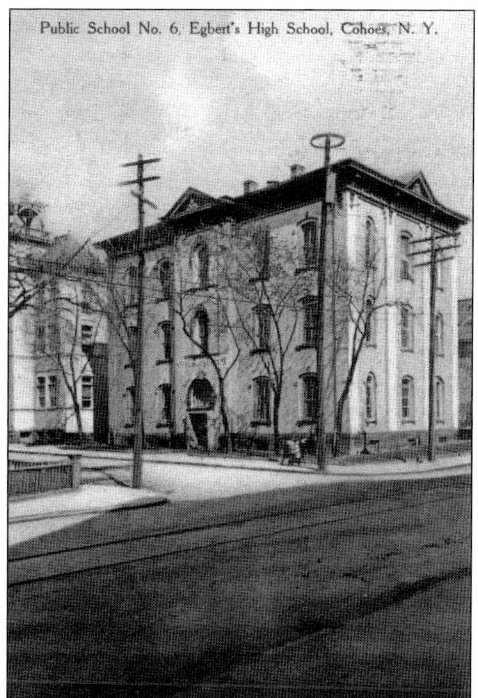


Public School No. 6, located on White Street next to Egberts High School, was built in 1871. The school, originally the White Street School, was the 3rd Ward grammar school until designated Public School No. 6 in 1897. Harriet Monk was the principal at this time. The village of Cohoes was among the first in the region to provide for free public education through local legislation passed in the 1850s.

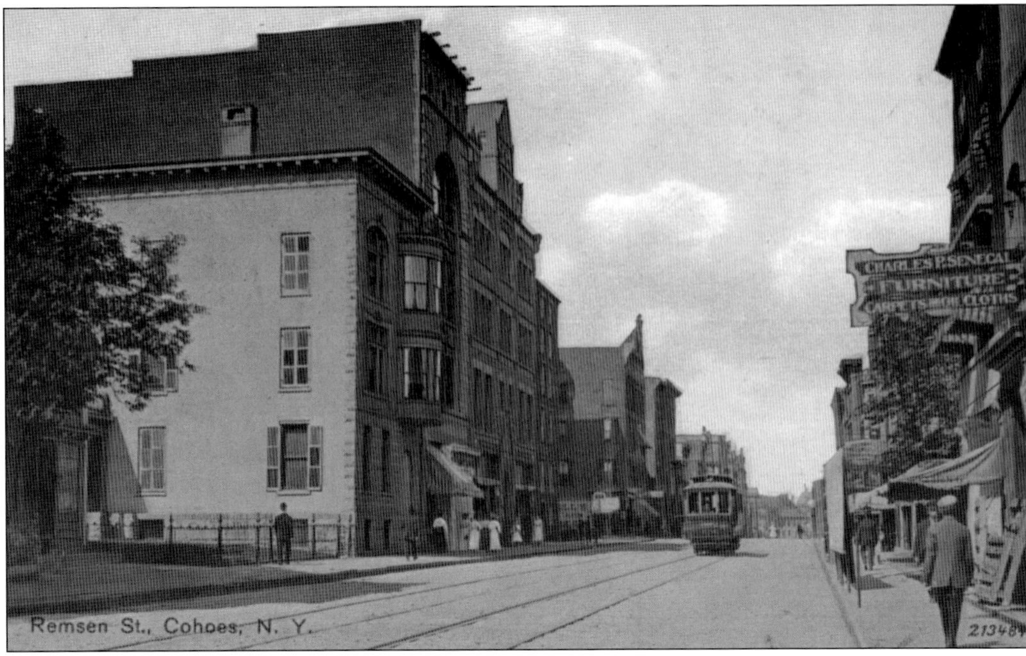


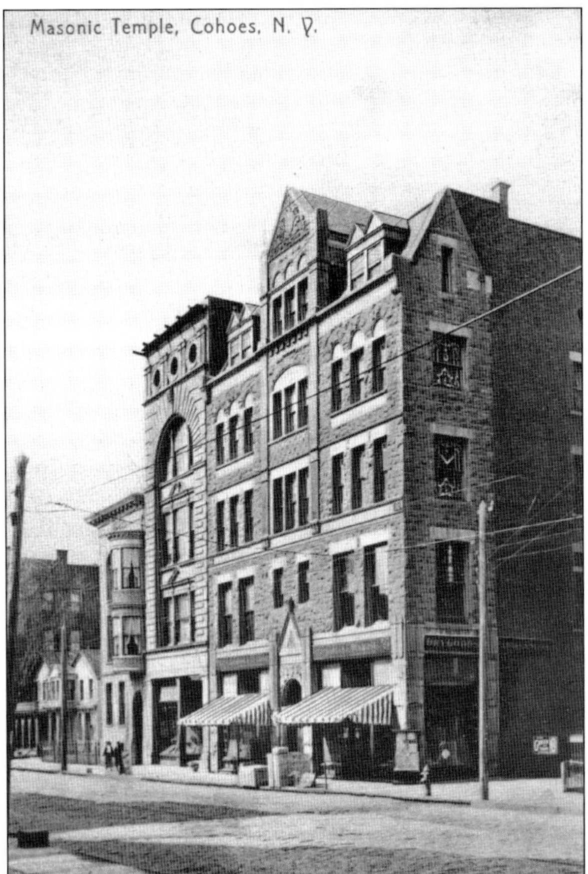


This block of Remsen Street contains the Masonic building, the opera house, and the Cohoes Hotel. The Cohoes Lodge of Masons was established in 1846, first meeting in a building at the corner of Factory and Remsen Streets. On August 21, 1895, the cornerstone for a building was laid at 128–130 Remsen Street, and 8,000 Masons participated in the ceremony. The temple, designed by architects Fielding and Mag from Troy, included a banquet hall on the fourth floor and a massive water-powered organ. Businesses occupied the first-floor storefronts. The Cohoes Opera House, opened in 1899, was a five-story brick-and-stone building between the Cohoes Hotel and the Masonic temple. Those appearing on its stage included the Barrymores, George M. Cohan, Eva Tanguay, Eddie Cantor, George Jessel, and Jimmy Durante. After vaudeville faded, the structure became a movie theater.

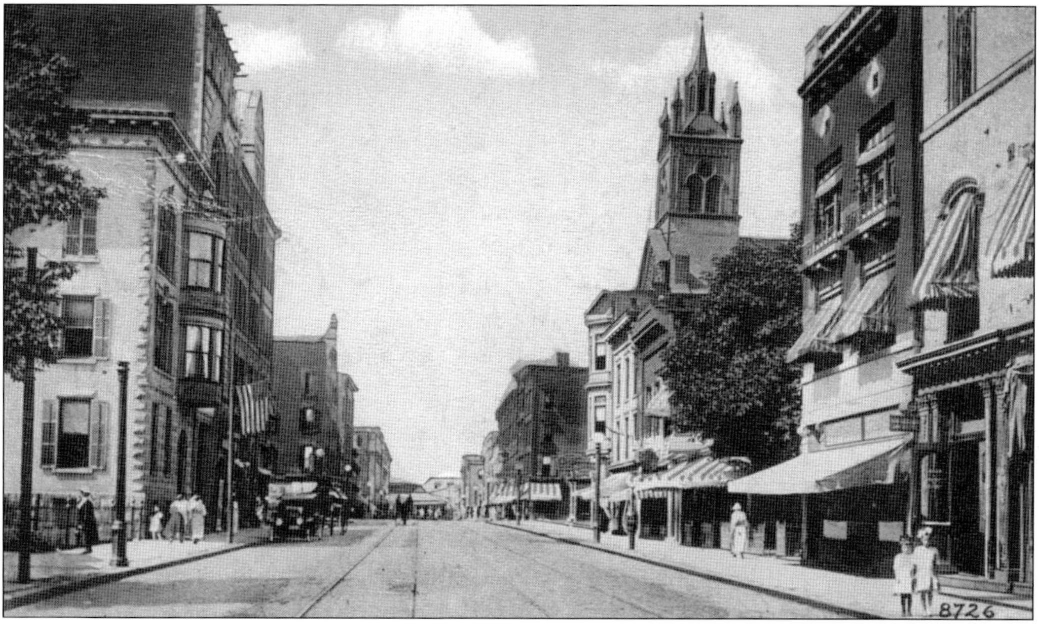

This view of Remsen Street shows the Cohoes Opera House and Cohoes Hotel on the left, and the Masonic building, which housed the Metropolitan Life Insurance Company. Opposite the Masonic building is the First Methodist Episcopal Church with its magnificent steeple. Along this section of Remsen Street, there were Ansel Carpenter's florist shop, Scotland & Munro Hardware dealers, and the jewelry and watch shops of Theodore Knoop and Thomas Timpane.

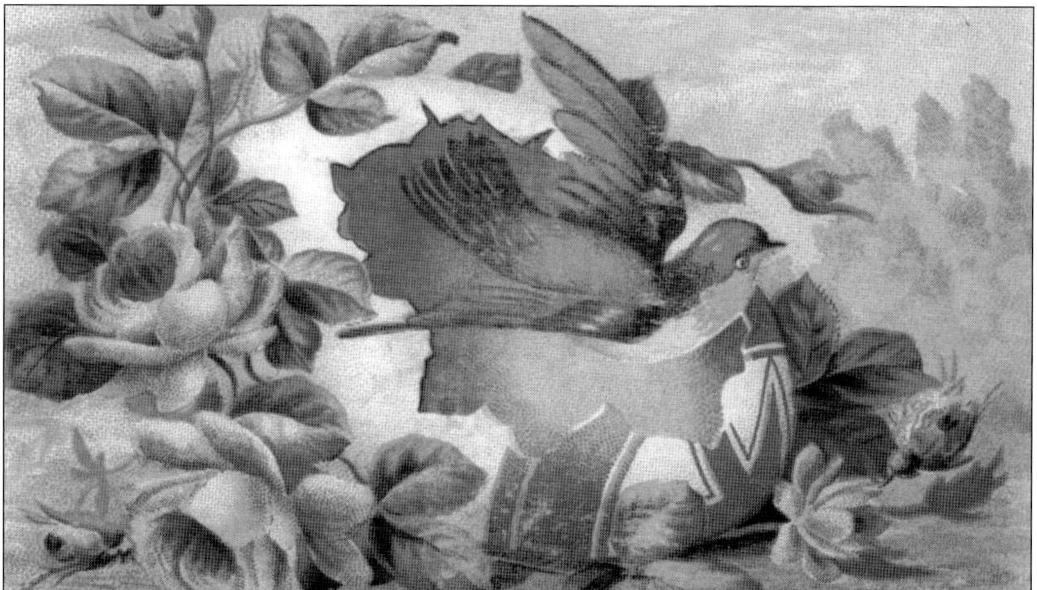

This trade card is from John Campbell's book and stationery store, located at 3 Adams Block on Remsen Street from the 1880s to 1900. He also dealt in clocks and silverware. The reverse of the card advertises Easter merchandise, including "the largest and most elegant variety of Easter Cards, fringed, satin and hand-painted" and a "large assortment of bibles, prayer books, hymnals, books, stationery and fancy goods."

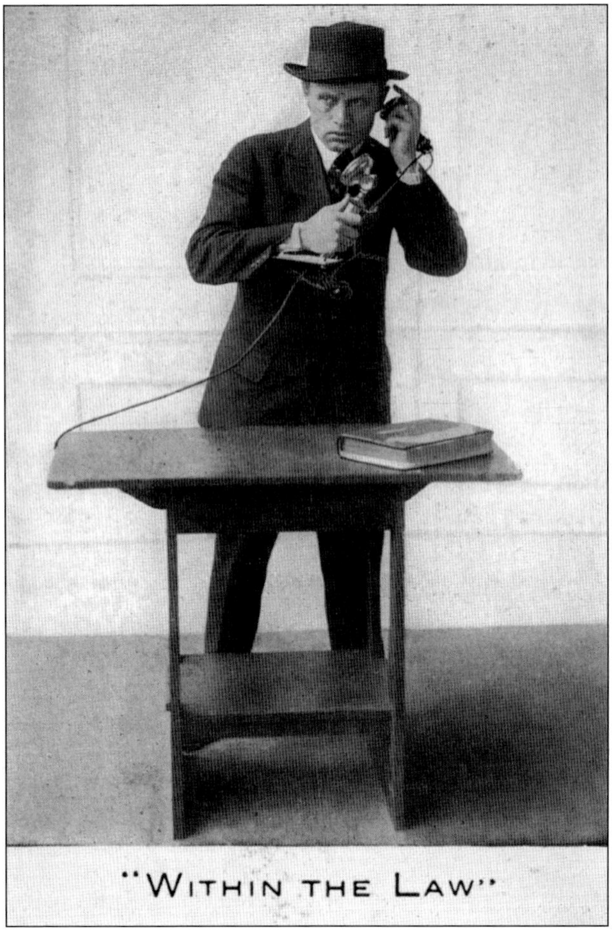


These postcards advertise *Within the Law*, a play by Bayard Veiller, presented on Tuesday, January 7, 1913, in Proctor's Theater. Frederick F. Proctor managed the theater in the Cohoes Opera House at 132 Remsen Street from 1910 to 1914. He was a former acrobat and aerialist who also managed and owned several other theaters in the Albany area. The Monday, January 6, 1913, *Troy Record* describes the play as "a modern play of metropolitan American life" and noted that "its originality of plot and elaborate investiture have brought only success in every city where it has been presented." The original Broadway production was in 1912, and films based on the popular play were produced in 1916, 1917, 1923, 1930, and 1939. The plot concerns a woman wrongly accused of theft and sent to prison who exacts revenge following her release.

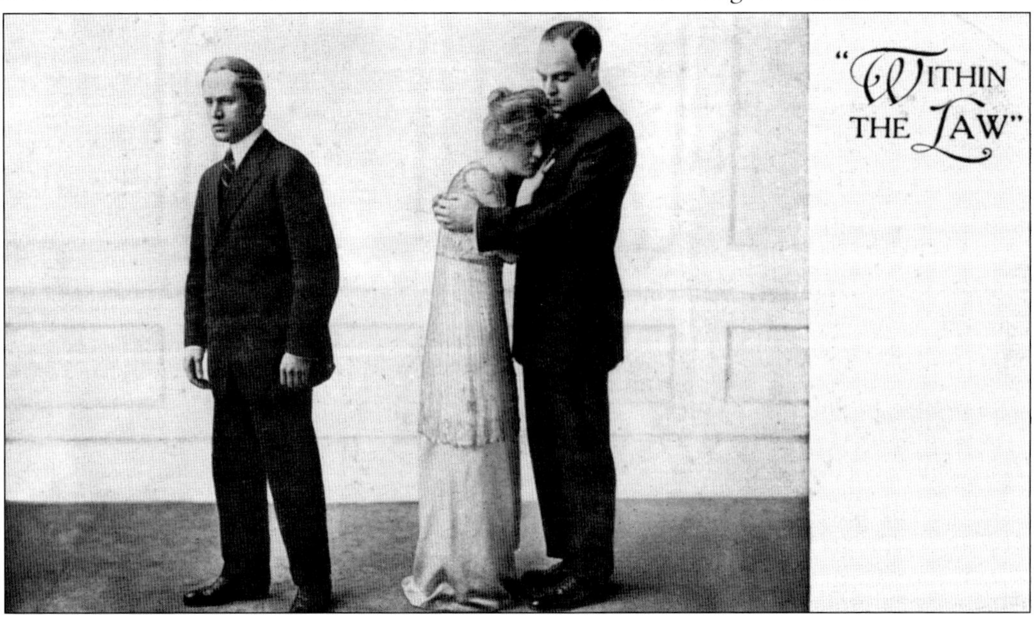

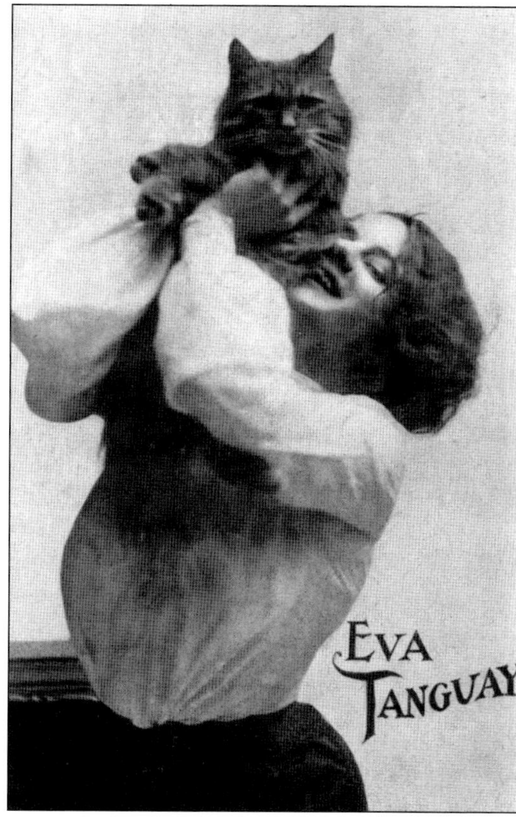


Eva Tanguay, the "I Don't Care" girl, was a vaudeville headliner born in Quebec in 1878; her family later moved to Cohoes. Stardom started in 1904, with Eva playing to capacity audiences, her salary ranging to $3,500 weekly. Her act was unique because of her songs, madcap humor, freakish costumes, and crop of tousled hair. It is lore that Eva first starred in an amateur hour at the Cohoes Opera House. Eva's daring songs like "I Want Someone To Go Wild with Me" and "It's All Been Done Before But Not the Way I Do It" had censors complaining while she was a box office smash. She said that one costume consisted of "two pearls." Fined for missing a matinee, she shredded a curtain and chided a manager onstage for lack of a large dressing room mirror. Eva died in 1947.

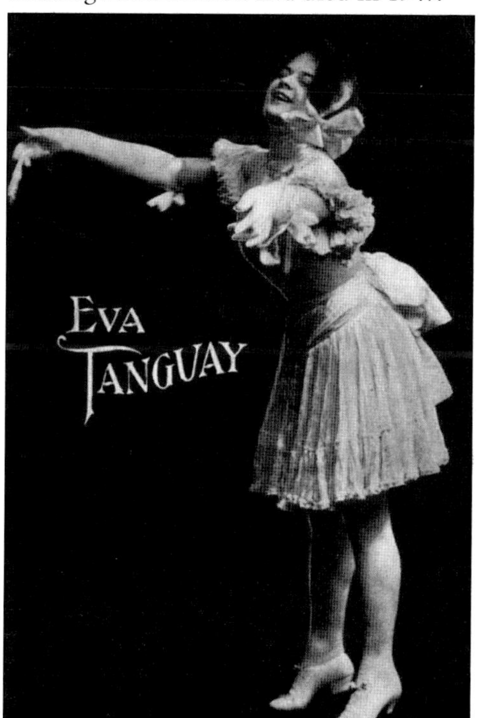

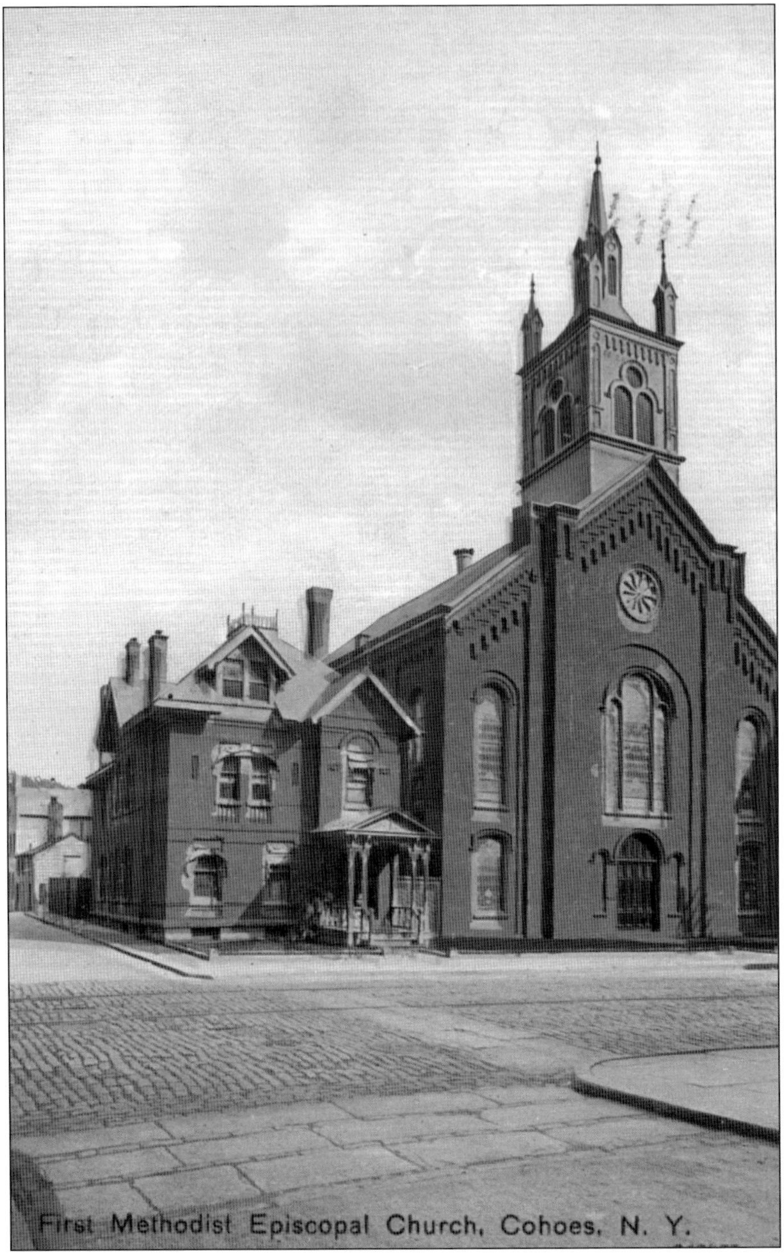


The First United Methodist Church on Remsen Street was dedicated in 1860. It replaced a smaller church built on the same site in 1848; the land on which the church was constructed was given to the congregation by the Harmony Company for the cost of $1, with the terms of the deed stating that the site be used only for religious or educational purposes. This church replaced an even earlier church on the other side of Remsen Street dedicated in 1841, two years after organization of the First Methodist Episcopal Society in Cohoes. The 1860 church building is still used as a house of worship, but the adjacent rectory on the corner of Remsen and Newcomb Streets was demolished. The Mechanics Bank Building, which later became Timpane's Jewelers, was built on the site. Just around the corner on Newcomb Street is an 1848 building that housed the Campbell Hose Co., the first firehouse in Cohoes.

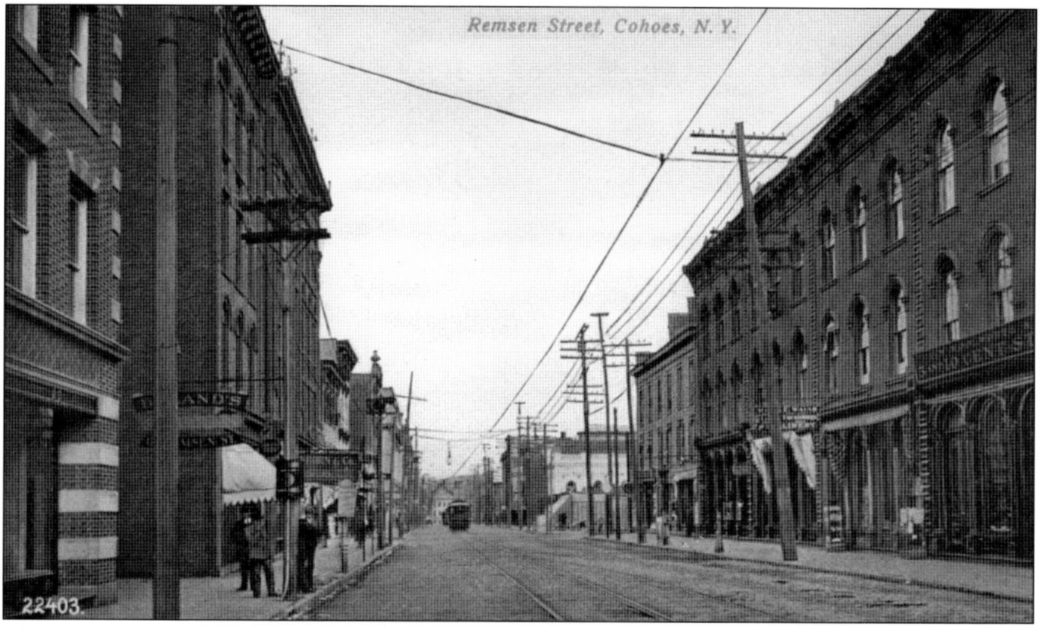


This view looks north on Remsen Street; the F.W. Woolworth five-and-dime store is on the right. Among other businesses in the block were N. Shaver, dealer in silks and dress goods, and Miss M. Craig, selling fashionable millinery. Remsen Street has been the center of the city's business district from the mid-19th century to the present. Note the trolley, tracks, and trolley power line.

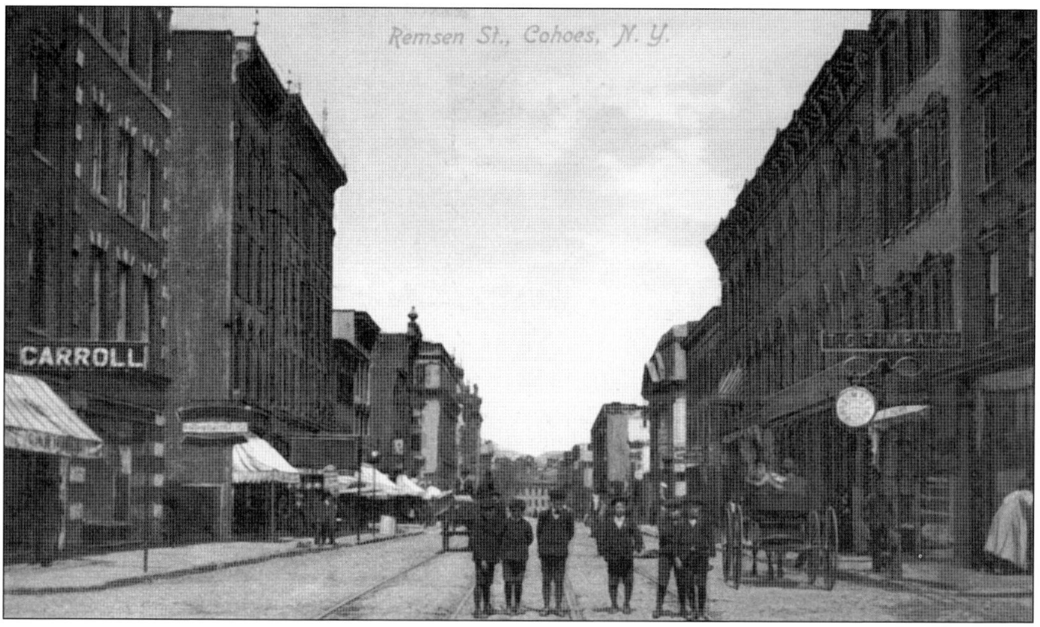


This c. 1910 Remsen Street view shows Carpenter's Florist Shop on the corner of Ontario Street and Knoop the Jeweler next door. Ansel Carpenter started Carpenter's in 1884 at 74 Younglove Avenue, relocating to 95 Remsen Street in 1909. Theodore Knoop opened a jewelry and watchmaking store in 1886 at 29 Remsen Street, later moving to 97 Remsen Street. His son Louis joined the business in 1908.

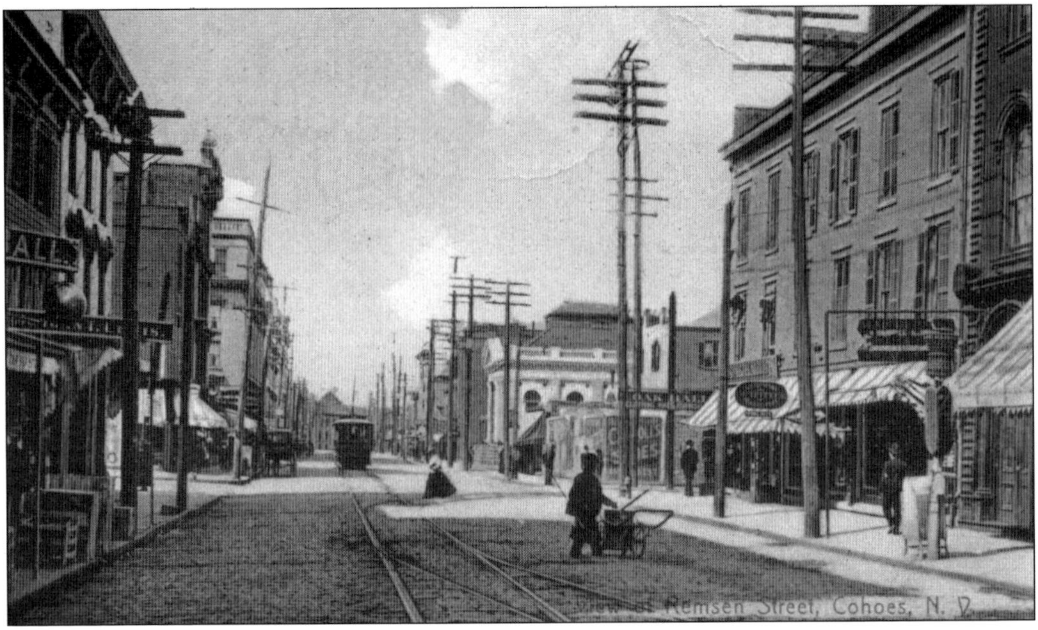


This c. 1900 view looking north on Remsen Street shows the Hayward feed mill at the corner of Ontario Street. On the right is the Adams Block, built in 1869. It was three stories tall and featured plate-glass windows, the first introduced in Cohoes, for the ground-floor businesses. James Carroll moved his boots and shoes store to Cohoes from Waterford in 1898, first opening at 129 Remsen Street.

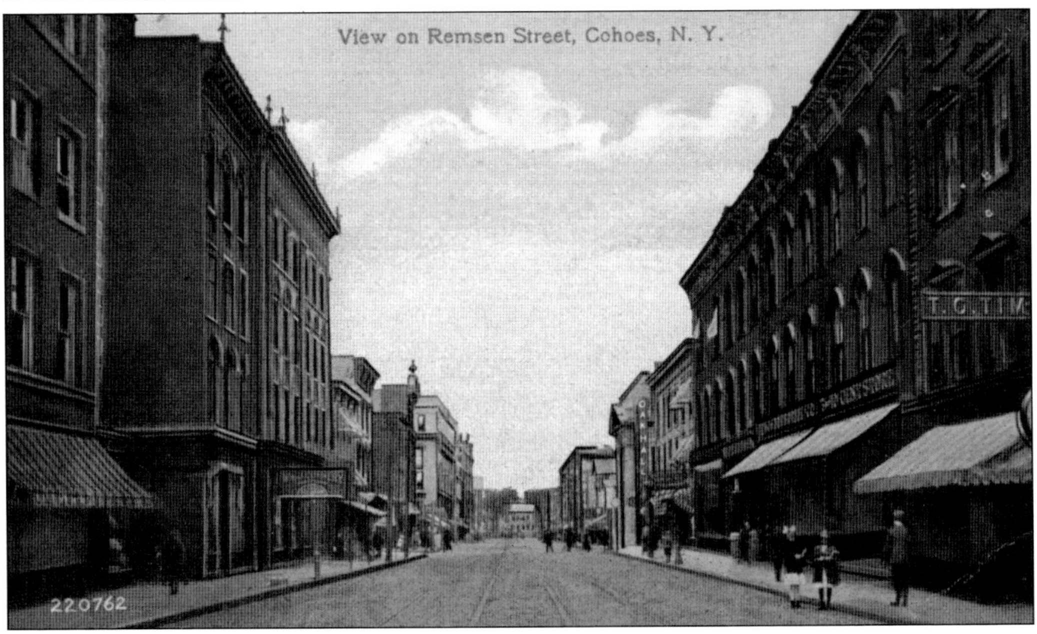


This later view of Remsen Street, around 1919, includes the People's Store, F.W. Woolworth & Co., and Timpanes on the right. Thomas Timpane began his jewelry business in 1894 at 57 Mohawk Street, moved to 71 Remsen Street in 1896, and then to 115 Remsen Street. In 1924, his son T. Brandon Timpane, an optometrist, joined him in business; in 1946, they relocated to 119 Remsen Street.

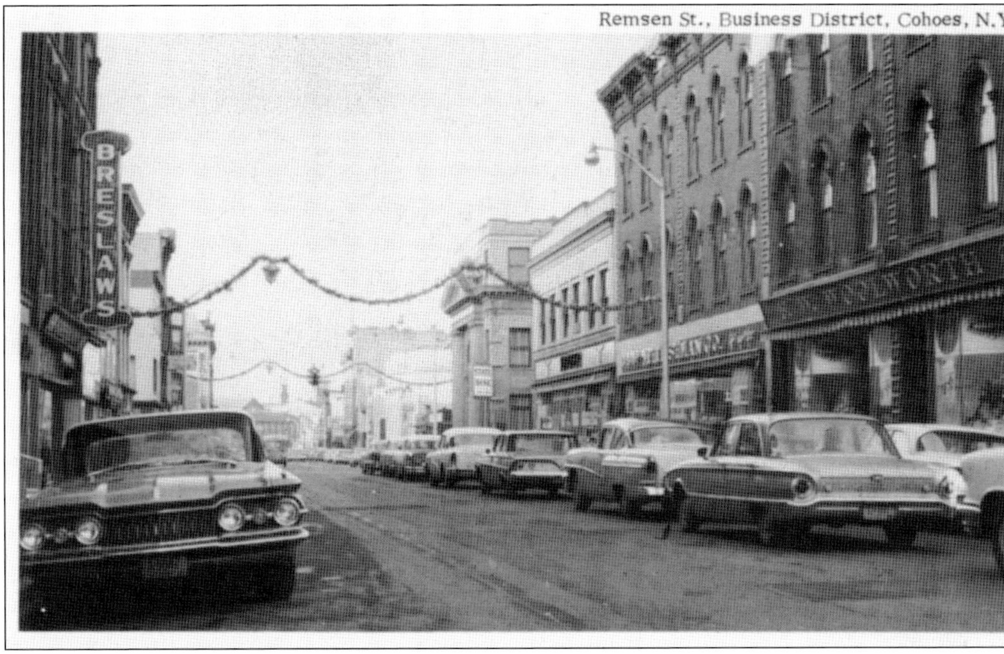


This mid-1960s postcard shows Remsen Street decorated for Christmas. Hundreds of electric lights were put up from Columbia Street to the north end to create "Santa Claus Lane." The merchants on Remsen Street stayed open every night in the month of December until 8:30. Businesses at the time included Irwin Jewelers, Cohoes Music Center, Carroll's Shoe House, Juliette's, Mr. Jules, Marra's Pharmacy, Miron's, Timpane's, Smith Electric, Breslaw's, Woolworth's, and Fishman's.

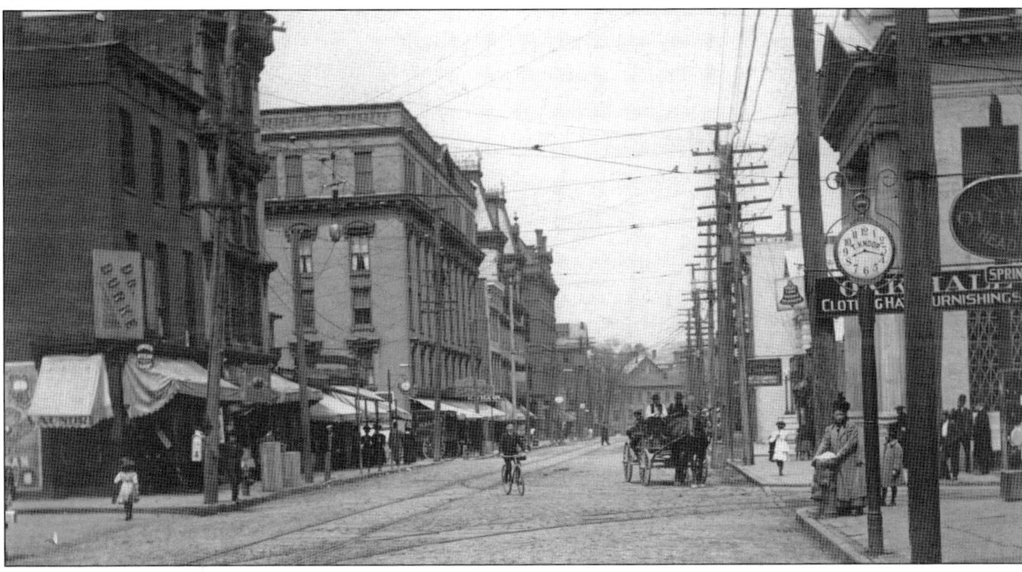

This view of Remsen Street dates from 1908, when Michael R. Burke opened his dentistry office at 94 Remsen Street, on the corner of Ontario Street. Across Remsen Street was the Oak Hall Clothing House, located in Granite Hall. The store opened in 1905 and remained in business until 1919. Dr. Burke moved his offices to 122 Remsen Street in 1920 and remained in practice until his death in 1956.

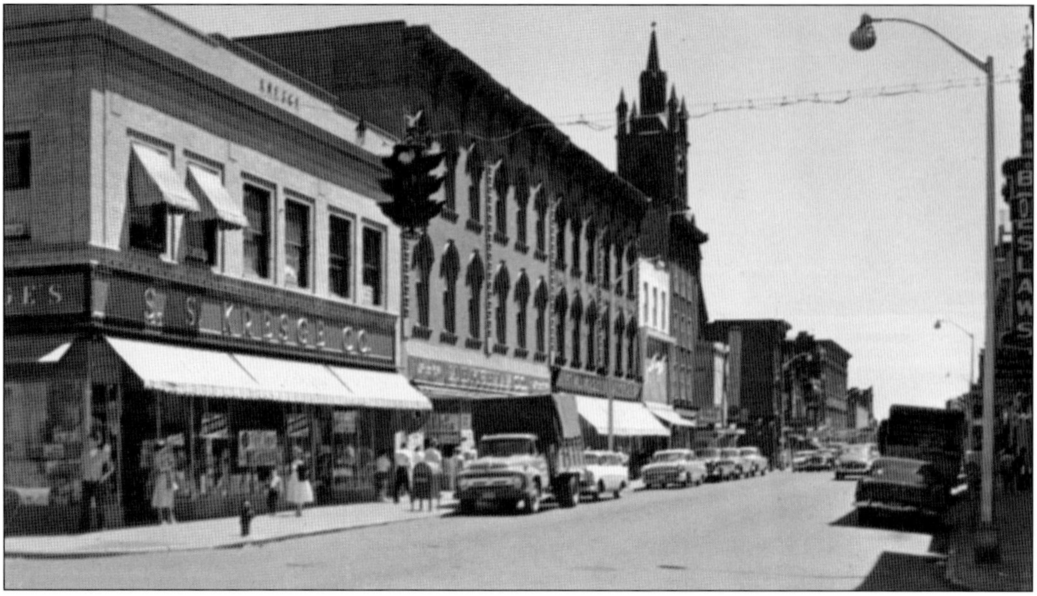


This early-1960s view of Remsen Street shows three of the city's long-standing department stores. From left to right are S.S. Kresge, M.H. Fishman, and F.W. Woolworth. Both Kresge's and Fishman's were at this location for over three decades, and Woolworth for over nine decades, closing in 1995. Kresge's was replaced by the Jupiter Department Store in 1964. Fishman's opened in 1946, managed by Samuel Fishman of Waterford.

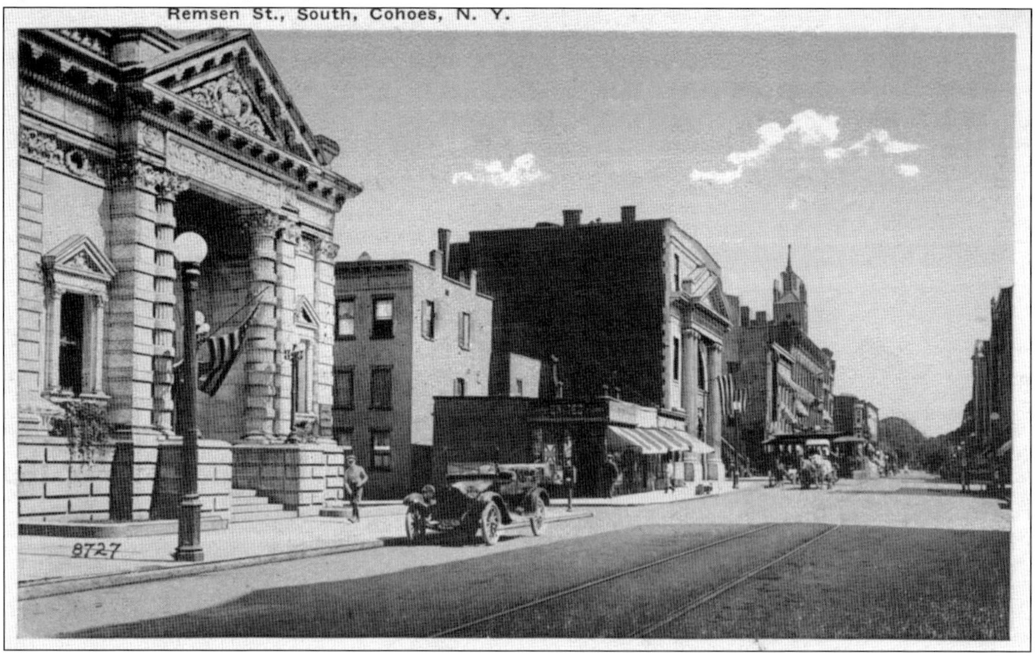


This c. 1920 view of Remsen Street looking south shows the Cohoes Savings Institution and the Manufacturers Bank. Businesses located between the bank buildings included C.A. Whalen Co., Inc., Cigar and Tobacco Dealer, which became the United Cigar Store Co. in 1919, and Edward A. Wallace Men's Furnishings. At 85 Remsen was Michael Vavaras, Bootblack, which became Mengepes Bros. Bootblack in 1920 and the New York Shoeshine Parlor in 1922.

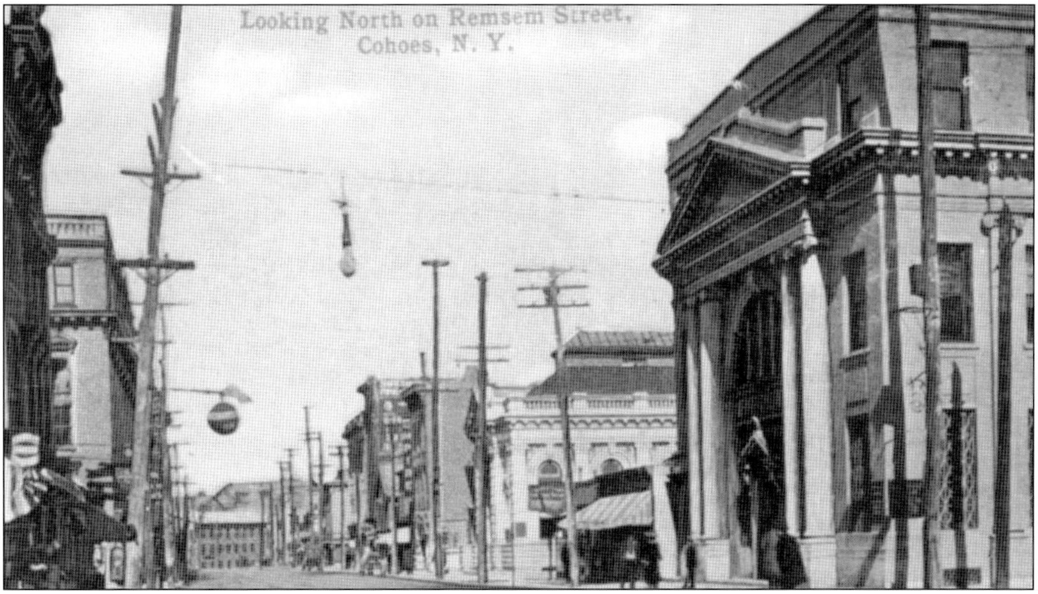


This view looks north on Remsen Street from the corner of Ontario Street. The Manufacturers Bank is on the immediate right, with the Cohoes Savings Bank and Empire Theater farther down the block on the eastern side of Remsen Street. The Wilcox & Co. Dry Goods and Carpet House is the large building on the left side of the street, across from the Manufacturers Bank. Note the electric arc lamp overhead.

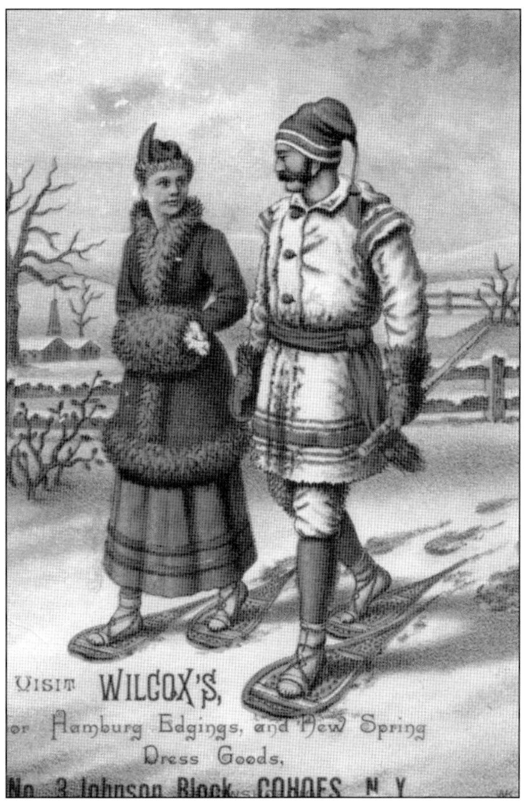


This 1882 trade card is from the Wilcox & Co. Dry Goods and Carpet House. The store was opened by Rodney Wilcox in 1878 at 64 Remsen Street, moved to 76 Remsen Street in 1886, and expanded to 74 Remsen Street in 1892. After Wilcox's death in 1920, his widow, Loretta, continued the business until 1923, when the store with the "widest variety of merchandise in the vicinity" closed.

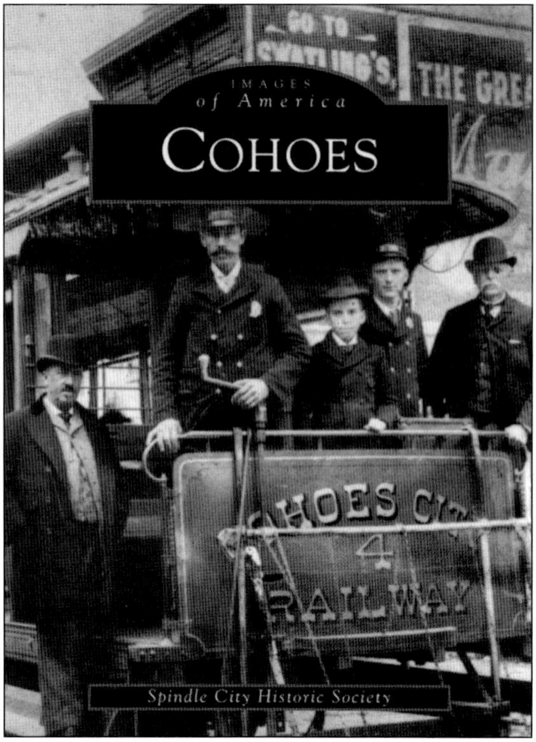



*Cohoes,* Spindle City Historic Society's first book, offers views of the city from the late 19th century through the 1940s. It chronicles the history of Cohoes in numerous images acquired from individual and group collections. It provides tremendous insight into how Cohoes got on the map as a canal-side village and later an industrial center, while acknowledging the many contributions over time of its citizens, both humble and well known.

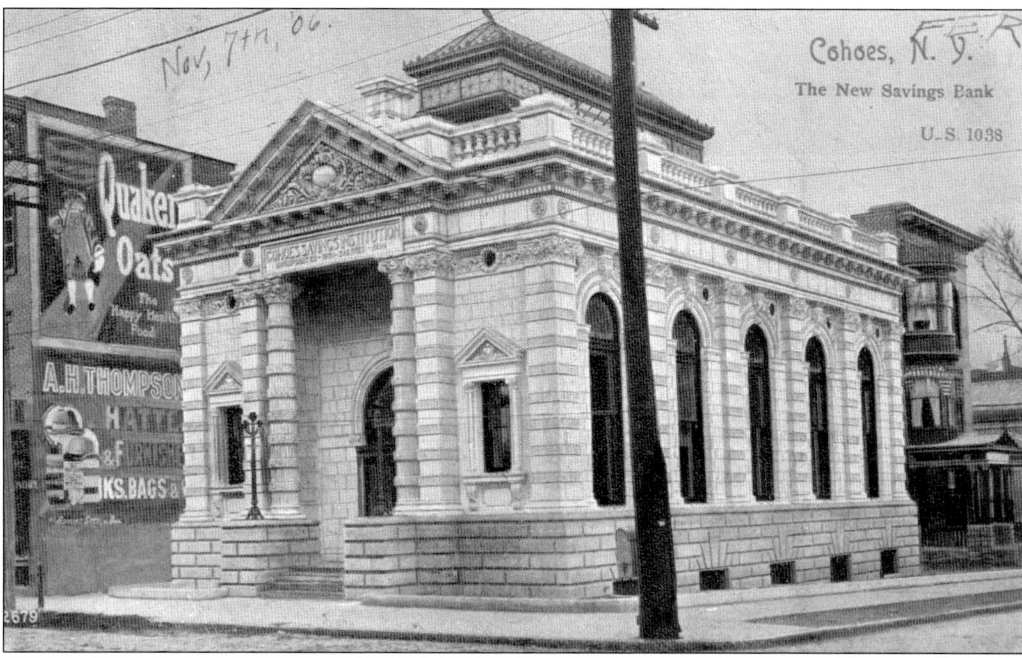



The Cohoes Savings Institution was established in April 11, 1851, as a bank owned solely by its depositors. It opened at 59 Oneida Street in 1853. Cohoes was a village of only 4,000 inhabitants, and local businesspeople founded the institution to serve themselves and their neighbors. The first president was Egbert Egberts. Although its first day deposits were $81 from three depositors, in four years, the deposits climbed to $29,248.78.

W.T. Eccles, dealer in boots and shoes, was located at 41 Remsen Street from 1878 to 1889. The business moved to 43 Remsen Street, where it remained until 1901. This trade card from the 1880s advertised men's calf shoes for $3 in balmoral, button, and congress styles, as well as "new style ladies' kid button boots, scallop top and fancy tip." Every pair of boots and shoes was warranted.

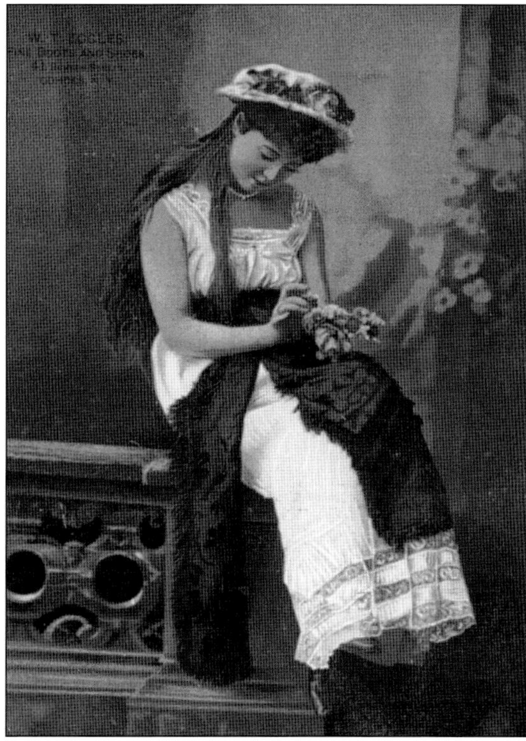

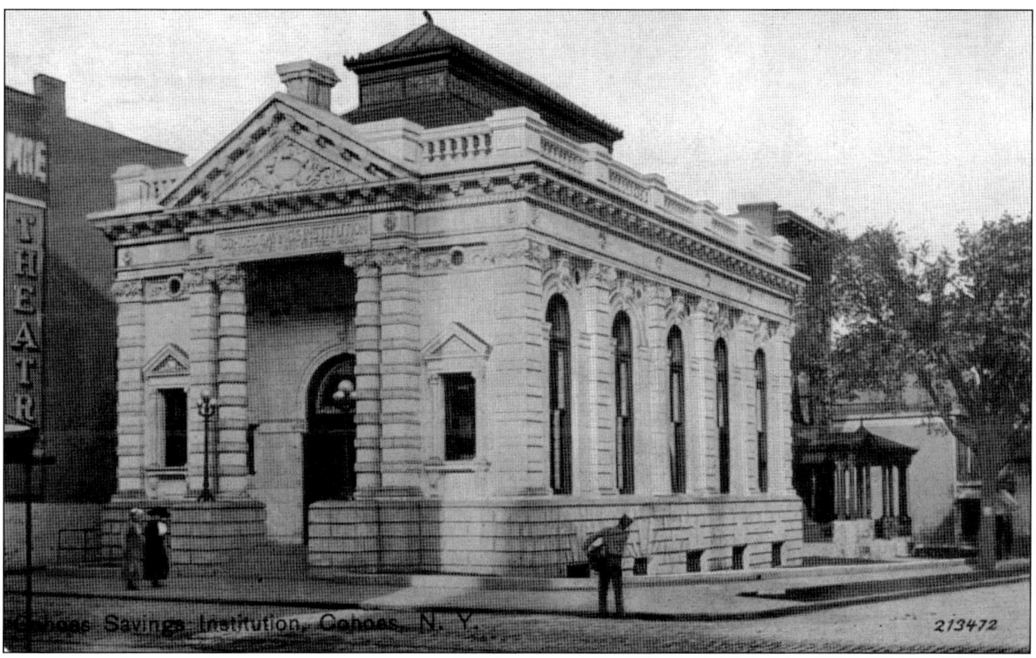


This postcard view of Cohoes Savings Bank on the corner of Remsen and Seneca Streets also shows St. Bernard's convent, adjacent to the bank on Seneca Street. The sisters, who taught at Keveny Memorial Academy, moved here after a 1939 fire at their convent, located on the corner of Mohawk and Ontario Streets. This Seneca Street building was later home to the Cohoes Senior Citizens Center from 1974 to 1978.

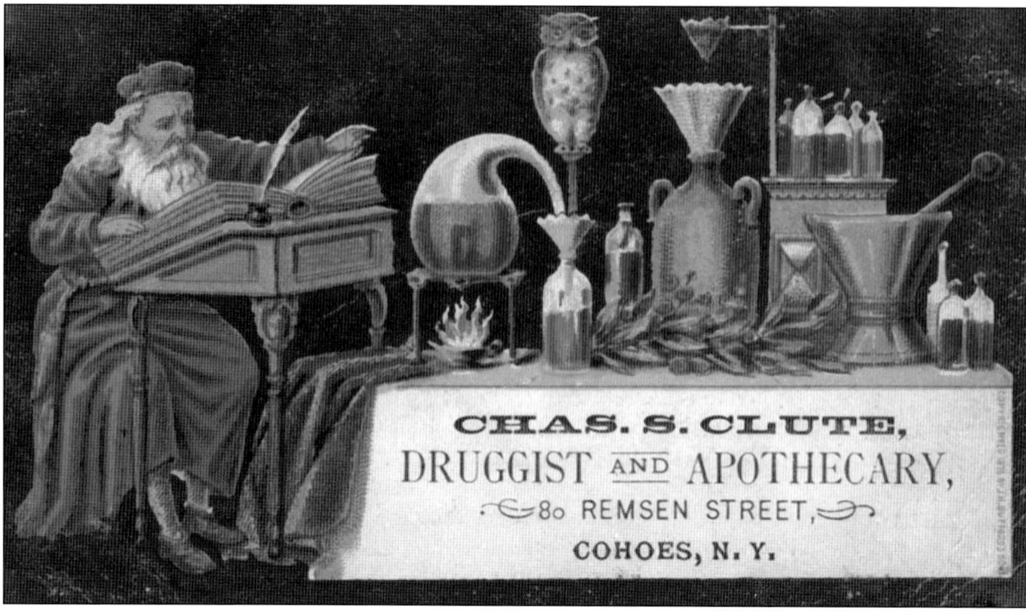


Clute and Baillie operated an apothecary at 80 Remsen Street. In 1883, Charles S. Clute took sole ownership of the business. The apothecary shop moved to 86 Remsen Street until its closing in 1888. The store filled prescriptions, "compounded with great care," and sold soaps, perfumes, hairbrushes, combs, hand glasses, powders, toilet waters, sponges, and chamois. Along with these items, the store offered pure wines, liquors, and cigars.

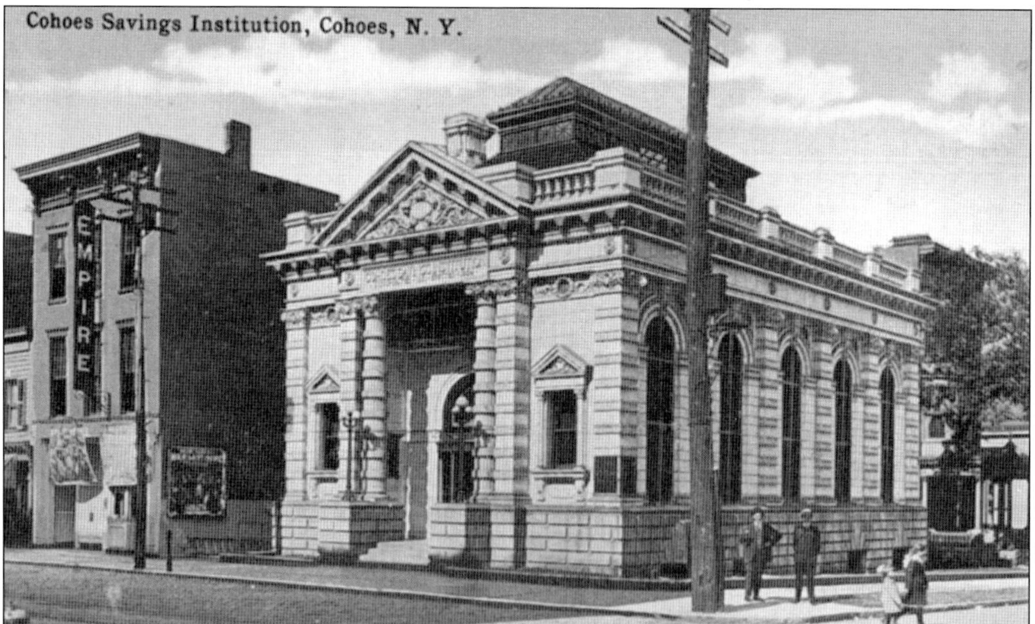


This view of Cohoes Savings Bank, a terra-cotta Beaux-Arts building constructed in 1905, also shows the Empire Theater, located at 77 Remsen Street, which opened in 1912. Thomas Timpane of Cohoes and J. Duffy of Troy owned the theater. In 1914, there was a fire at the theater, and 100 people safely exited the burning building. The estimated loss due to the fire was $5,000.

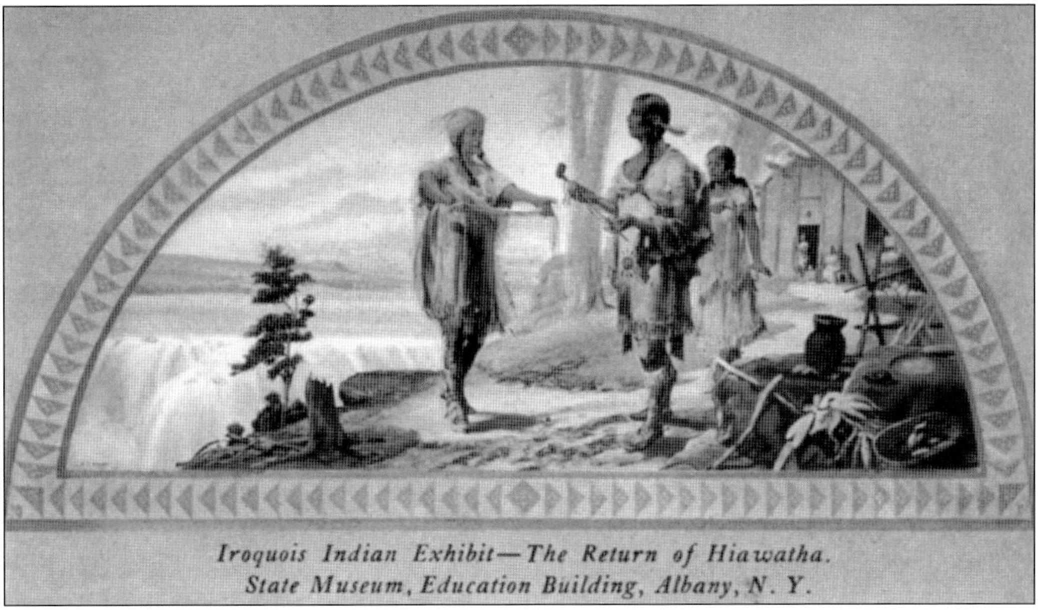


In 1950, under the presidency of James Calkins, the office of Marcus T. Reynolds, architects, did remodeling of the Cohoes Savings Bank. The project included murals by David Cunningham Lithgow, depicting Indian legends and the falls, the coming of Europeans, the birth of industry, and the discovery of the Cohoes Mastodon. In 1951, the bank produced booklets describing the murals and bank's history. These murals are intact today.

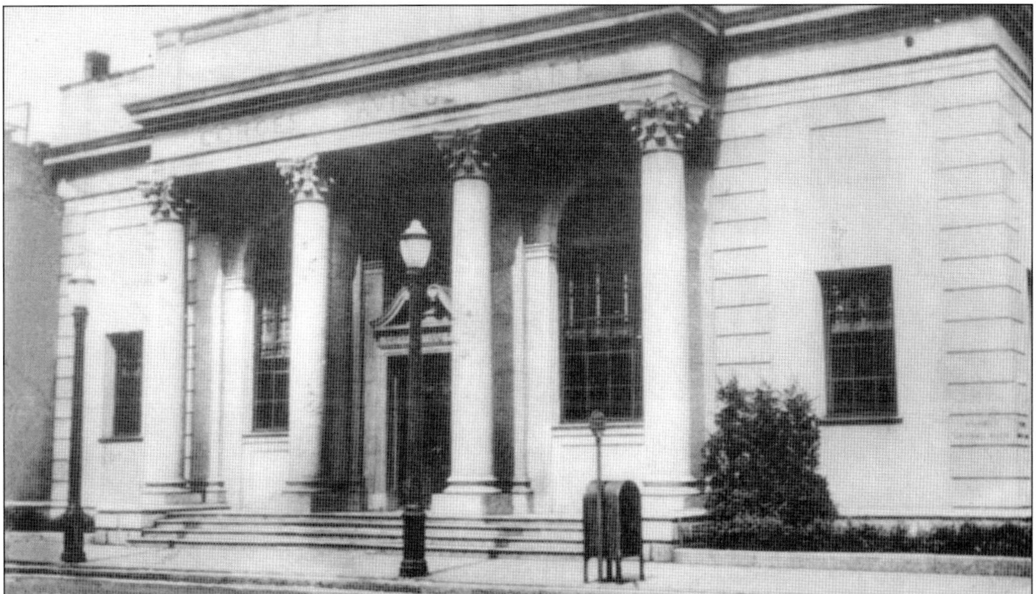


The lot at the corner of Remsen and Seneca Streets was purchased and a new building for the Cohoes Savings Institution was completed in 1905. The Cohoes Savings Institution was renamed the Cohoes Savings Bank in 1922. In December 1923, bank president George McDowell realized that the bank's quarters were inadequate, so an adjoining plot at 75 Remsen Street was purchased and an addition to the existing building was erected.

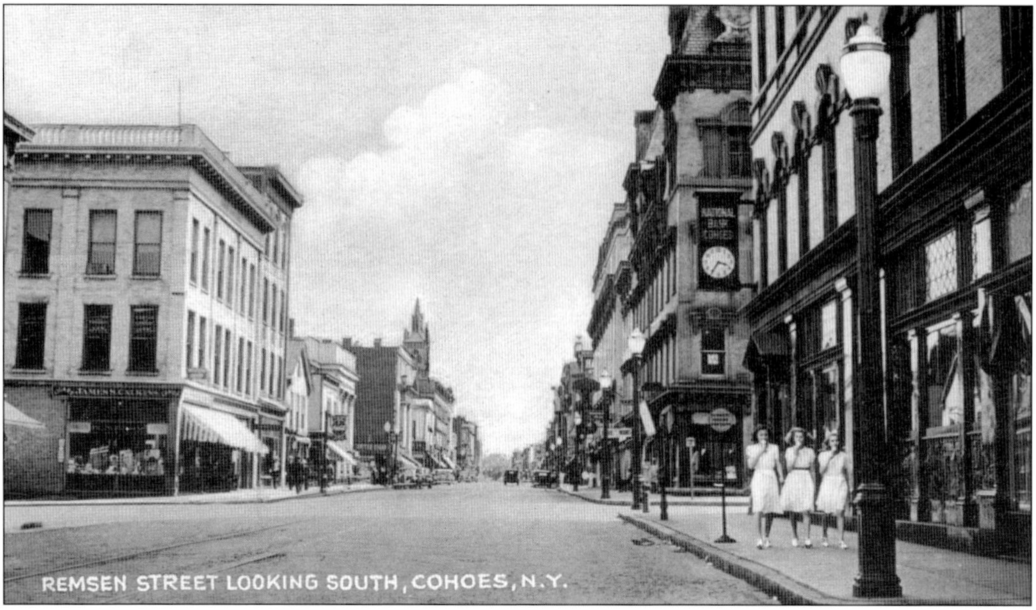


Three young women, in the 1940s, are walking past the National Bank Building on Remsen Street with ice cream, likely from the Wilfrid LaMarche Confectionery Shop across the street. The LaMarche store remained in business at the Germania Building through the beginning of the 21st century. The Buchanan and Wilcox Buildings are just to the south of the bank. Note the Coca-Cola sign on the east side of the street.

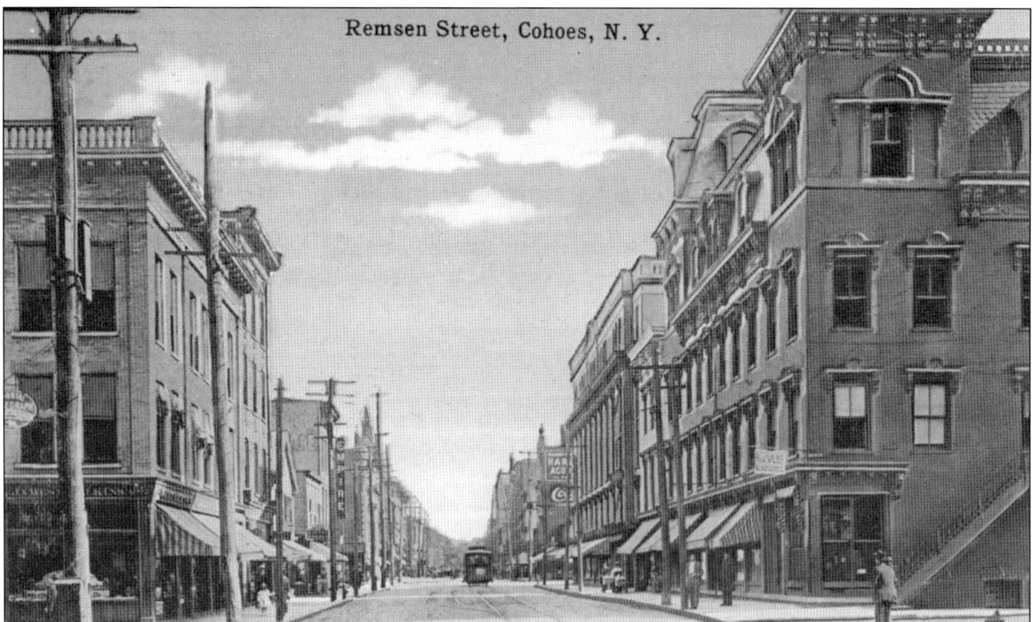


This earlier view of the same section of Remsen Street brings fond recollections of the Cohoes Conservatory of Music, established in 1924 by sisters Marie and Eugenie Lajeunesse. It was on the second floor of 63 Remsen Street in the Carter Block, designed by Cohoes architect Aaron Goddard. Many Cohoesiers learned to play piano there and performed in annual recitals. Calkins Pharmacy was on the ground floor of the building.

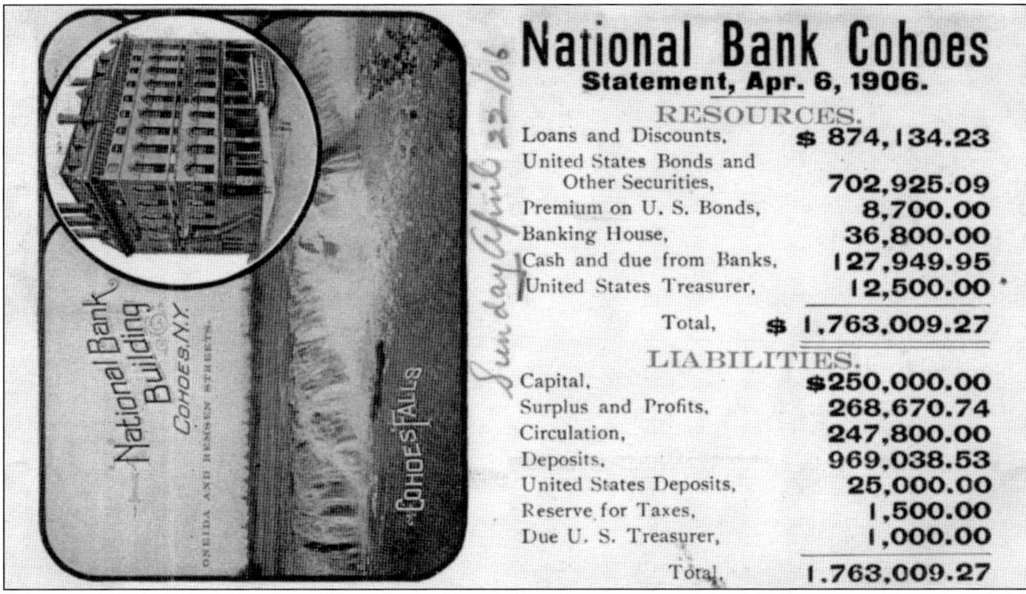


# National Bank Cohoes

**Statement, Apr. 6, 1906.**

RESOURCES.

| | |
|---|---|
| Loans and Discounts, | $ 874,134.23 |
| United States Bonds and Other Securities, | 702,925.09 |
| Premium on U. S. Bonds, | 8,700.00 |
| Banking House, | 36,800.00 |
| Cash and due from Banks, | 127,949.95 |
| United States Treasurer, | 12,500.00 |
| Total, | $ 1,763,009.27 |

LIABILITIES.

| | |
|---|---|
| Capital, | $250,000.00 |
| Surplus and Profits, | 268,670.74 |
| Circulation, | 247,800.00 |
| Deposits, | 969,038.53 |
| United States Deposits, | 25,000.00 |
| Reserve for Taxes, | 1,500.00 |
| Due U. S. Treasurer, | 1,000.00 |
| Total, | 1,763,009.27 |

In 1873, William Acheson and James Masten (the brother-in-law of Pres. Chester Arthur) erected a building at Remsen and Oneida Streets. The total cost of construction was $60,000. The building included a first-floor post office and shops, second-floor offices, and the third-floor music hall. It was later home to the National Bank of Cohoes (note the 1906 statement with the Cohoes Falls). The first bank officials in 1859 included Egbert Egberts, Daniel Simmons, T.G. Younglove, Wm.G. Caw, W.F. Carter,, and C.H. Adams. In 1882, the bank moved to the first floor of the music hall. D.J. Johnston was president in 1893. The bank took ownership of the building in 1905 and was forced to close the music hall for safety reasons. In 1968, the bank transferred the building to the City of Cohoes for $1. The hall was restored and reopened in 1975.

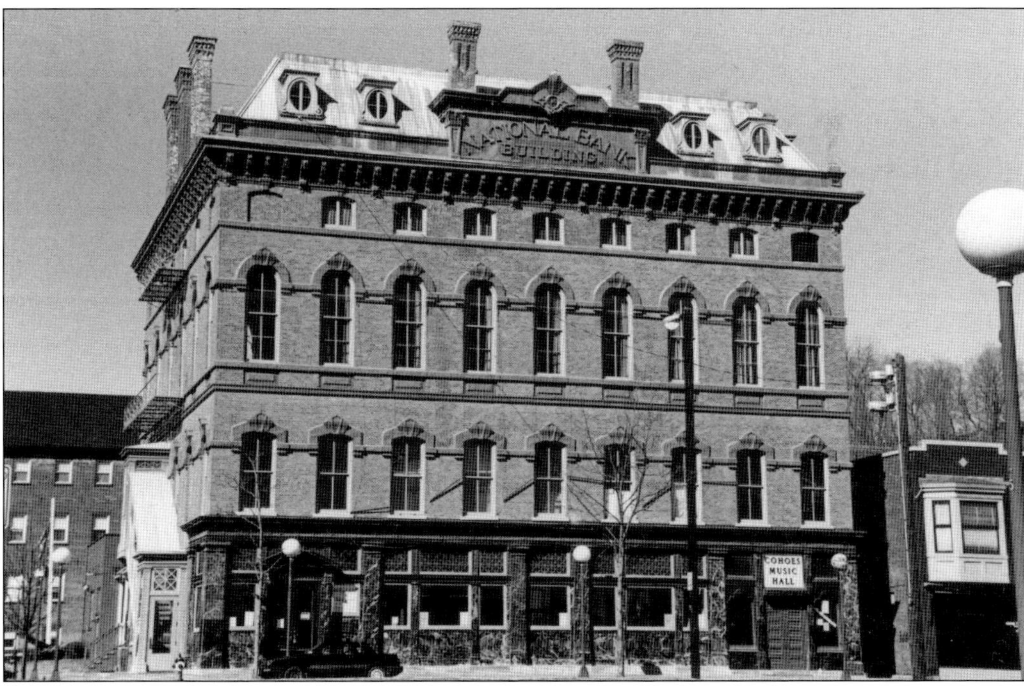

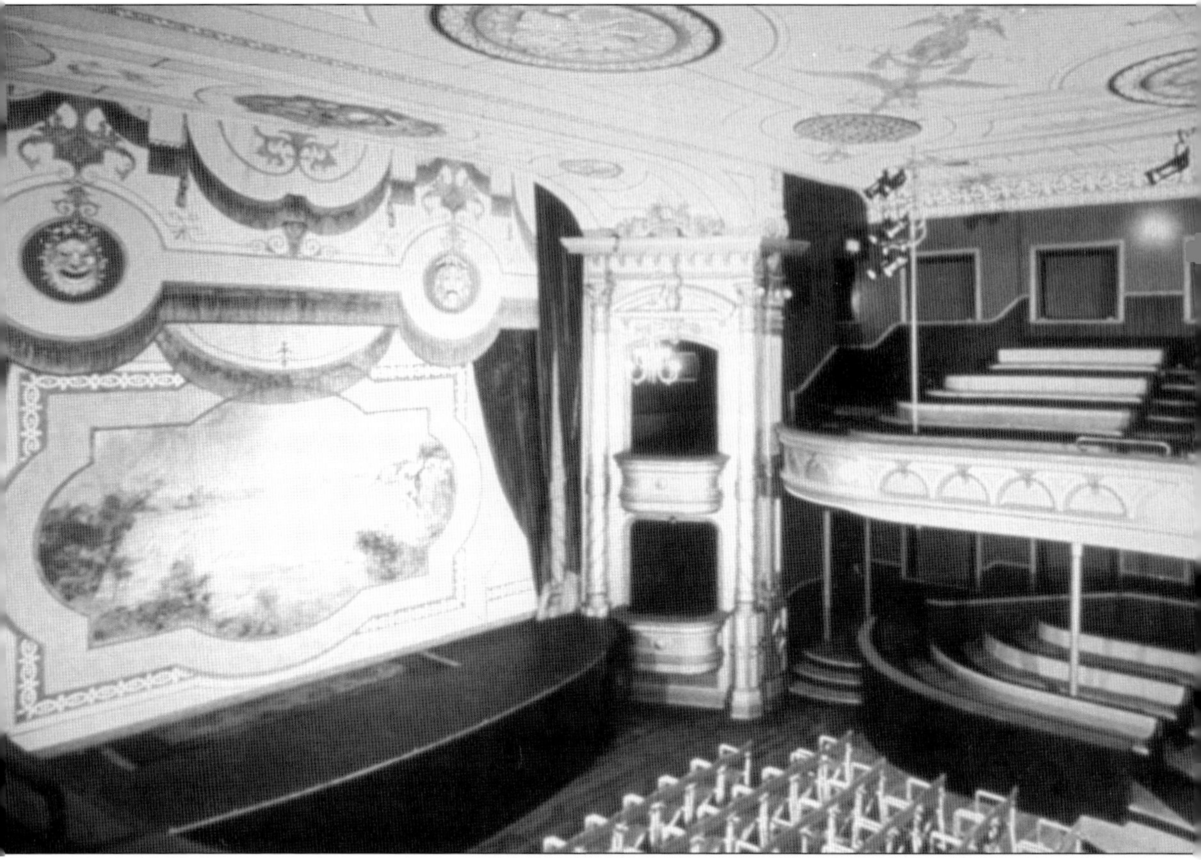

The music hall grand opening was on November 23, 1874, with a performance of *London Assurance*. The decor was a fine example of 19th-century French Renaissance style in pearl and gold, lit by gas, seating 475. The drop curtain had a scene of Lake Lugano, Italy. The building's redbrick exterior was manufactured in Cohoes. Notable performers included Buffalo Bill Cody, John Philip Sousa, General Tom Thumb, P.T. Barnum's baby elephant Hunky Punky, La Petite Adelaide, and Clarence Darrow. In 1969, the City of Cohoes began to restore the hall. Reconstruction was done within five years, and the drop curtain now depicted the Cohoes Falls. The theater was reopened on March 7, 1975, with a revival of *London Assurance* from 1874. The first floor is for the Cohoes RiverSpark Visitors Center and the home of the Spindle City Historic Society. The music hall remains an architectural jewel and is one of the oldest professional theaters operating in the country. It is a living link to 19th-century Cohoes and an asset for the future.

The *Cohoes Daily News* began publication at No. 1 Granite Hall on September 22, 1873, with Edward Monk as editor and proprietor of the newspaper and Clark & Foster as the printers. It was published daily at noon except on Sundays. The newspaper cost 1¢ per copy. In 1879, James H. Masten, who was Cohoes's postmaster, became proprietor of the newspaper with Edward Monk, and in 1881, he became its sole owner.

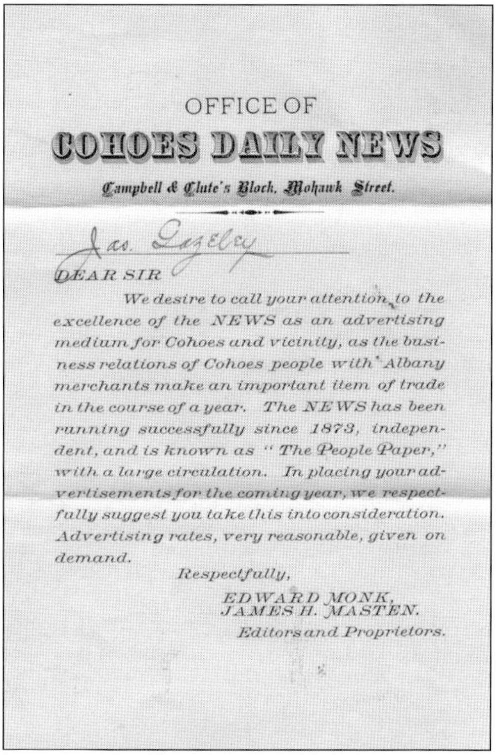

OFFICE OF

COHOES DAILY NEWS

Campbell & Clute's Block, Mohawk Street.

Jas. Gazeley

DEAR SIR

We desire to call your attention to the excellence of the NEWS as an advertising medium for Cohoes and vicinity, as the business relations of Cohoes people with Albany merchants make an important item of trade in the course of a year. The NEWS has been running successfully since 1873, independent, and is known as "The People Paper," with a large circulation. In placing your advertisements for the coming year, we respectfully suggest you take this into consideration. Advertising rates, very reasonable, given on demand.

Respectfully,

EDWARD MONK,
JAMES H. MASTEN.
Editors and Proprietors.

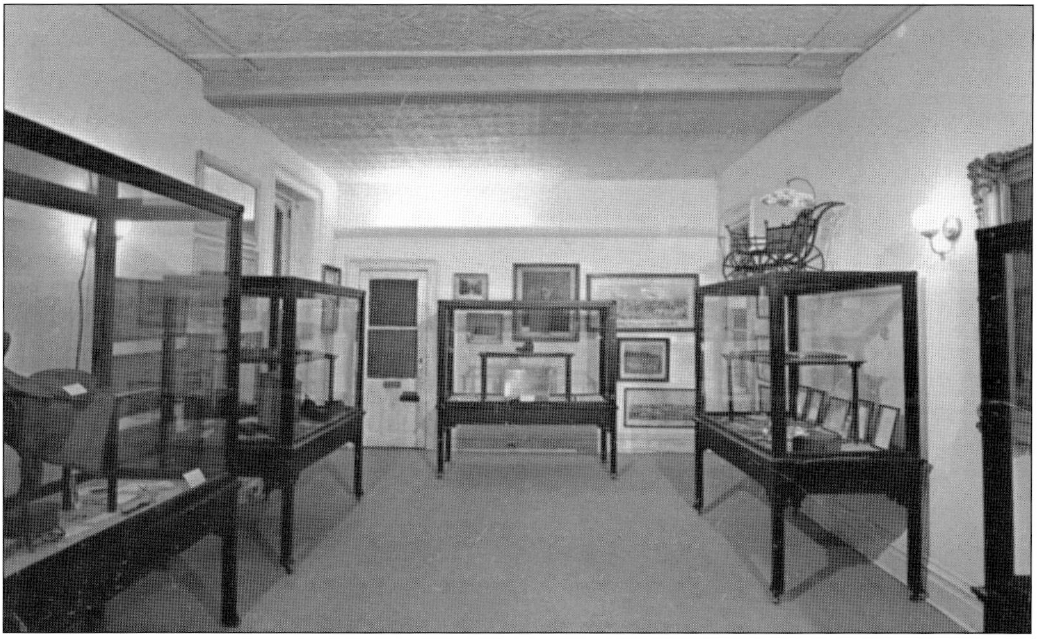

This room, located in the National Bank Building, housed the collections of the Cohoes Historical and Cultural Society. The society was organized in 1964 to promote the cultural and historical assets of Cohoes and create a museum. In August 1968, the society was granted a lease by the city to use this space as a museum and headquarters. Group members were instrumental in the restoration of the music hall.

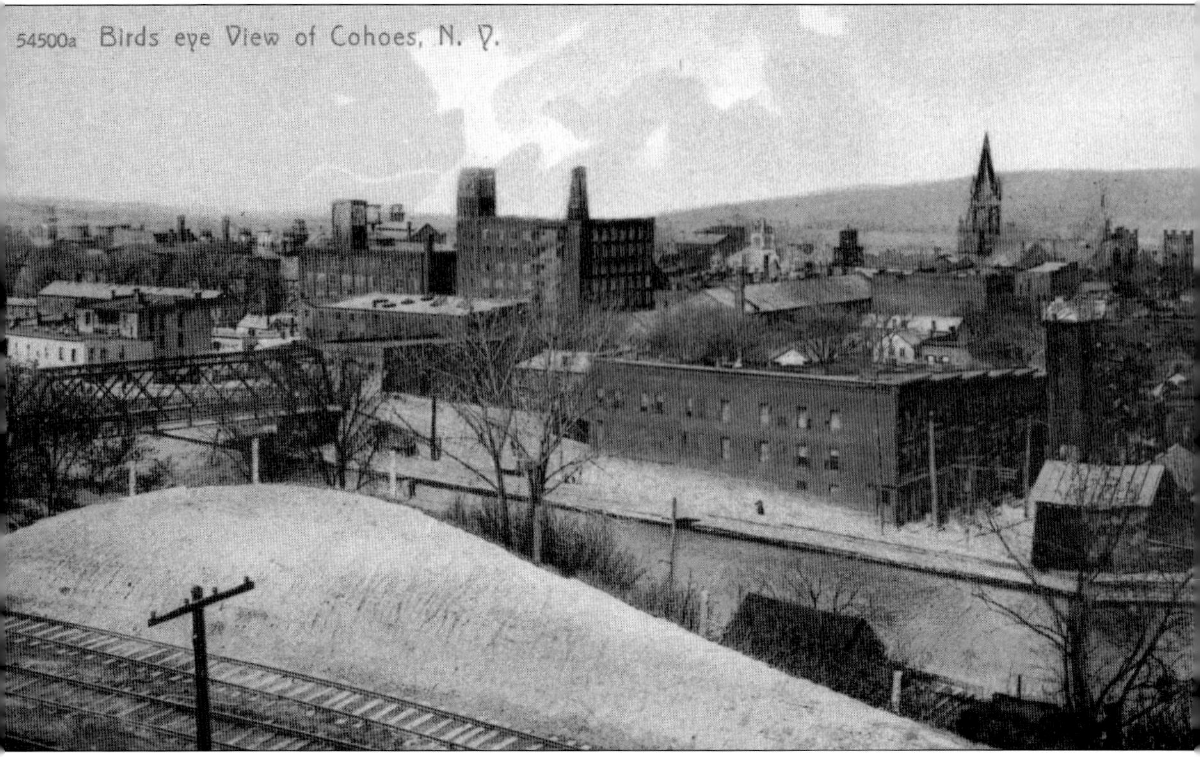


This panoramic view of downtown Cohoes looking eastward shows many of the city's landmarks. The tracks of the Troy & Schenectady Railroad are in the foreground, and the enlarged Erie Canal and Lock No. 13 are just beyond. The High Street Bridge is on the left. The brick row houses to the right of the bridge still stand at the head of White Street. The railroad bed is now the route of the Mohawk-Hudson Bike Trail. The Victor Knitting Mill (Cohoes

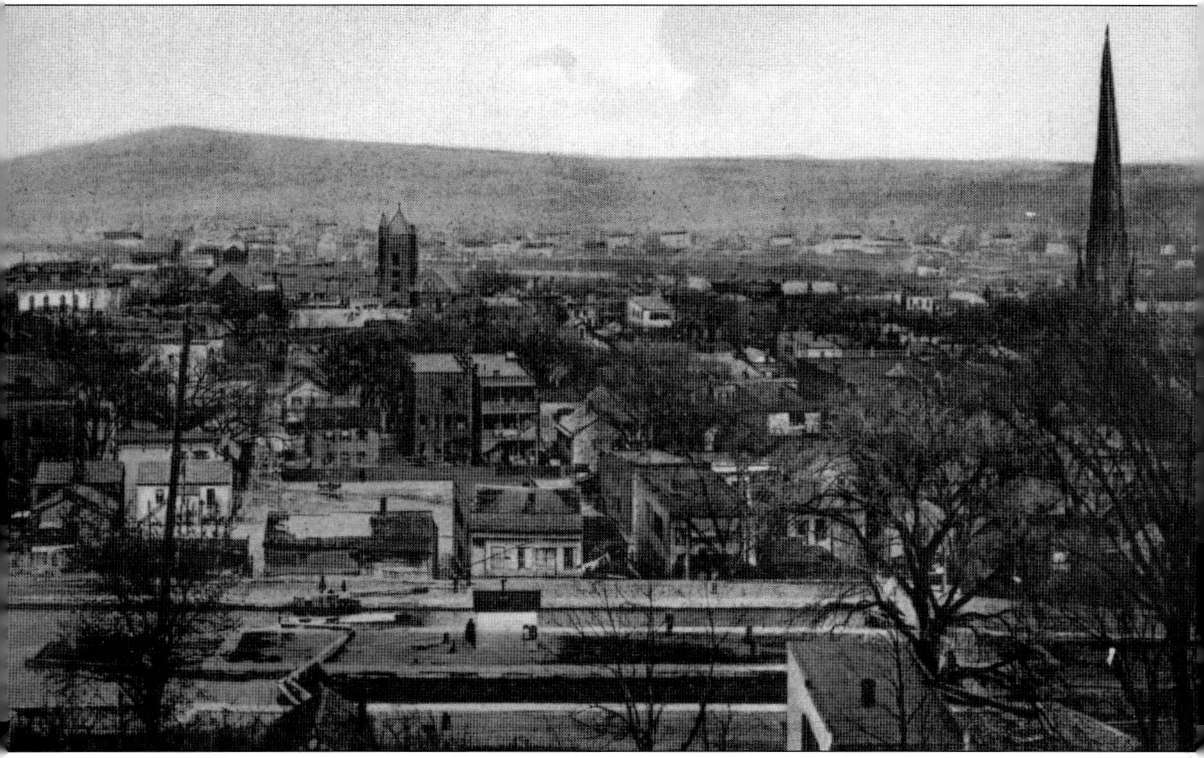

Carrybag) is in the center of the left panel, and city hall is to its right. To the left of the Victor Mill are the Ogden Mill and the large group of factories that once occupied the northern ends of Mohawk and Remsen Streets. Six of the city's churches—Silliman Memorial, St. Bernard's, Dutch Reformed, the Baptist church, St. John's, and St. Joseph's—are also visible.

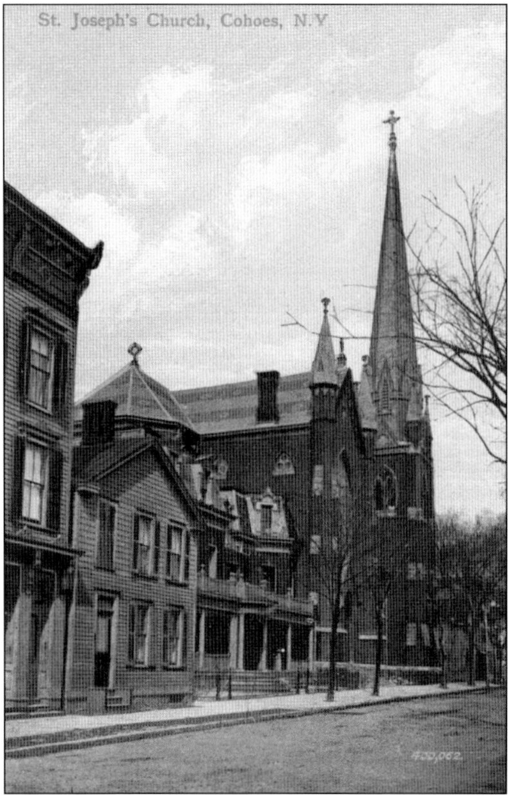


This postcard shows St. Joseph's Church and rectory prior to Father Lavigne's pastorate. At that time, there were houses on both sides of the church and rectory. What is now St. Joseph's Place, between Lancaster and Congress Streets, had numerous houses and a business, so the church entrance was on Congress Street rather than its present location. The bricked-in outline of the original entrance can still be seen today.

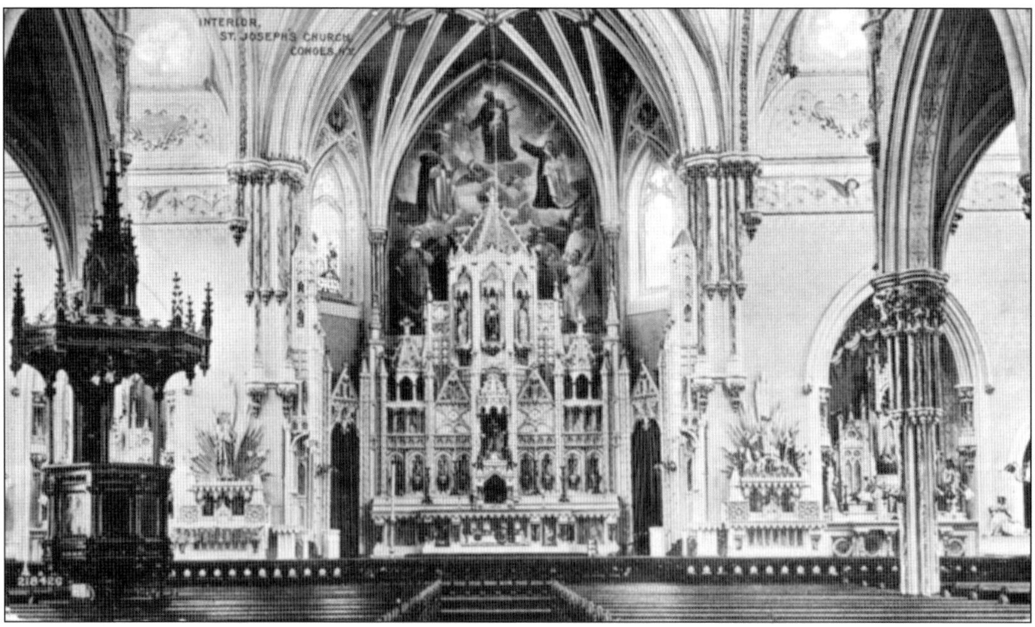


This interior view of St. Joseph's shows the main altar and three of the six side altars. Behind the main altar is a painting of St. Joseph in heaven. The artist is unidentified, but it is claimed that people of the parish were used as models. The pulpit was outside of the sanctuary among the first rows of pews, bringing the priest closer to the congregation while delivering his sermon.

This 1908 postcard, printed to celebrate the 40th anniversary of St. Joseph's, shows, clockwise from center and starting at the bottom, Monsignor Dugas; the rectory, as it appeared before a later addition; the church's second convent; the church; and the school. Both the school and convent had been rebuilt following a 1901 fire. The church was also the second church on the site, as the original church had been demolished in 1874 after it was determined structurally unsound.

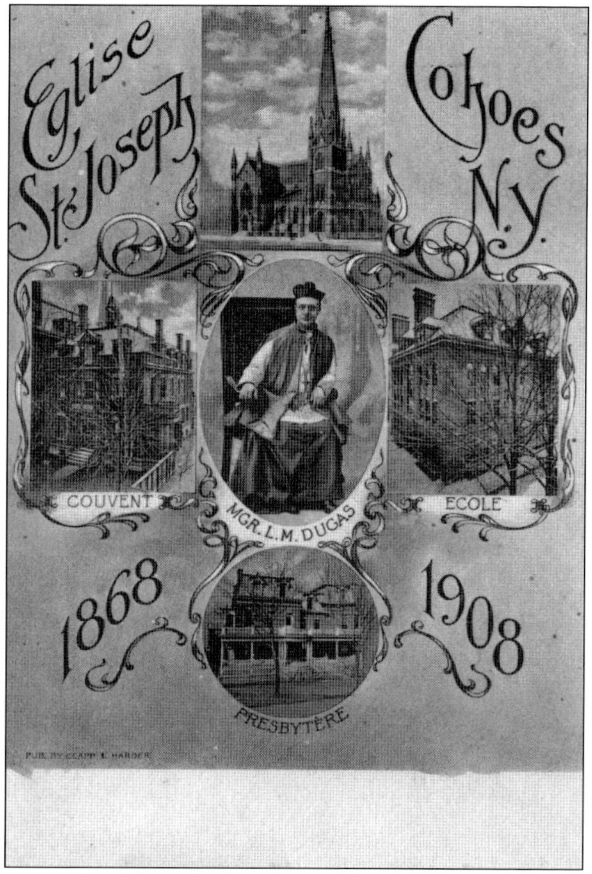


This postcard shows the church and enlarged rectory after removal of the houses shown in the postcard on the previous page. Father Lavigne was instrumental in these changes to the neighborhood, the opening of the street named St. Joseph's Place, and relocation of the church's main entrance. He served as pastor of the church from 1915 to 1946. During his tenure, the church interior was renovated and a new organ was installed.

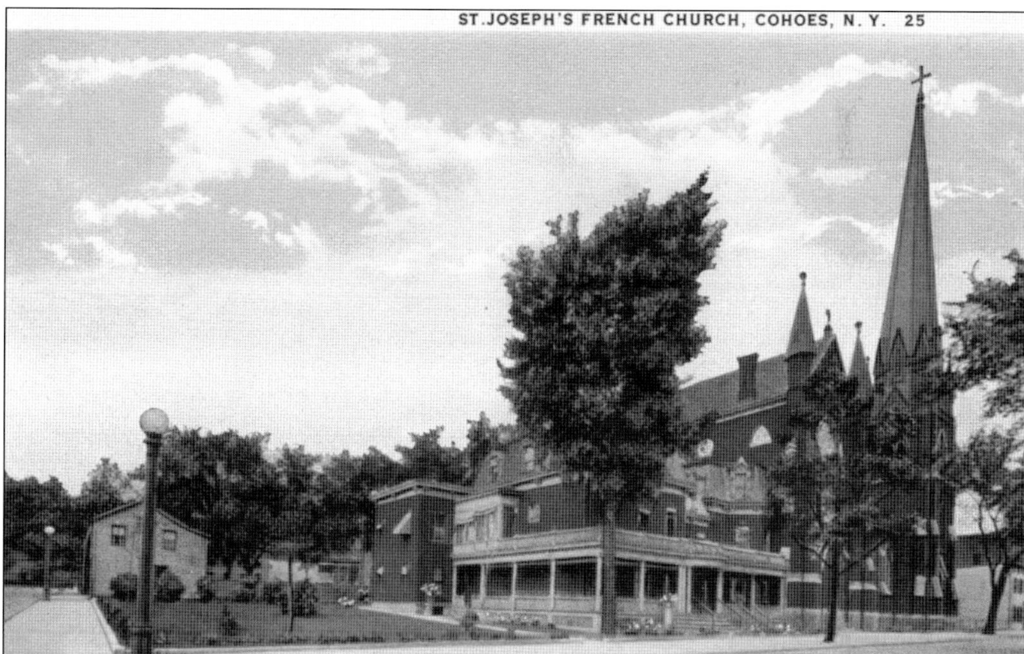

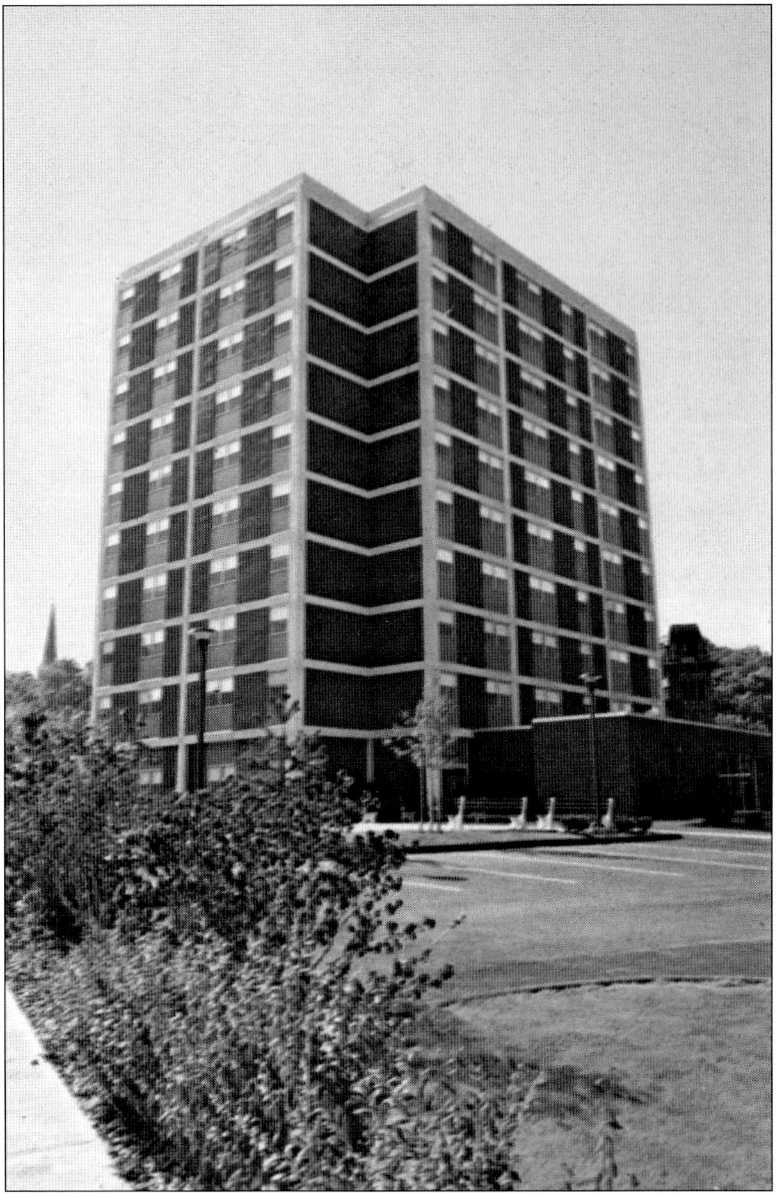

In 1969, ground was broken for construction of the Dr. Jay McDonald Towers near the intersection of Remsen and Cayuga Streets. This nine-story, 95-unit building, developed as part of the Cohoes Model Cities plan, was completed in 1972 and provides housing for senior citizens. Dr. McDonald was the driving force of the Cohoes Citizens Party, a grassroots group that gained control of city government by defeating the Democratic Party establishment that had been in power for four decades. Dr. McDonald served as mayor of Cohoes from 1964 until his death in June 1969. As a tribute to his many years of service to Cohoes, his wife, Virginia McDonald, who later served as mayor and was the first woman elected mayor in New York State, was presented with the Dr. Jay McDonald memorial flag. The symbols on the flag represented the Model Cities and All-America City programs, Dr. McDonald's service as mayor, and his three decades as a physician. The flag was to be flown annually at city hall on June 22, the anniversary of his death.

The Manufacturers Bank was established on March 12, 1872. The first bank headquarters was at 70 Oneida Street. The officers were W.E. Thorn, president, and J.V.S. Lansing, vice president. Directors included D.H. Van Auken, G. Campbell, D.J. Johnston, N.J. Clute, W. Moore, and P.R. Chadwick. The bank relocated to 91 Remsen Street to a building called "the old clapboard mill." Built in 1846, it was originally a machine shop for constructing equipment for the Ogden Mill and later became a knitting mill. The building shown in the postcards was erected in 1906 and included a large hall for meetings or performances on its top floor, as did many banks of the time. In this meeting space on January 18, 1914, Fr. Peter Kohanik celebrated the first Divine Liturgy for the Russian Orthodox faithful of Cohoes, and the large attendance encouraged the establishment of St. Nicholas Parish in Cohoes.

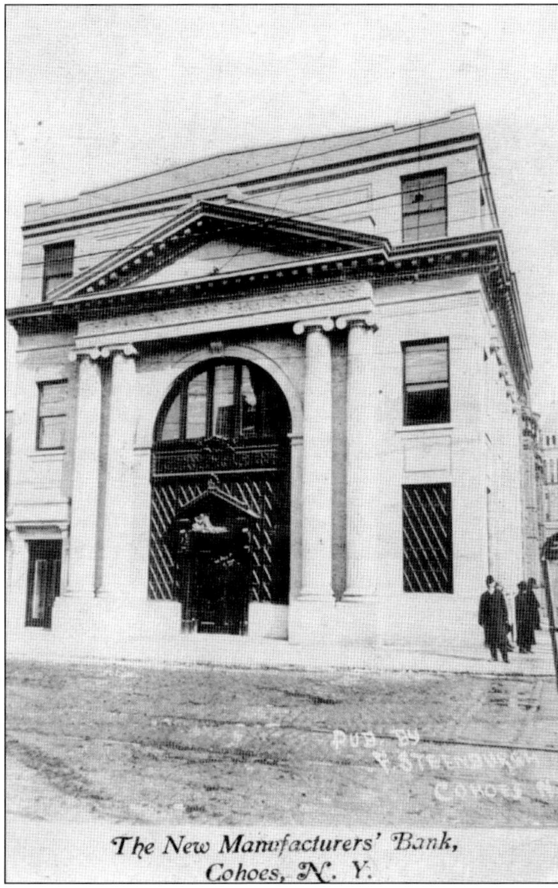

The New Manufacturers' Bank, Cohoes, N. Y.

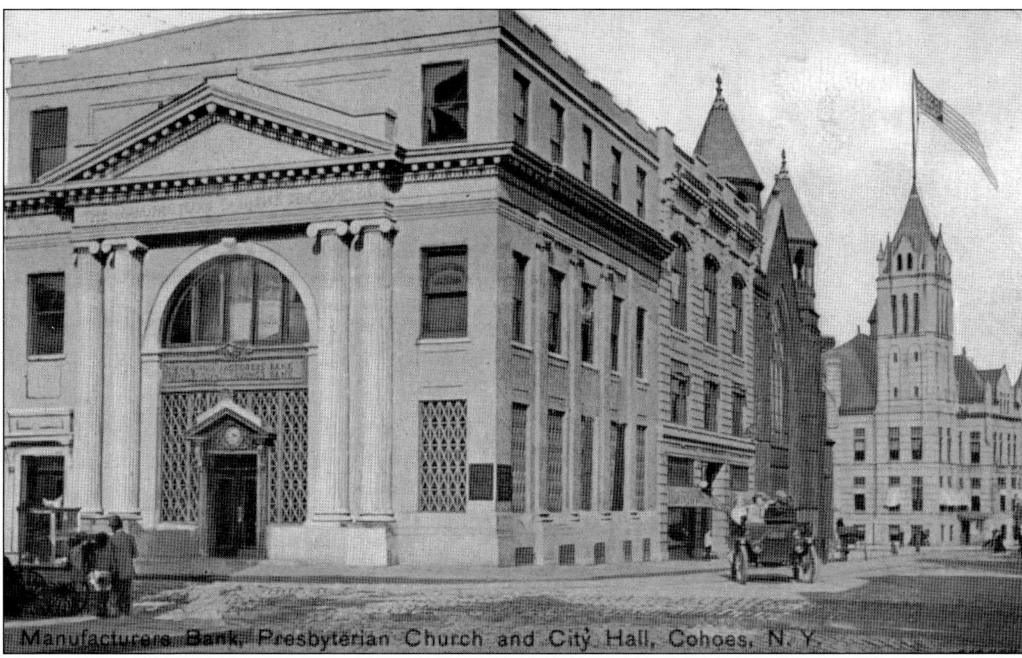
Manufacturers Bank, Presbyterian Church and City Hall, Cohoes, N. Y.

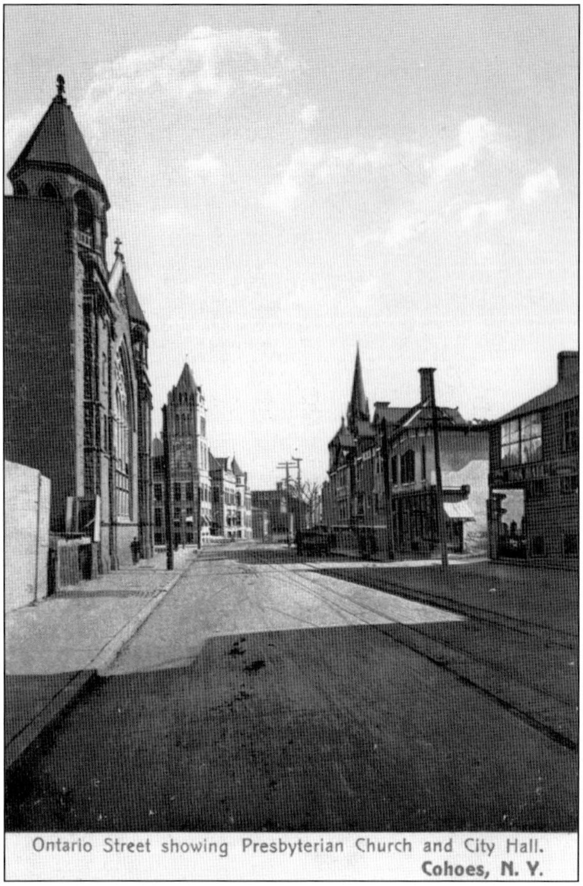


These views of Ontario Street show Silliman Memorial Church and city hall. On the right, at the corner of Remsen and Ontario, is Granite Hall. The Granite Hall Block was built by a Mr. Baker in 1847 and was the Cohoes showplace of its day. Four stories high, with step gables, a large hall on the top floor, and storefronts at street level, Granite Hall had a long history of important social functions and popular commercial tenants. The last owner, Dale Carpenter, sold the building to the Kresge Company when he moved his florist business to Columbia Street, and a five-and-dime store was built on the site. A building, visible in the postcard on page 81, was constructed in 1913 on the lot between the Silliman and the Manufacturers Bank and became the Cohoes Moose Lodge in 1924. The lodge had a large moose head hanging on its facade.

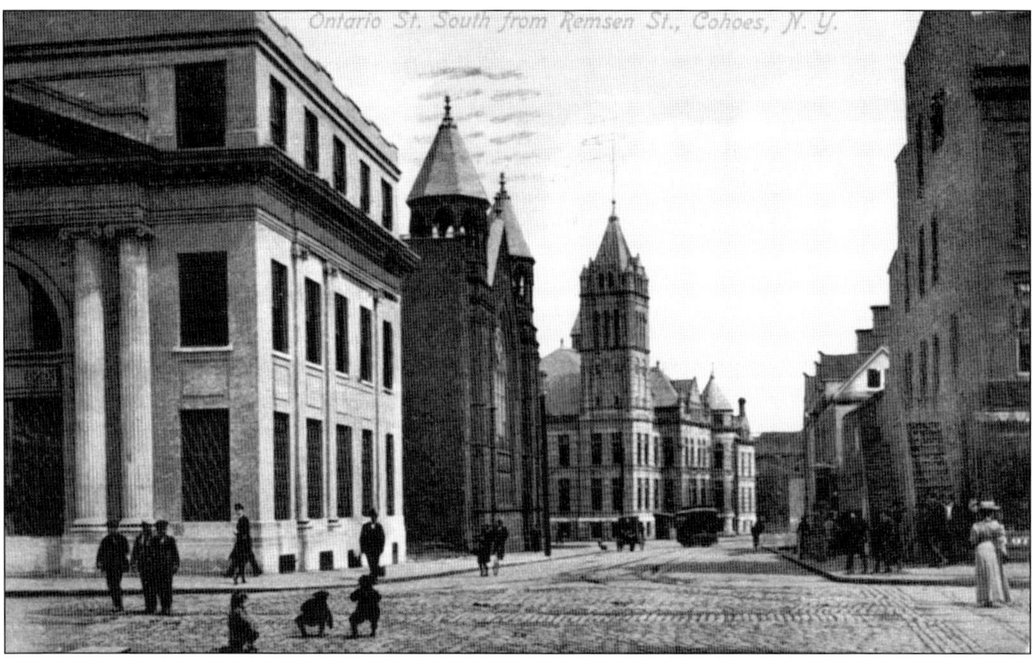

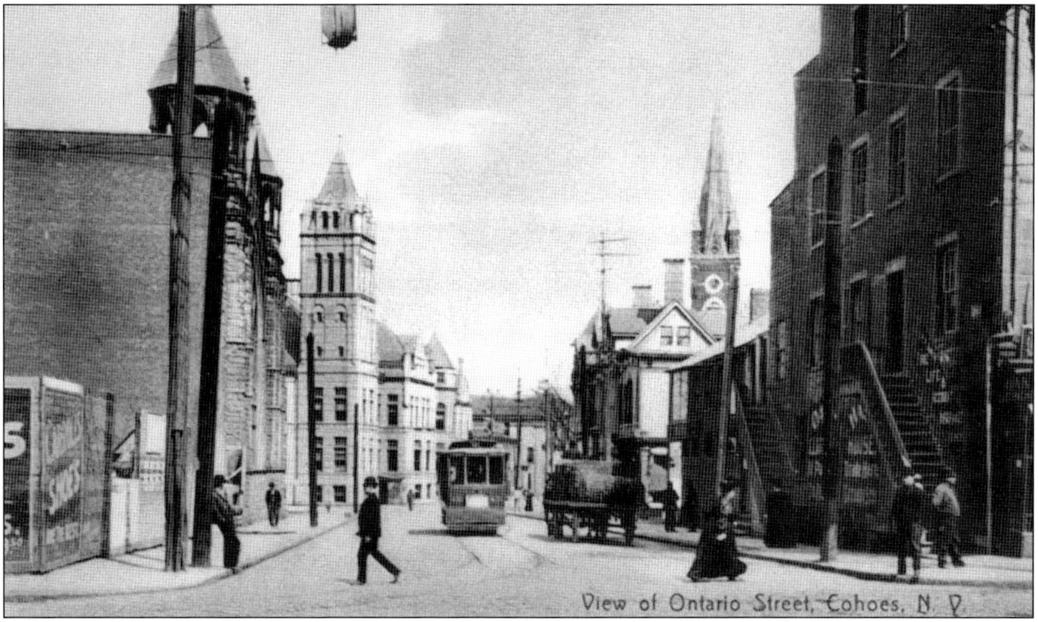


In a view heading east on Ontario Street, one sees the Silliman Memorial Church and Cohoes City Hall on the left. On the right at the corner of Remsen Street is the Oak Hall Clothing House. The shop was in business at Granite Hall from 1904 to 1919. This image is from just before the construction of the Manufacturers Bank Building in 1906. In the distance are St. Bernard's steeple and St. Bernard's School.

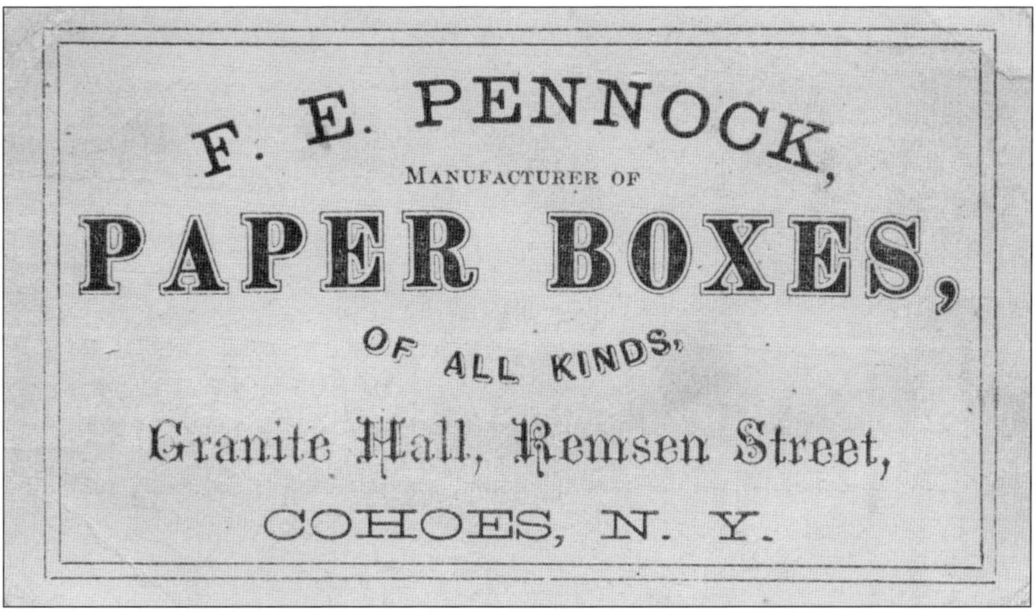


Francis E. Pennock established a paper box factory in 1868 at 98 Remsen Street. The factory was at 13 Factory Street in 1882 and expanded to 11, 15, and 18 Factory Street (now Cayuga Street) by 1885. He ran the business with his wife, M.A. Pennock. They relocated to Pittsfield, Massachusetts, in the late 1880s. There were five paper box factories in Cohoes in the 1870s.

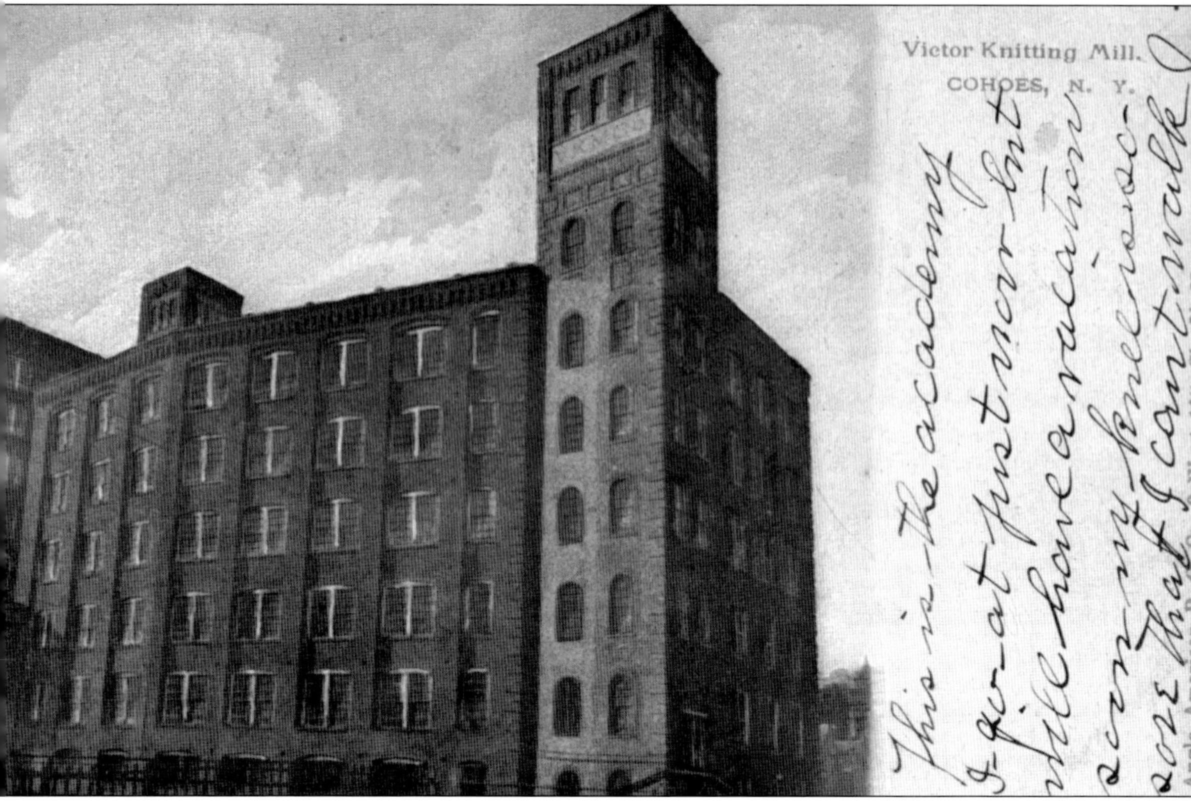


The Victor Knitting Mill was established in 1886 at 100 Ontario Street. The mill specialized in women's hosiery and sleepwear. In the early 1890s, the mill moved to the corner of Olmstead and Ontario Streets. This building would later be occupied by the Cohoes Carrybags Company, which had its origin as the Cohoes Envelope Company. In 1936, a Mr. Lackey founded the Cohoes Envelope Co. at 60 Olmstead Street. The company produced bags and envelopes for businesses. In July 1946, a US trademark was filed for Cohoes Carrybags by the Cohoes Envelope Co., Inc. The Cohoes Carrybags Co. eventually settled at 308 Ontario Street, a massive building at the corner of Olmstead Street, which, at one time, also housed the *Cohoes American* newspaper. In the inscription on the postcard, the writer, in referring to working at the Victor Mill, states, "This is the academy I go—at just now but will have a vacation soon. My knee is so sore that I can't walk."

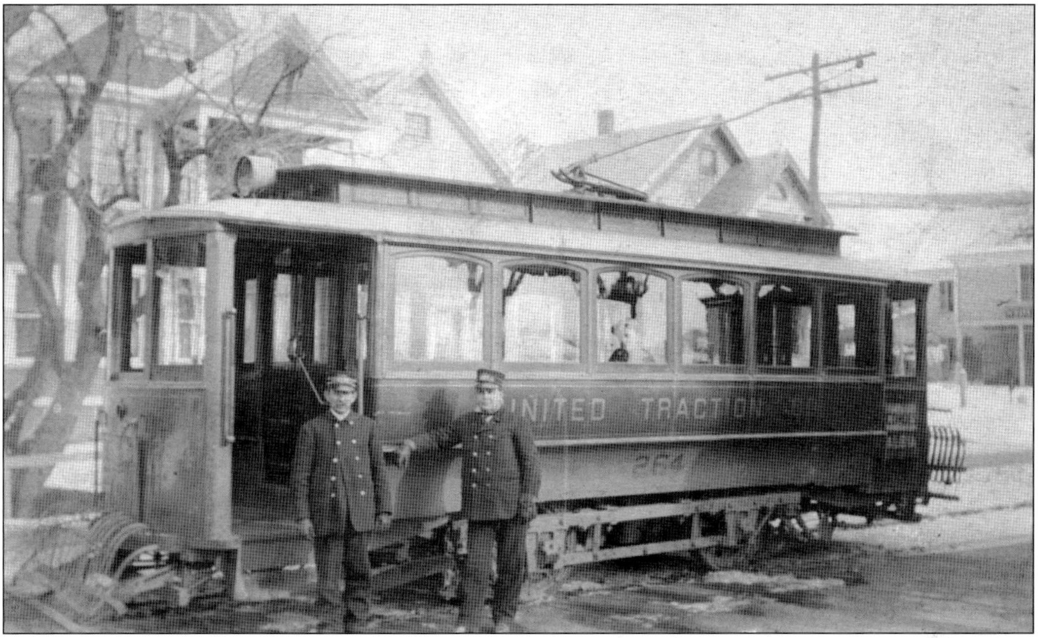


In 1899–1900, the streetcar systems connecting Cohoes were consolidated as the United Traction Co. It cost 5¢ to ride within the city limits or 7¢ for a longer ride. Troy cars were red, Troy-Cohoes cars were white, Cohoes-Lansingburgh cars were blue and white, and Cohoes-Waterford were green; the lines were referred to by these colors. The White Line crossed Green Island to Troy, then Congress Street to Albia.

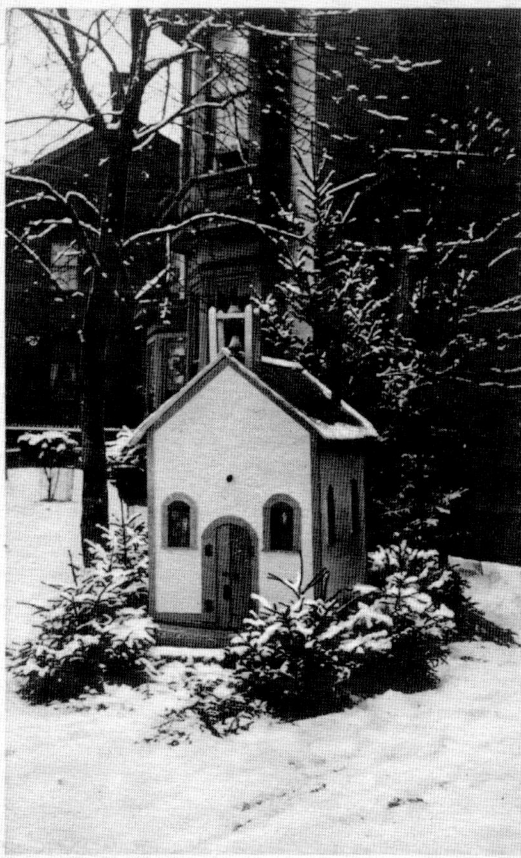

W. Jennings Funeral Home, Phone Cohoes 1081

In the 1930s or 1940s, funeral director William Jennings built this Christmas display for the lawn of his home and place of business at 174 Mohawk Street and used this postcard image as an advertisement. The miniature church stood about five feet tall, and music was paired with it. Jennings and his wife, Emma, were both funeral directors, and their business is listed as far back as 1916 in Cohoes directories.

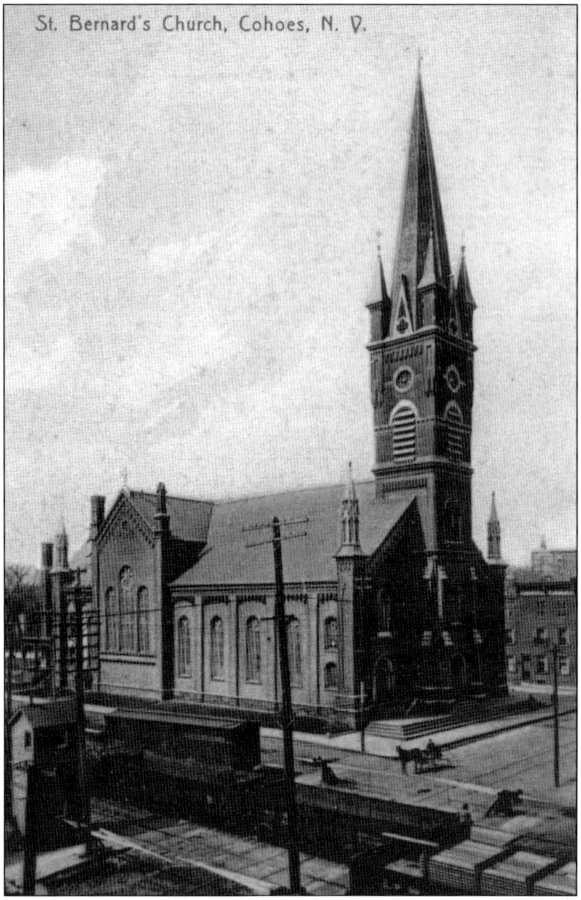


In November 1847, Bishop John McCloskey laid the cornerstone for St. Bernard's, the first Catholic church in Cohoes. Its site would later be occupied by the Keveny Memorial Academy. By 1855, the congregation had outgrown the original building, and its then pastor Fr. Thomas Keveny bought land across the street. The cornerstone of this building (pictured) was laid in 1863. It was opened on October 14, 1866, with a grand concert. In February 1876, a violent storm caused the 200-foot church spire to break from its brick base, and it crushed part of the roof and landed on the Delaware & Hudson Railroad tracks east of the church. The spire was rebuilt the following year, but the bell chimes were never replaced. In 1956–1957, the church building was renovated, and the tower was lowered in height by 20 feet and a granite Celtic cross was put in place.

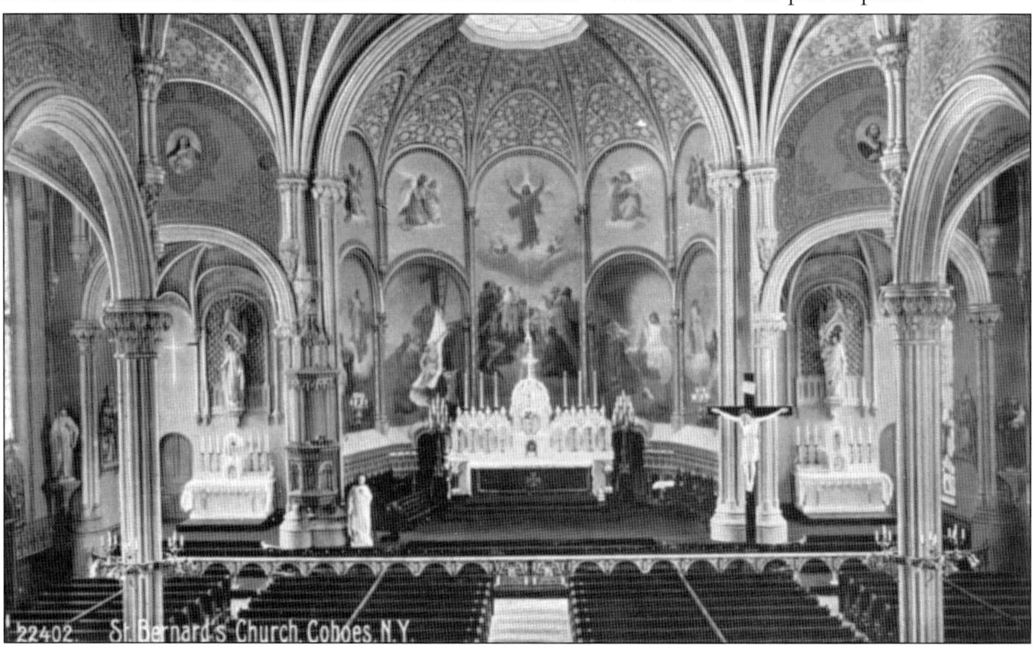

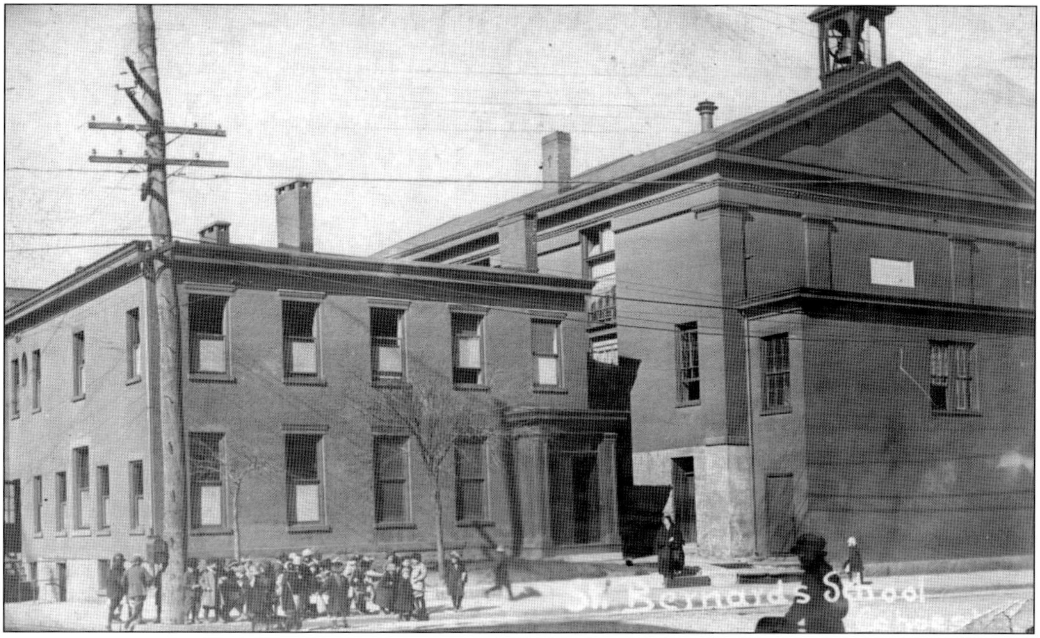


In 1860, six members of the Sisters of St. Joseph were sent to St. Bernard's Parish in Cohoes to establish a school. This was the oldest school conducted by the Sisters of St. Joseph in the present Diocese of Albany. The sisters also taught an evening school for students who were employed in the mills during the day. The school was on Ontario Street, next to the old church and across the street from the present church building. The school became known as St. Bernard's Academy in 1898. In 1929, a new school building was constructed on the same site. The name of the school was changed to the Keveny Memorial Academy to honor its founder, Fr. Thomas Keveny. During its existence, Keveny was both an elementary school and a high school. In its last years in the 1970s and 1980s, it was solely a high school. The school was closed in 1986.

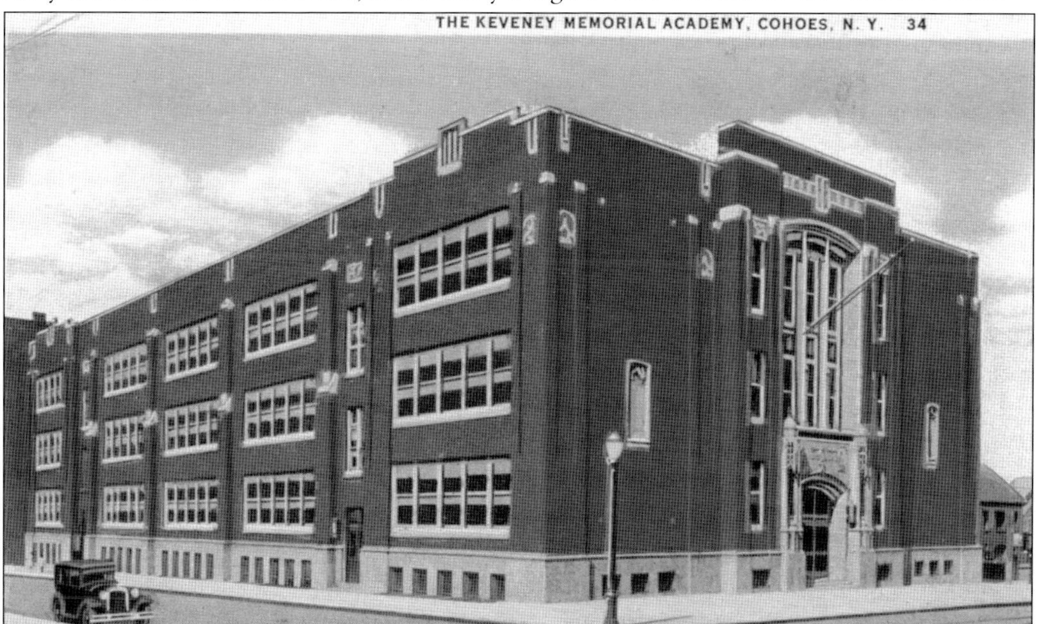

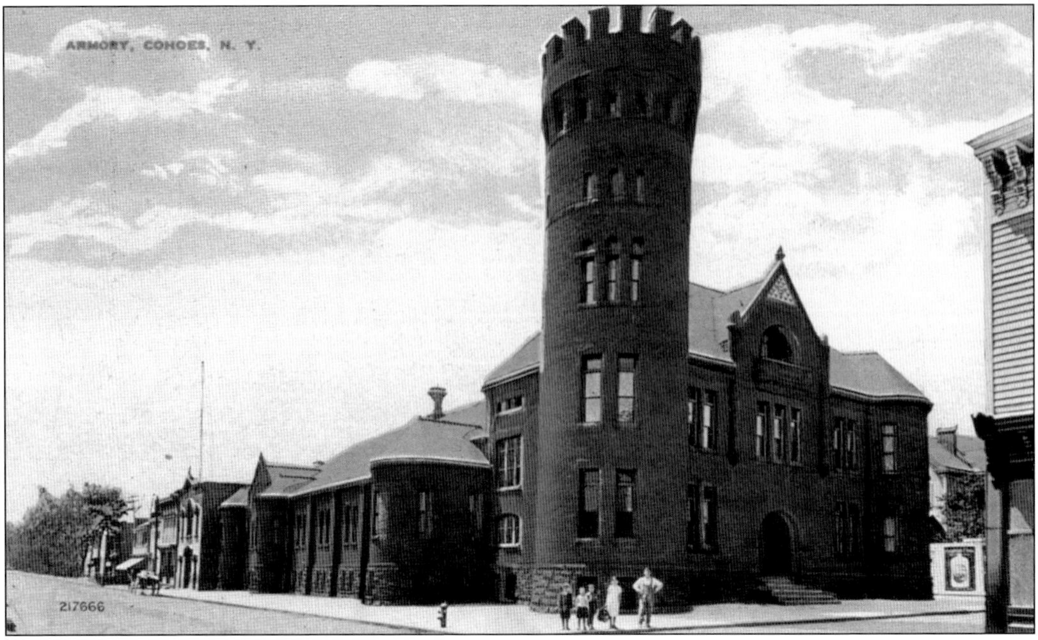


The Cohoes Armory was built in 1892–1893. Architect Isaac Perry designed this and about 30 other armories in Upstate New York. These structures were used as training centers and staging areas for reserve troops. Cohoes's Company B of the 105th Infantry was accepted into the National Guard in 1876. During the industrial revolution of the late 19th century, the National Guard was often used to quell union riots. Company B first went on duty in July 1877 during a railroad strike in Troy. The armory housed the 7th Separate Company, which was reorganized in 1898 as part of the 2nd Regiment for service during the Spanish-American War. Company B, as part of the 27th Division, was called into active duty during World Wars I and II. The National Guard vacated the armory in 1964. In 1972, it was purchased by Oscar Cramer, whose retail store called Cramer's Armory occupied the building until 1997.

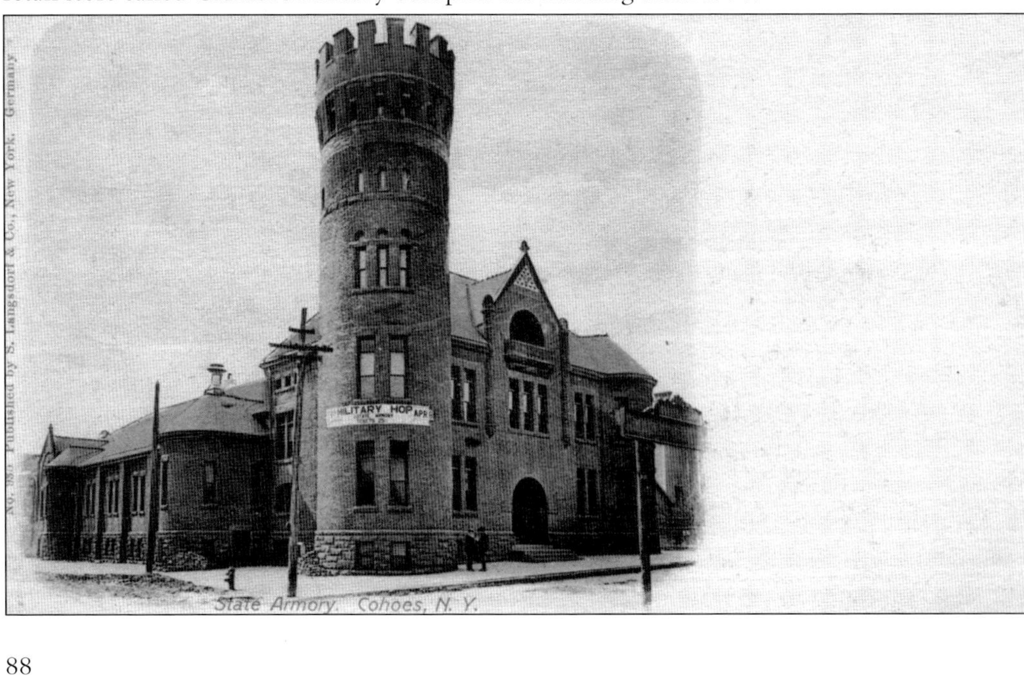

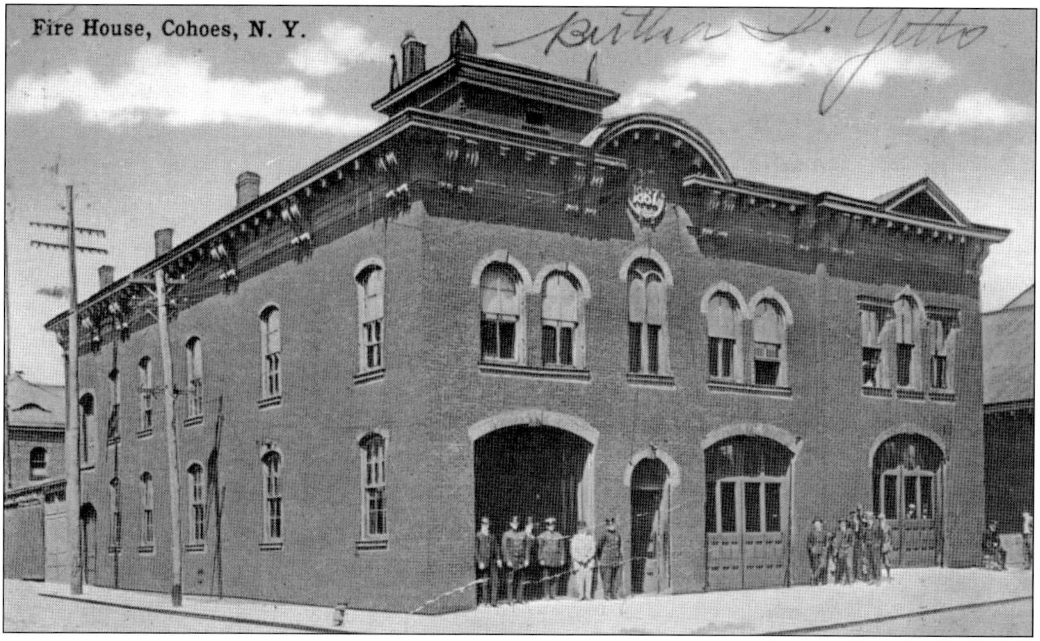


Charles H. Adams, who became the first mayor of the city in 1870, purchased the first steamer for fighting fires in Cohoes in 1867. The fire company formed to take charge of the engine and constructed an engine house on Oneida Street east of Canvass Street, which is shown in the postcard above. The fire company had 36 members but no horses to pull the steamer. In February 1873, a fire started at the Erie Mill, which received great damage before the firemen arrived. A few months later, Cohoes purchased a team of horses for the steamer, along with the services of an engineer and driver. The postcard below shows fire chief T.C. Collin and driver Bob Murray in a carriage pulled by the fire department's horse Dolly Gray, in front of their firehouse on Main Street next to the Cohoes Armory (seen on page 88).

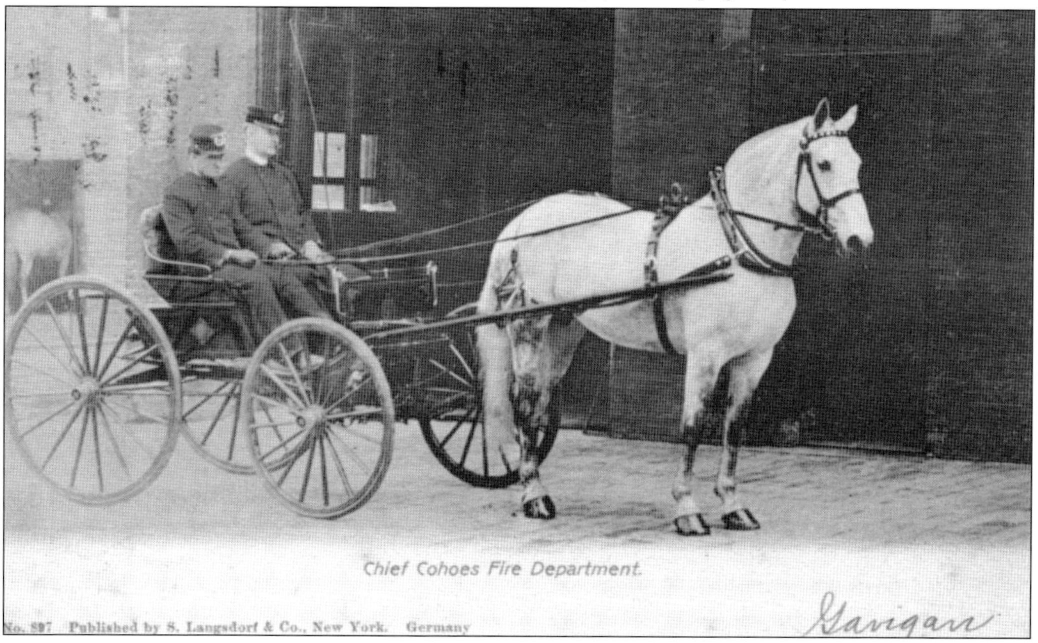

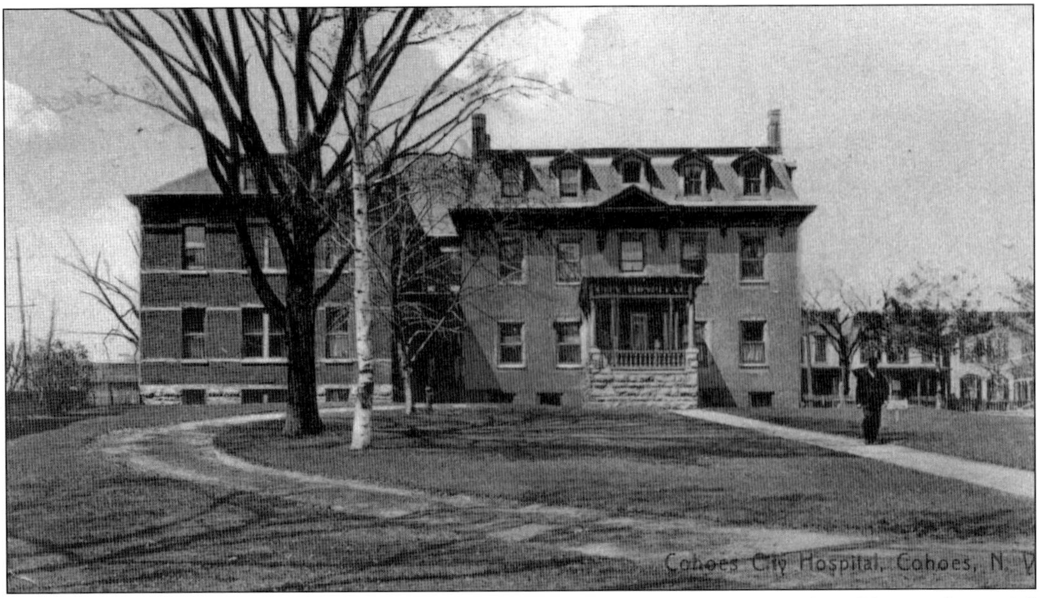


The first Cohoes Hospital was established in February 1872 but lacked sufficient financial support and closed. In 1897, a committee met to create a replacement in Cohoes, as interest in having a hospital remained. The proposed location was on Main Street. The building on the site was constructed in the 1790s for the Lansing family as a summer residence. It became the property of John Scott, a mill owner. On February 1, 1898, the Cohoes Hospital Association formed; plans were drawn up and accepted. On June 23, Dr. Bulmer, a pathologist, agreed to do microscopic work at the hospital free of charge. By September 1898, the hospital's D.J. Johnston Memorial Room, named for the Harmony Mill superintendent, was completed, and on November 9, philanthropist and industrialist Horace B. Silliman donated $700 to the hospital to establish a surgical department.

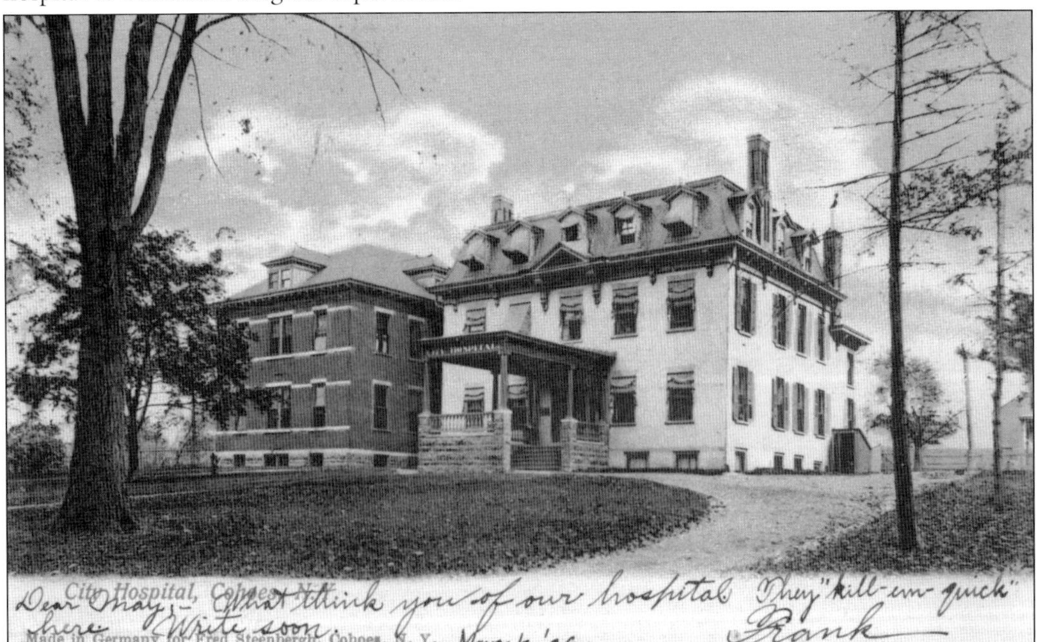

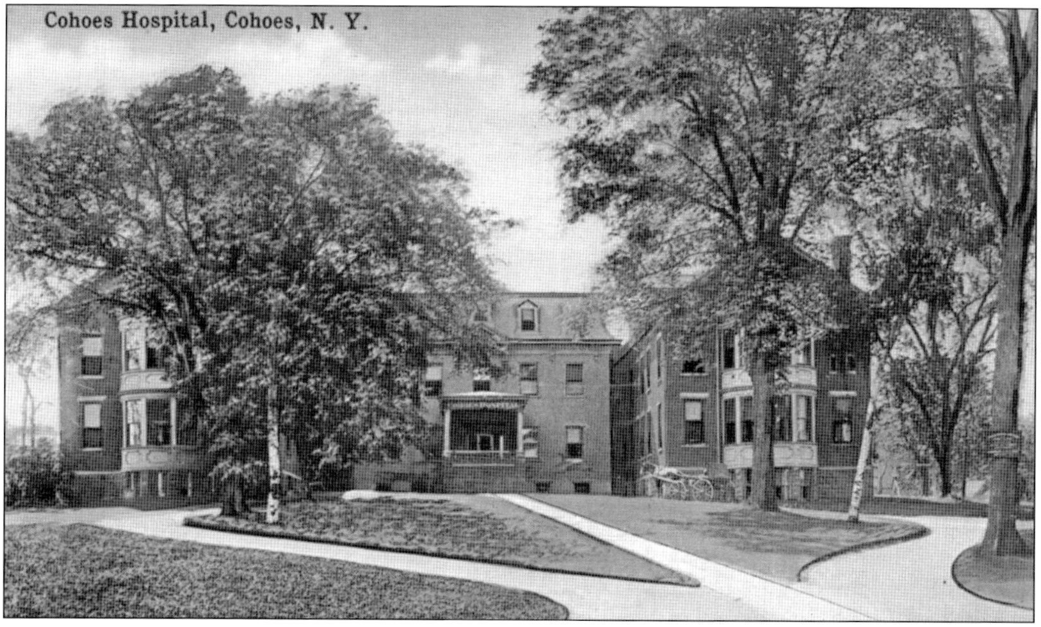


The new Cohoes Hospital was first used on Labor Day in 1898, when a horse-drawn trolley crossed the path of a Delaware & Hudson Railway train. The trolley, carrying passengers home from an outing at Rensselaer Park, was smashed, scattering passengers and wreckage, with 14 people killed and 25 injured. The accident victims were cared for in the new hospital, which was still under construction. In July 1899, ground was broken for an annex to the hospital, and a nursing school was established. Its first graduate was Lina B. Loron in 1903. The nursing school existed until 1938. The Cohoes Hospital was recognized as one of the finest in the area. However, according to Frank (see lower postcard, page 90), they "kill-em-quick" here. By the 1950s, overcrowding and obsolescence of the existing buildings made it clear that a new facility was needed (see page 117).

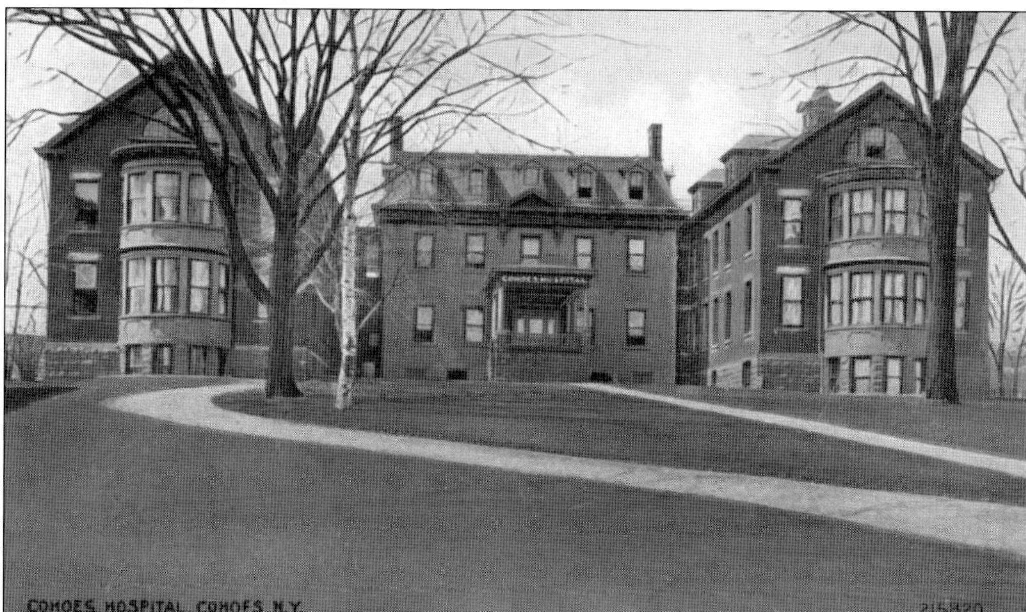

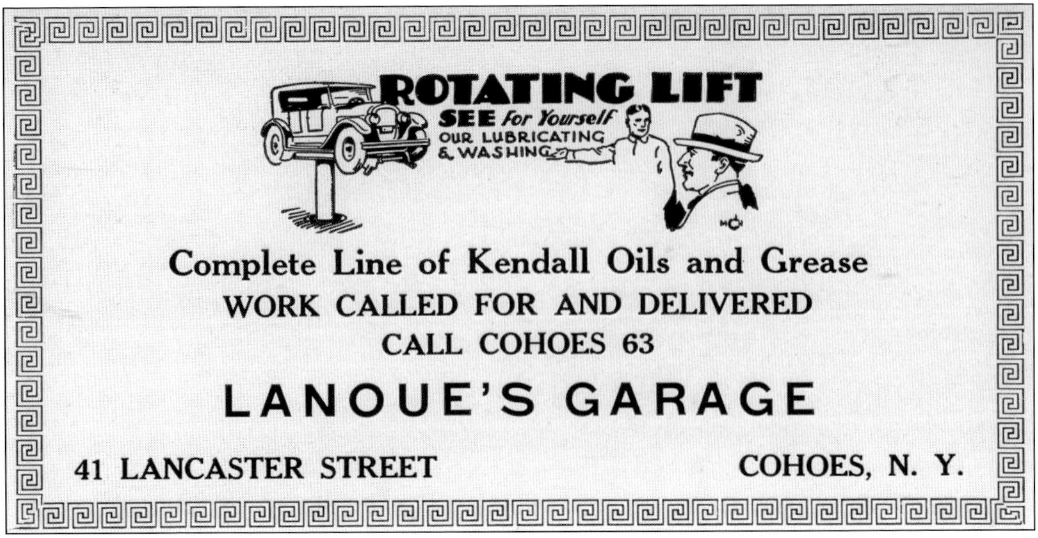


John J. Lanoue opened Lanoue's Garage in 1939 at 41 Lancaster Street. His shop was at this location until 1945, when he moved the business to 55 Sargent Street. He retired in 1985. Lanoue was a member of the Cohoes Masonic Temple and a veteran of the Coast Guard. On this ink blotter, he advertises a rotating lift in his shop.

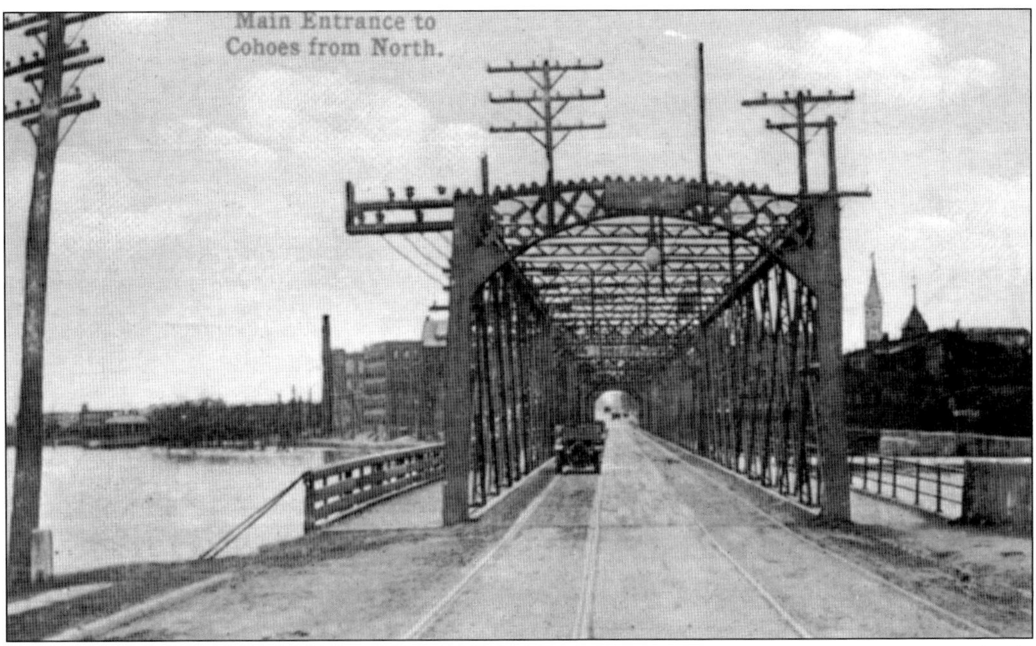


In this view looking south is the bridge over the Mohawk River, connecting the Northside section of Waterford with Cohoes. The first bridge in this area, built in 1795, was a wooden covered toll bridge. Following damage by ice jams on the river or by fire, that bridge was replaced by subsequent structures in 1806, 1826, 1832, 1854, 1872, and 1887. The 1887 bridge in this postcard was replaced in 1932.

# *Four*
# The Island

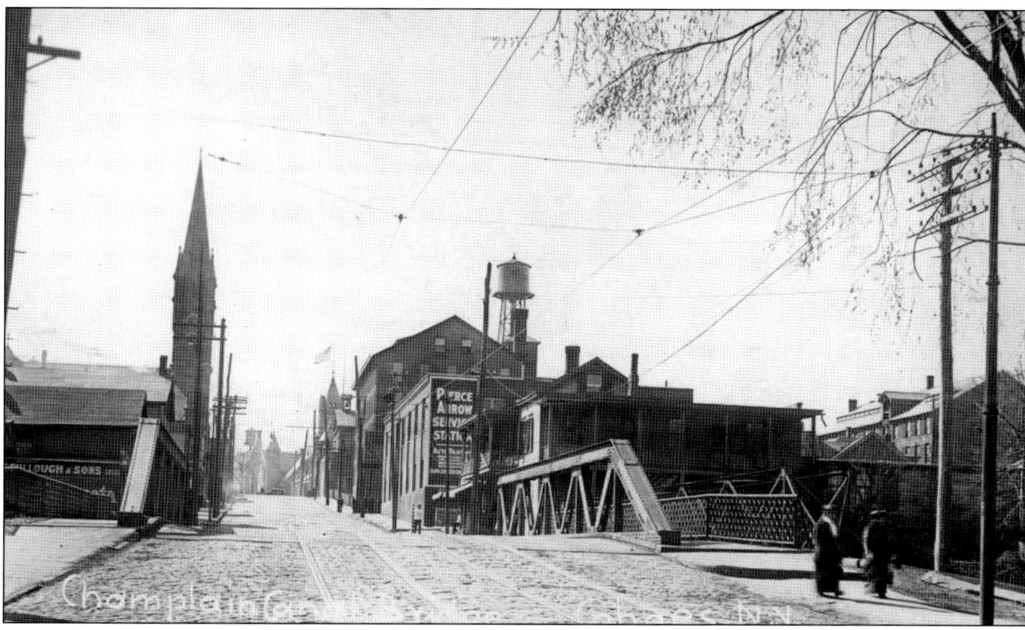


The view in this postcard takes one west on Ontario Street and across the Champlain Canal. Several Cohoes landmarks can be seen, including St. Bernard's Church, city hall, and a Pierce-Arrow service station (an unaffordable car for most folks). The N&S Shirt Company is to the right. The Champlain Canal, opened in 1823, served Cohoes until it was replaced by the New York State Barge Canal in 1918. New York State Route 787 is along the canal's path today.

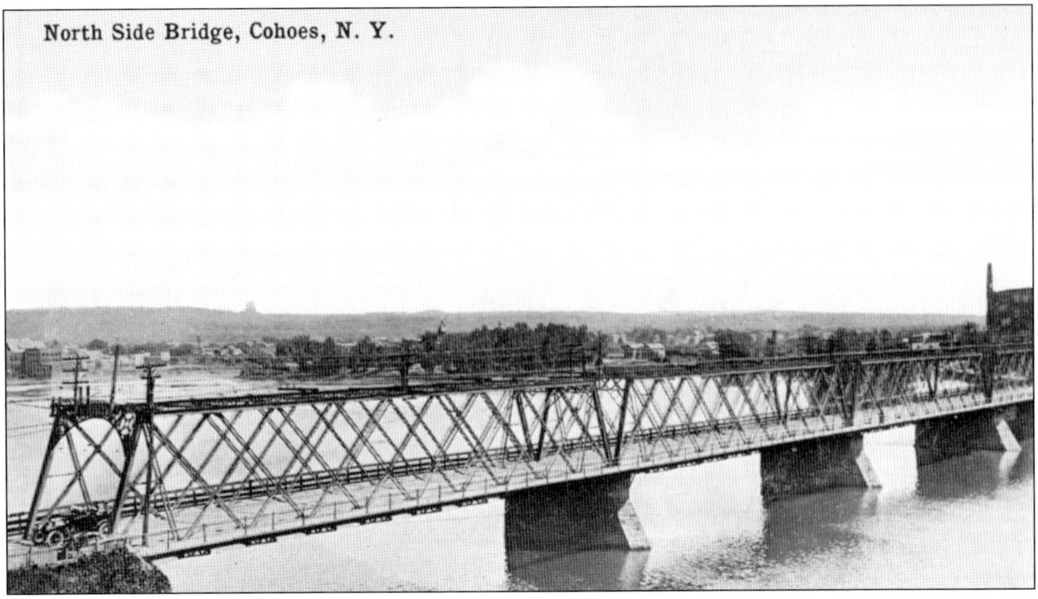


These postcards show the Cohoes-Northside Bridge, which opened in 1887. This steel bridge replaced one with a wooden plank roadbed, known as the Combination Bridge. It was built in 1871 as a replacement for a covered bridge, which, according to the *Cohoes Cataract* newspaper, Cohoesiers never considered a first-class structure and "were in constant dread of having to cross." The 1887 bridge was replaced by a concrete arched structure, dedicated on November 15, 1932. New York governor Franklin D. Roosevelt, who was elected president the week before the bridge's dedication on November 15, 1932, had authorized funds for the new bridge in 1931. Several thousand people attended the dedication ceremonies, which began with a parade of dignitaries from city hall to the bridge, decorated in red, white, and blue bunting for the occasion. Cohoes politician Michael T. Smith was in the first automobile to cross the bridge.

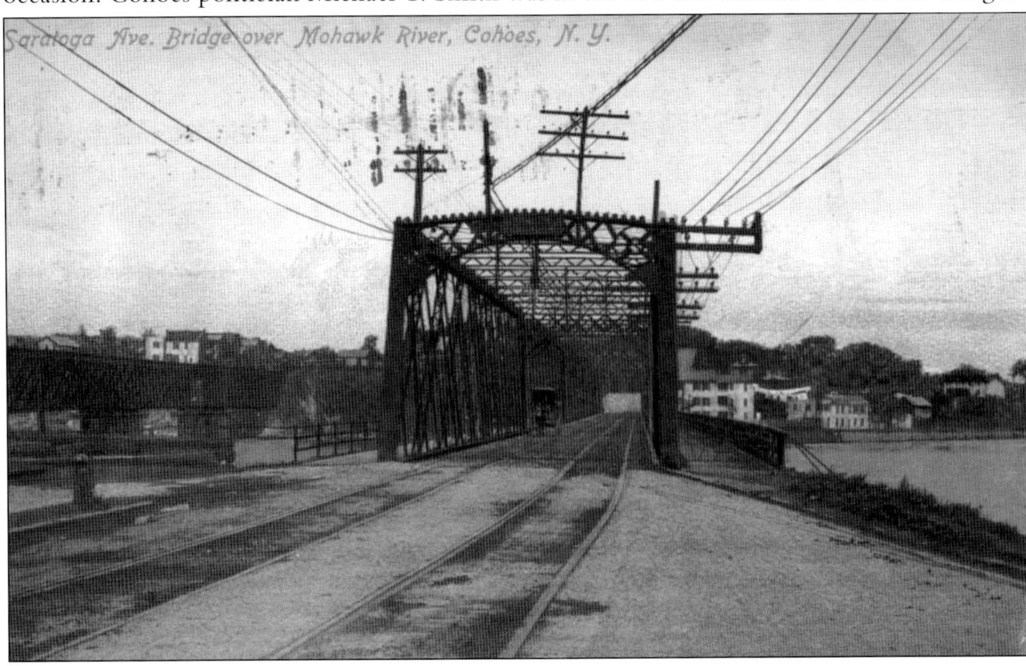

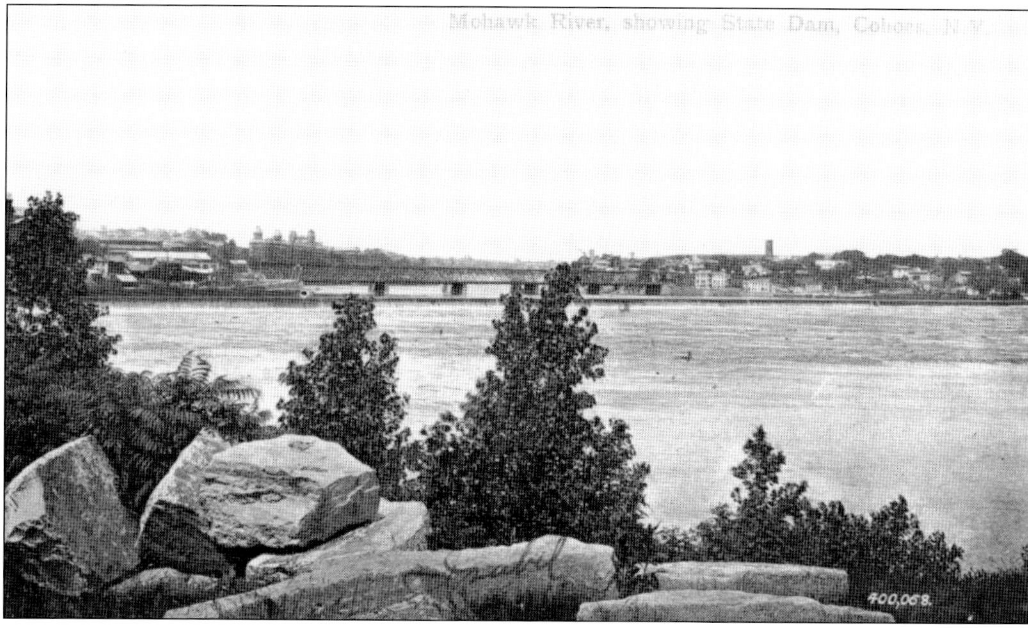


These postcard views show a branch of the Mohawk River, with the state dam, the Cohoes-Waterford Bridge, and railroad bridge spanning the Mohawk River. The postcard below shows the area east of Simmons Island, where Daniel Simmons manufactured highly regarded axes. Simmons selected this site because of its location next to the Champlain Canal, which delivered iron shipments from the Adirondacks. An adjacent lumberyard provided handles for the tools. The axe works flourished there from 1834 throughout the 19th century and was one of the nation's earliest producers of axes and edge tools. Simmons, as a blacksmith in Albany, was among the first to apply a borax flux method to produce axes that held a very durable cutting edge. An increasing market for these axes led him to move his shop to Cohoes, with its abundant waterpower and transportation network.

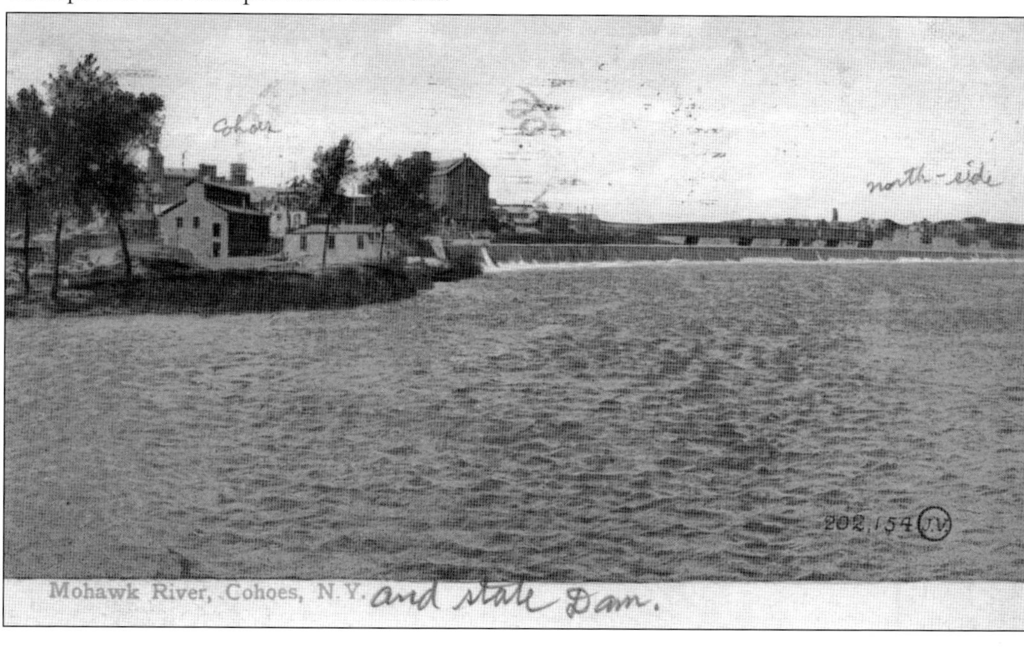

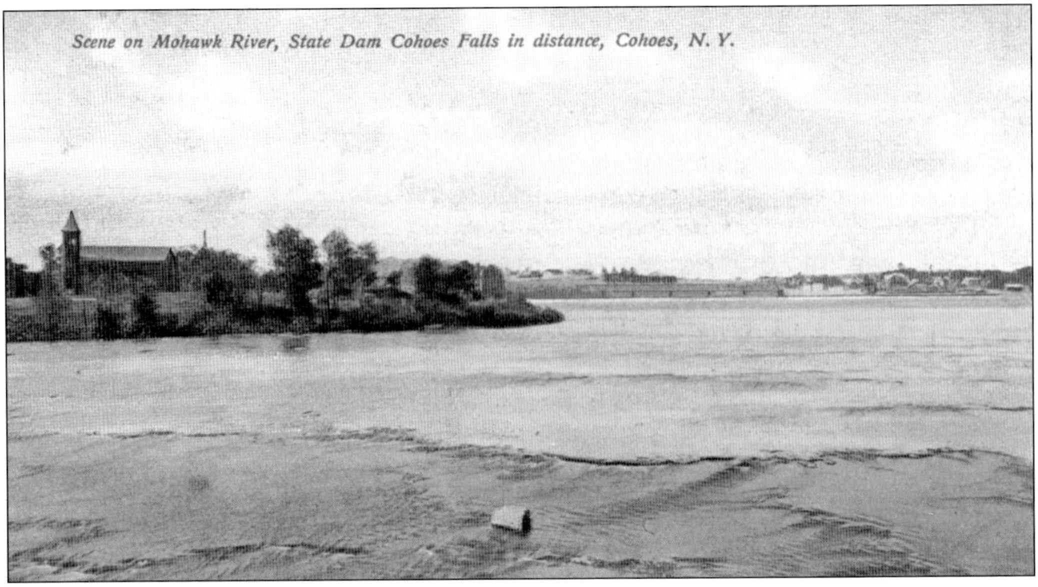


Rev. Valentine Gierlacki arrived in Cohoes in December 1903 to organize a Polish parish to serve the city's growing Polish and Slovak populations. A church planning committee was formed, and it chose a site on Page Avenue on Simmons Island. Construction began the day after Labor Day in 1903. Every evening, parishioners volunteered to dig the foundation to save money for the parish. This work was often done after a hard day's labor in the mills. The cornerstone of the church was laid on October 2, 1904, with more than 1,500 in attendance. The first building had a school on the first floor and the church on the second level. In December 1924, the church was damaged by fire. A new church, which still stands today, was dedicated on Sunday, November 29, 1925. The postcard below shows its interior. Over the years, additional stained-glass windows and a new entrance were added.

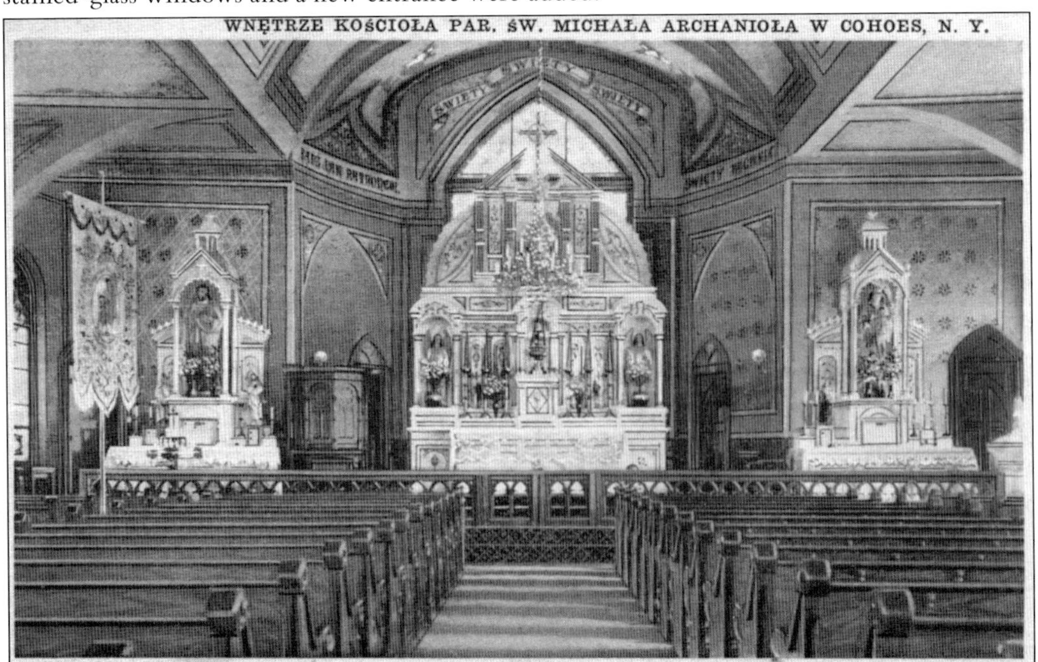

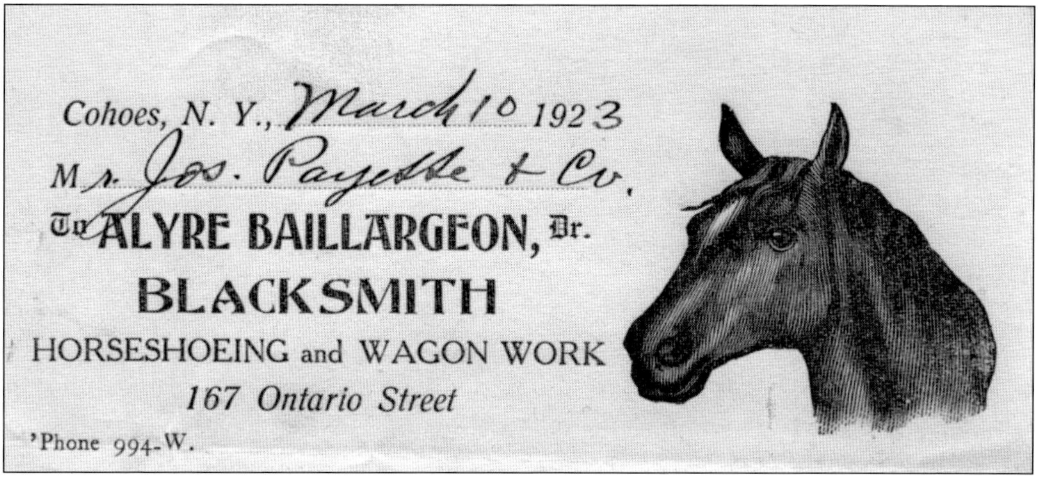
Cohoes, N. Y., March 10 1923
Mr. Jos. Payette & Co.
To ALYRE BAILLARGEON, Dr.
BLACKSMITH
HORSESHOEING and WAGON WORK
167 Ontario Street
'Phone 994-W.

Alyre Baillargeon owned a blacksmith shop located on Simmons Island at Ontario and Clark Streets. The shop had previously been at 104 Saratoga Street from 1907 to 1916. His shop was on the first floor, and the upstairs portion of the building was a residence for his family. With the growing popularity of motor vehicles, he gave up his blacksmith business in 1925 and became an automotive valve maker.

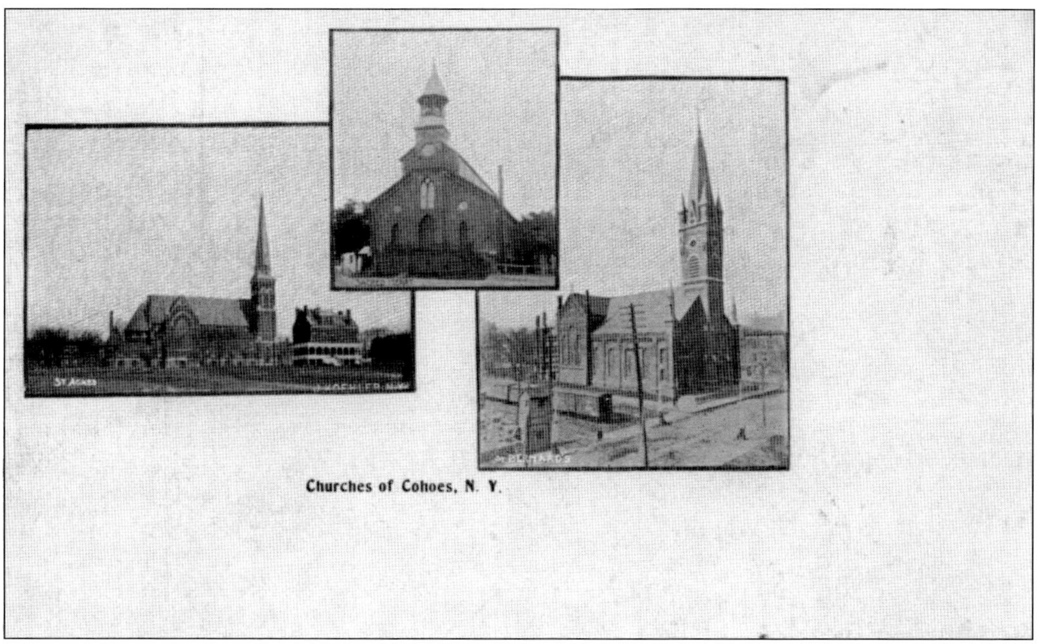


Sacred Heart, St. Agnes, and St. Bernard's were three of the nine Catholic churches in Cohoes. The churches reflected the immigration patterns that shaped the city. They were the center of social life for immigrant groups and helped maintain cultural traditions, language, and customs. Sacred Heart Parish, originally a mission of St. Joseph's Parish, became an independent church in 1887. Like St. Joseph's, the church preserved French Canadian language and culture.

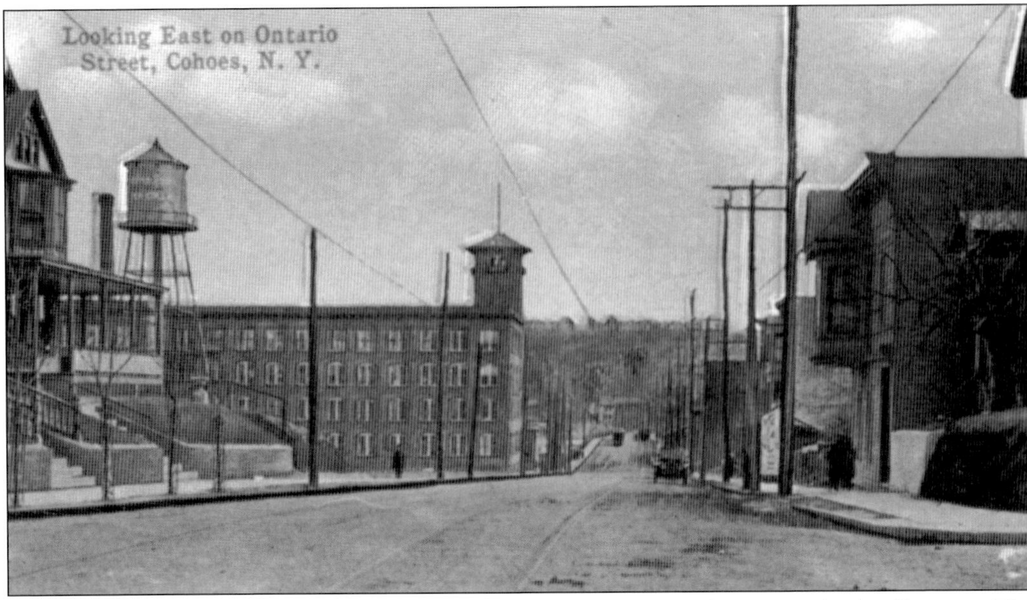


In this view looking east on Ontario Street, the 112th Street Bridge is seen in the distance. The James E. Cunniff variety store, which was open until 1939, was in this section of the street. Industries included the Rensselaer Valve Co., Peterson & Packard Coal Co., and Corliss, Coon & Co., which is also shown in the postcard below. Corliss, Coon & Co. began in Troy in 1838. The company, a manufacturer of men's linen collars and cuffs, became Coon & Co. in 1883 and was located on Fulton Street. In 1904, the company became Corliss, Coon & Co. and relocated to 31 Ontario Street in Cohoes in 1905, where it remained until 1942. In Cohoes, it produced linen collars and cuffs for both men and women. The popularity of the company's products was so widespread that it had salesrooms in Chicago, Boston, Baltimore, St. Louis, and New York City.

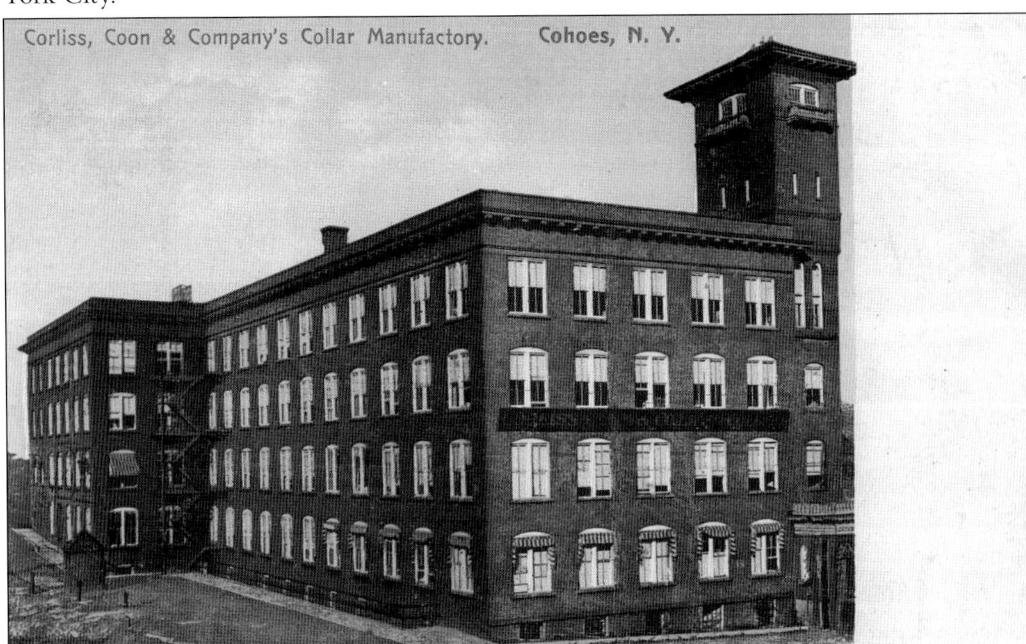

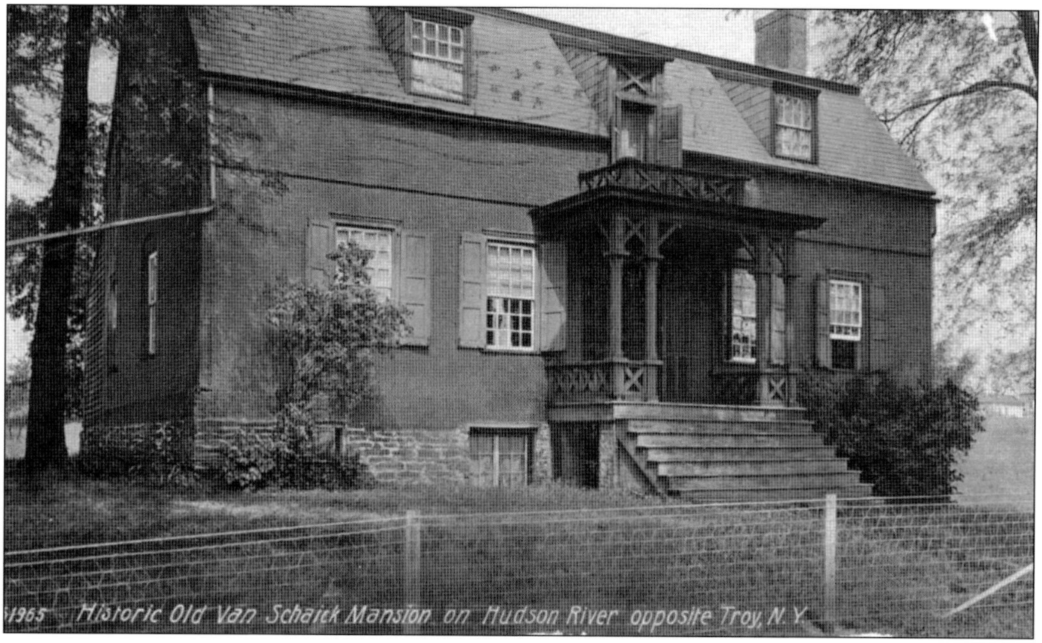


Anthony Van Schaick built the Van Schaick Mansion in 1735. The 15-room house overlooking the Hudson River was constructed using materials imported from Holland and bricks made on Van Schaick Island. The mansion is best known for its key role during the Revolutionary War. It was the army headquarters of the Continental Army, Northern Department, from June to October 1777. Maj. Gen. Philip Schuyler and his aides planned the first Battle of Saratoga here. Schuyler's main army camped on Van Schaick Island, just behind the house. George Washington also visited the mansion twice. In August 1777, Gov. George Clinton consulted with military leaders and remained for three days at the mansion; during this period, the Van Schaick mansion was considered the state capitol. It is the only place in New York where the governor's official flag can be unfurled when the governor himself is not present.

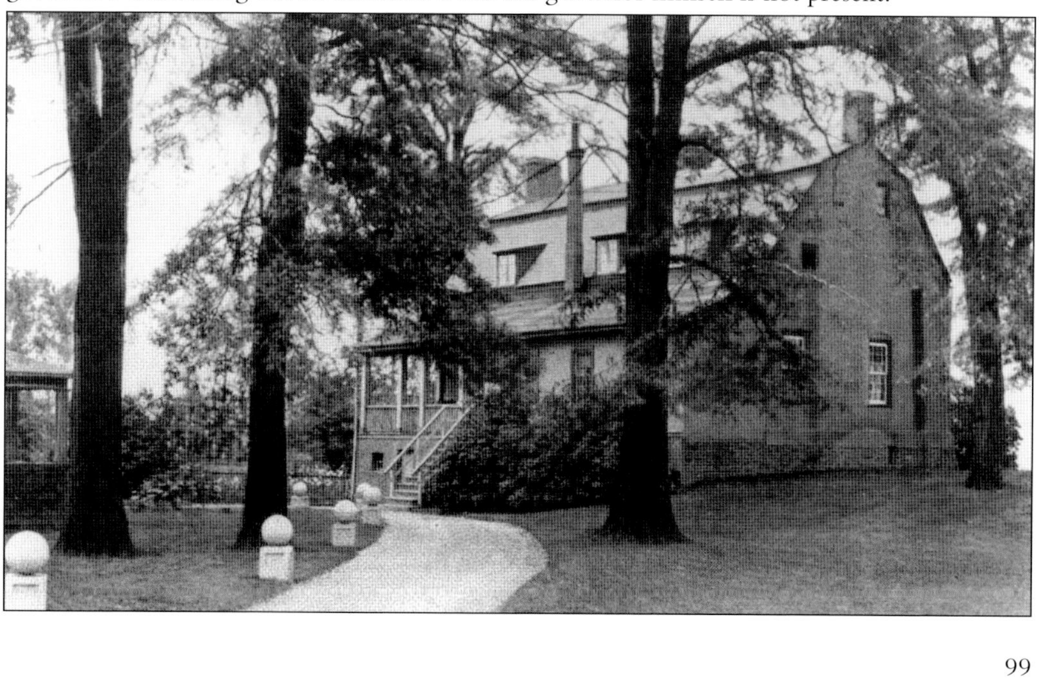

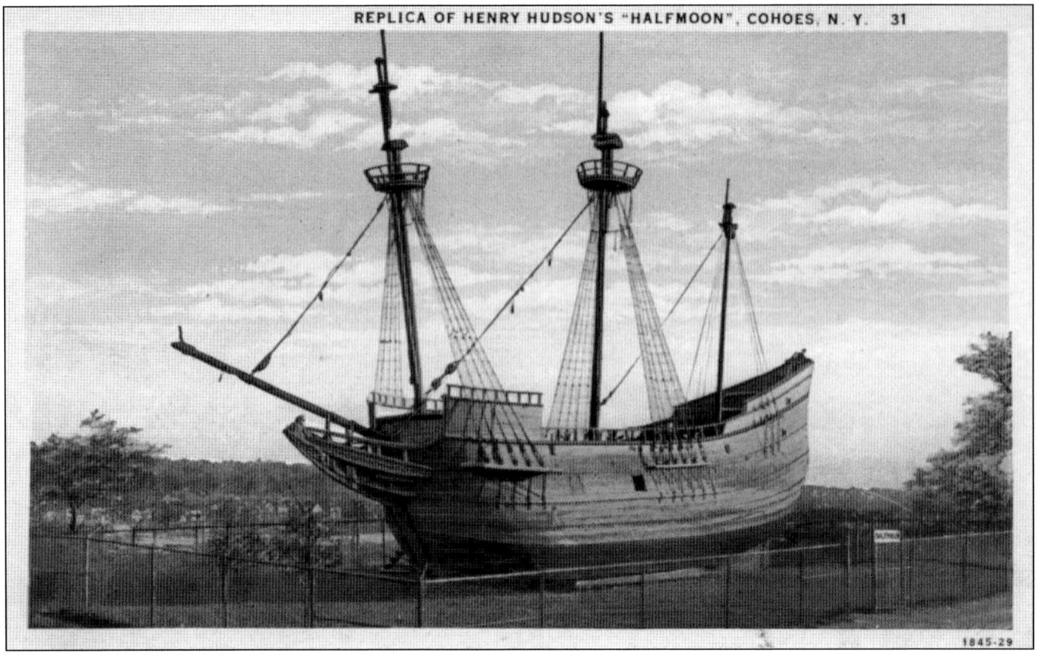


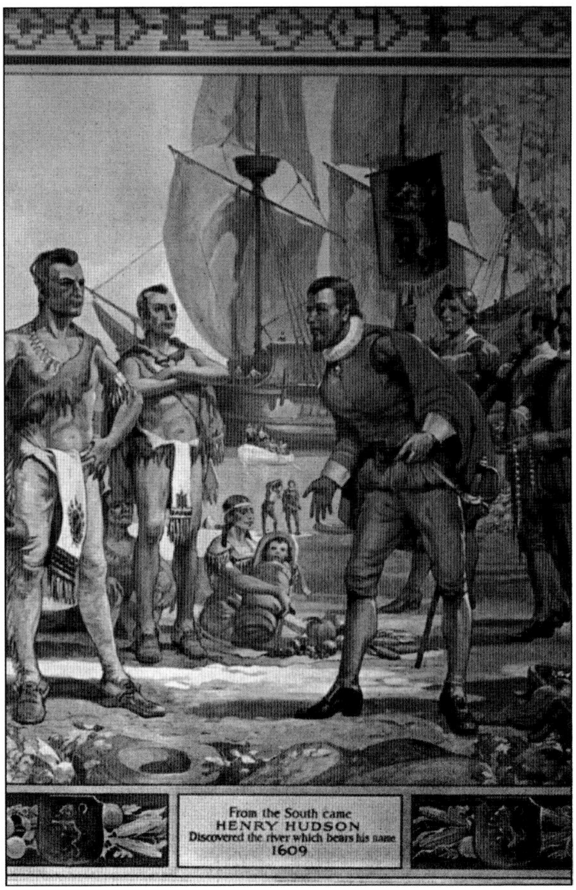


This replica of Henry Hudson's ship, the *Half Moon*, was built in the Netherlands for the 1909 Hudson-Fulton Celebration, and was presented to the State of New York. The celebration commemorated the 300th anniversary of Henry Hudson's exploration of the Hudson River. The ship led a maritime parade of vessels in Brooklyn Harbor to kick off the massive 16-day celebration in New York City and the Hudson Valley. The concluding ceremonies were held in Cohoes on October 11, 1909. The ship was constructed using information from journals written by a member of Hudson's crew along with detailed shipbuilding plans for the ship *Hope*, the *Half Moon*'s sister vessel. During the celebration, 20 crew members of the Dutch warship *Utrecht* were enlisted to portray Hudson's crew. The ship flew flags of the Dutch East India Company and the Dutch state's crest.

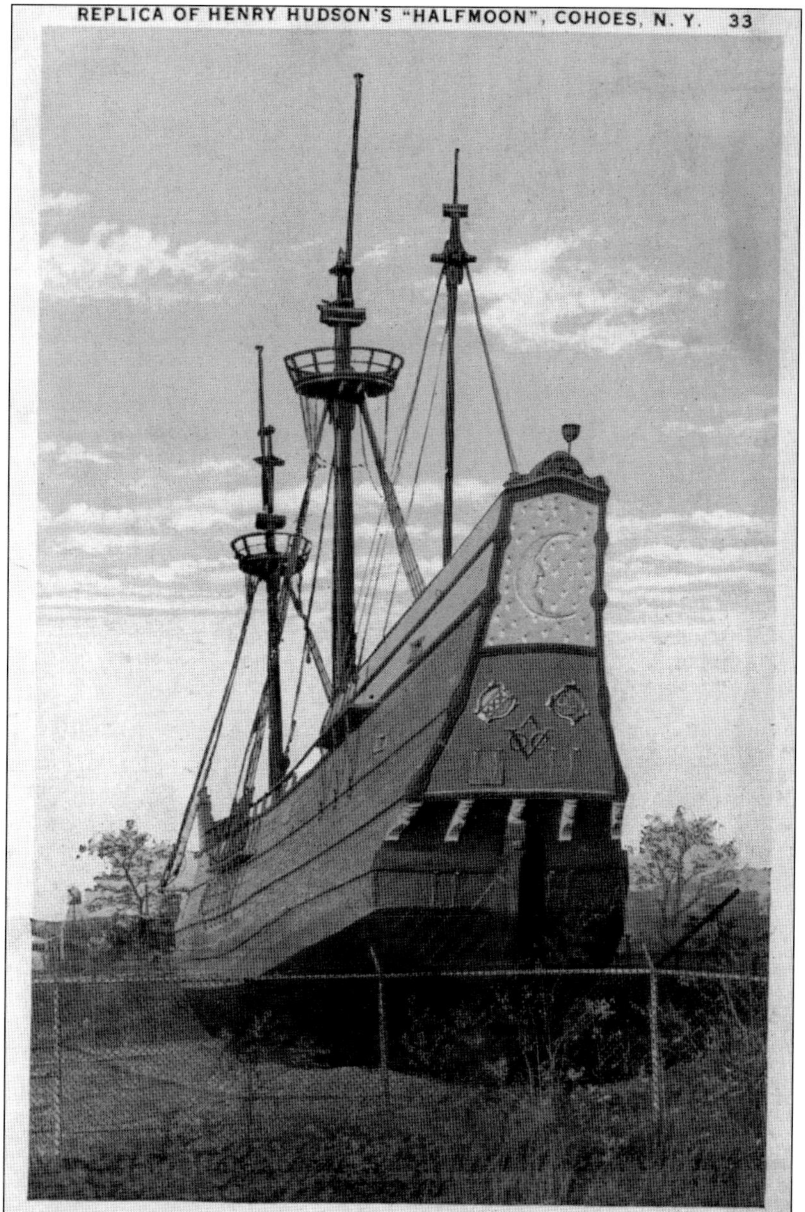


Cohoes lawyer Daniel Cosgro, who would be elected mayor of Cohoes in 1921, was one of 15 members of the local organizing committee for the 1909 Hudson-Fulton Celebration. After the festivities, the *Half Moon* replica was moored near Kingston and fell into disrepair. A battle ensued for the ship's custody between Albany, Cohoes, and New York City. Through the efforts of Mayor Cosgro, the *Half Moon* was brought to Cohoes in 1924 and anchored off Van Schaick Island. After undergoing repairs at the Matton Shipyard, it was put on display in Van Schaick Park near the pond. The ship was a popular attraction in the late 1920s, when it was open to the public during the summer months. In this view, the rear portion of *Half Moon*, painted sky blue and white with a half-moon with the profile of a man in the moon in the crescent, can be seen. The ship had a device on the main deck called the "silent servant," a post shaped like a man with a pulley system and lines that assisted in raising and lowering sails.

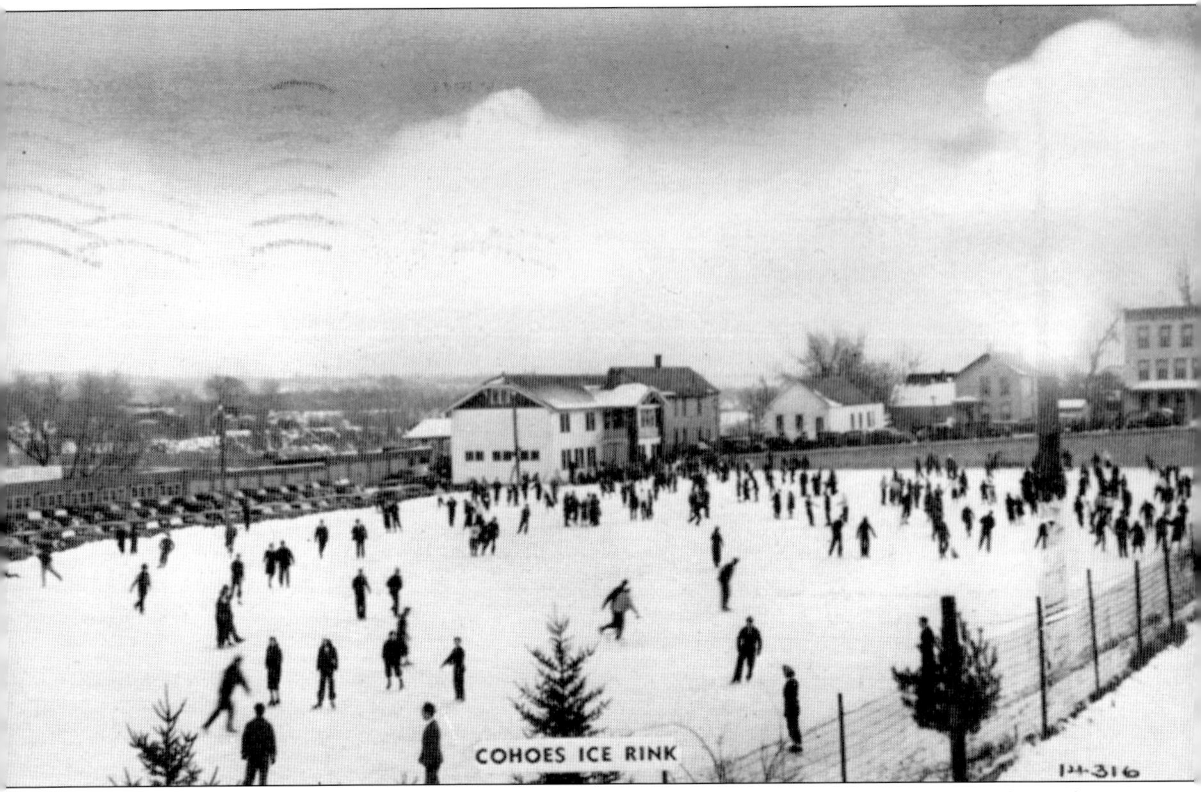


Iver Carlson ran Carlson's Ice Rink for 40 years starting in 1910, when he purchased the Cohoes Ice Rink. Thomas Wallace, who owned the *Cohoes Republican*, an early Cohoes newspaper, originally established the rink on Ship Street in 1892. The first Rensselaer Polytechnic Institute (RPI) hockey game, a contest against Williams College on January 25, 1902, was played at the Cohoes Ice Rink. Carlson's Ice Rink remained open until 1971 and was operated in its last two decades by Iver Carlson's son E. Iver Carlson. Carlson's drew the city's children for skating in part because of the actions of Cohoes mayor Daniel Cosgro. Cosgro was alarmed at the number of youngsters who lost their lives each winter skating on the city's canals, so he contracted with Iver Carlson in the 1920s to provide free skating for schoolchildren each winter afternoon.

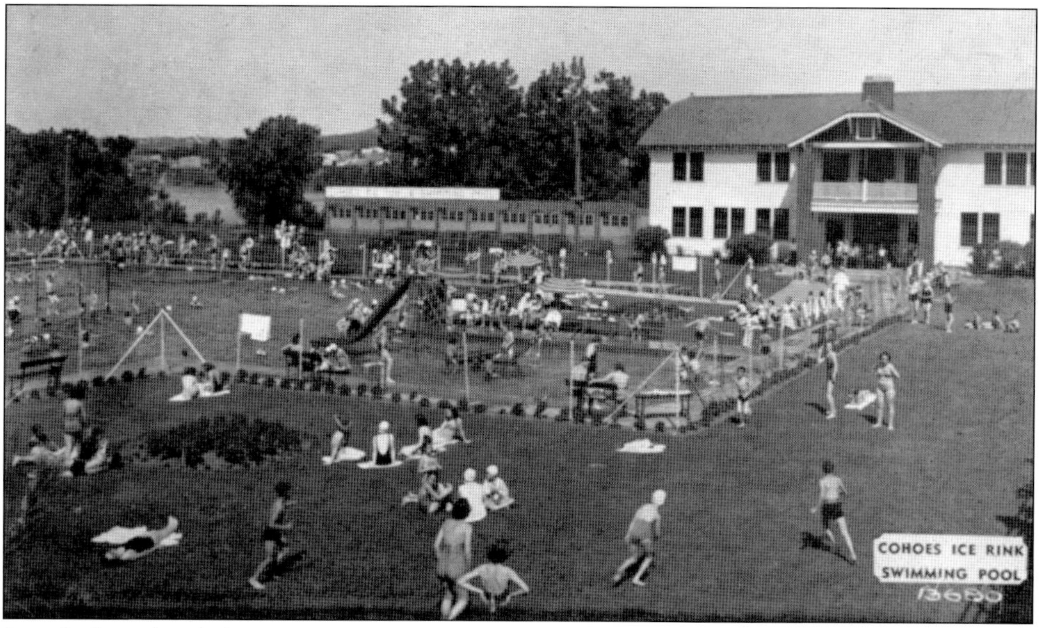


Iver Carlson decided to open a swimming pool in 1924 due to the success of the ice rink, and Carlson's became a summer destination for city residents. In 1950, E. Iver Carlson purchased the business from his father, Iver, and operated the pool until its closing in 1975. Many people purchased season passes for the pool, and the site also had a basketball court and playing fields for pickup games of baseball or football. Generations of Cohoesiers participated in the "learn to swim" classes at Carlson's. The building used as the bathhouse, shown in the postcard above, was later converted into a restaurant after the closing of the pool. The restaurant, called the Sassy Swede, was run by Iver Carlson's granddaughter Linda Plowman, with her mother, Doris, E. Iver's wife, as chef.

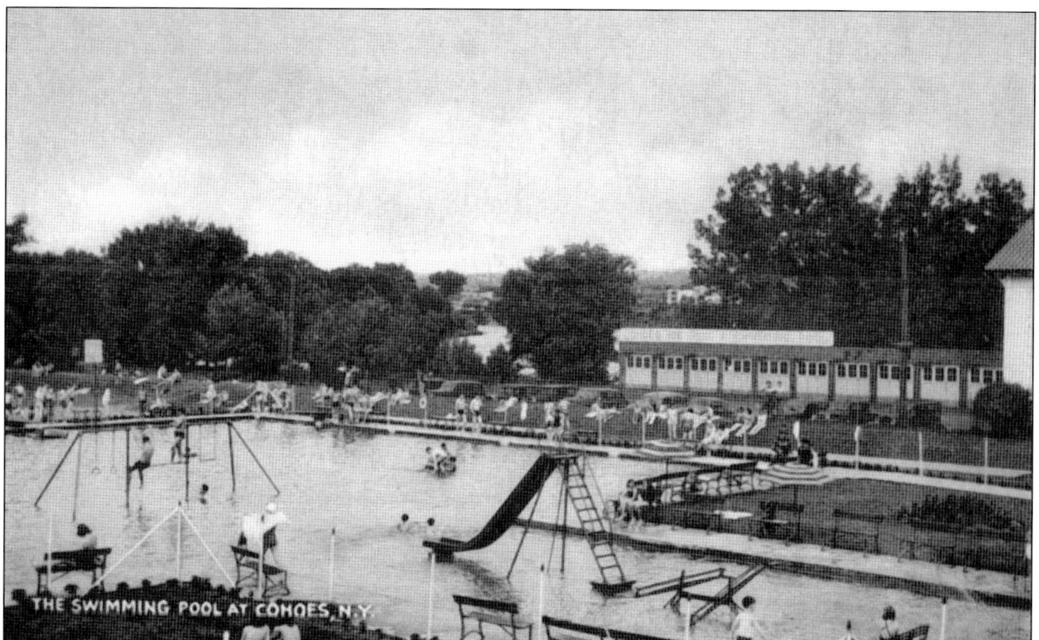

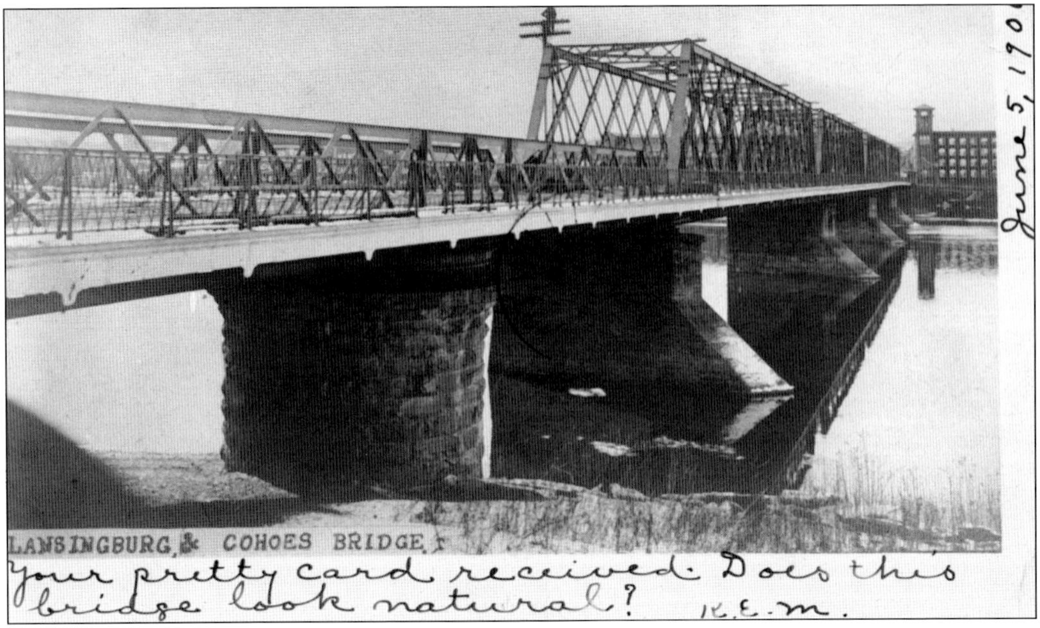


In 1872, Thomas Knickerbocker constructed a covered bridge at this location spanning the Hudson River between Cohoes and Lansingburgh. It was replaced with an iron double-intersection Warren truss bridge, shown on this postcard, which was opened on May 18, 1880. Initially a toll bridge, it became free to cross in 1914. The bridge was owned by the Troy and Cohoes Bridge Company, which also owned the Waterford and Congress Street Bridges over the Hudson River. On March 4, 1920, the bridge's deck caught fire from sparks from a trolley, and the span collapsed. To provide pedestrians with a place to cross at 112th Street, a temporary suspension bridge was constructed using the first three piers of the old bridge; the easternmost truss was not damaged in the fire. This bridge was in service for three years until a replacement could be built.

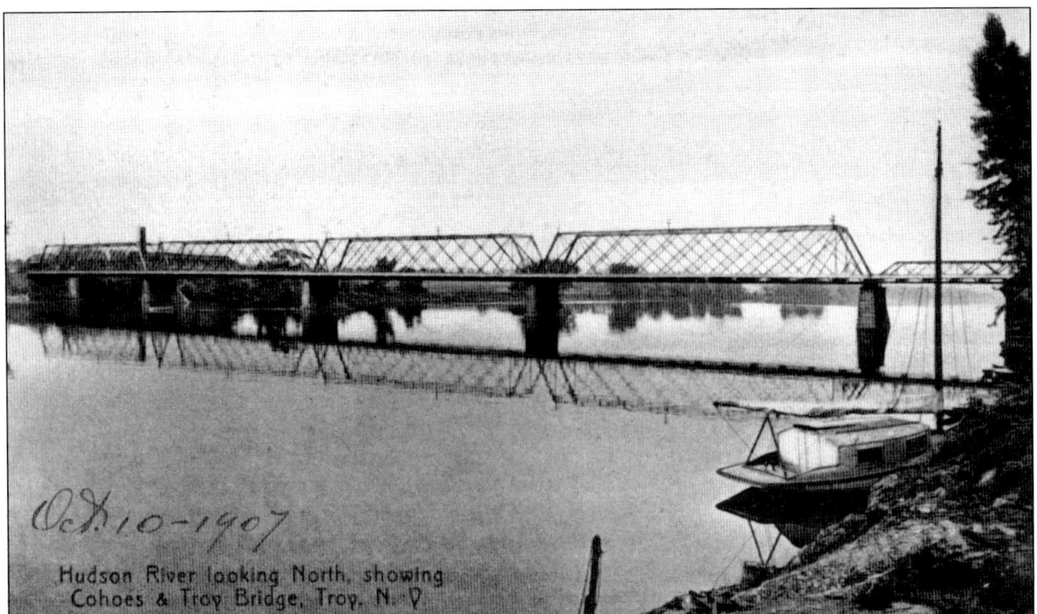

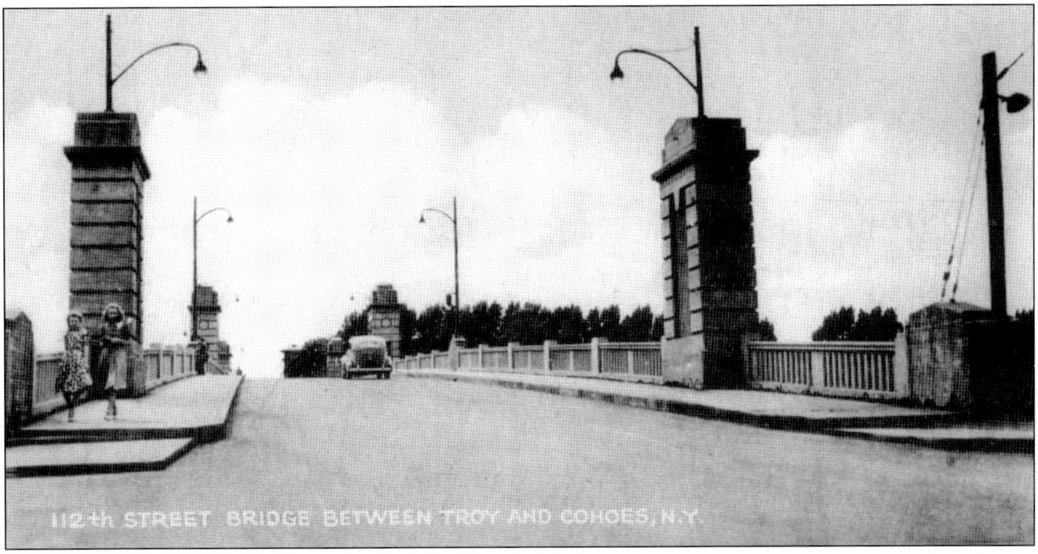


The replacement span that crossed the Hudson River between Cohoes and Lansingburgh was a bascule bridge, or drawbridge, with concrete approach spans. It was opened on October 23, 1923, and was extensively ornamented, with decorative light stanchions and graceful open-spandrel concrete arches. The Chicago-based engineering firm of Joseph B. Strauss, the engineer for the Golden Gate Bridge, constructed the 200-foot bascule span, which could be lifted to allow boats through, notably those from the nearby Matton Shipyard. B.H. Davies of the New York State Department of Public Works designed the bridge. The overall length of the structure was 803 feet. A plaque from the 1880 bridge was set into concrete on the Cohoes side of the new bridge. By 1998, the bridge was in disrepair and was replaced by a steel multigirder bridge, designed and built by Harrison & Burrows; design elements in the new structure echo the earlier bascule bridge.

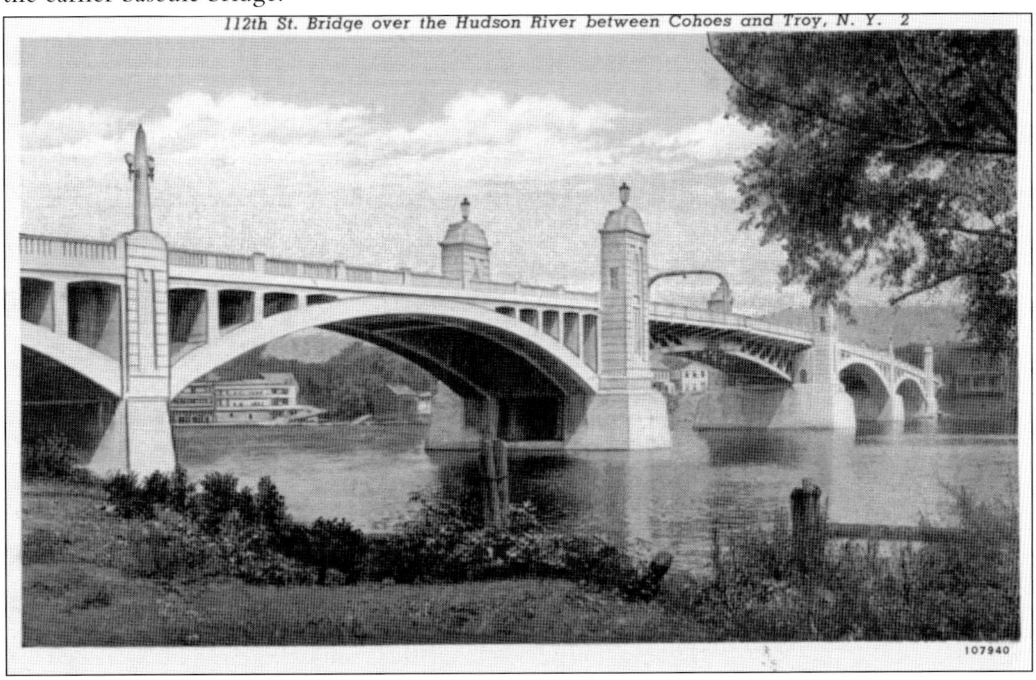

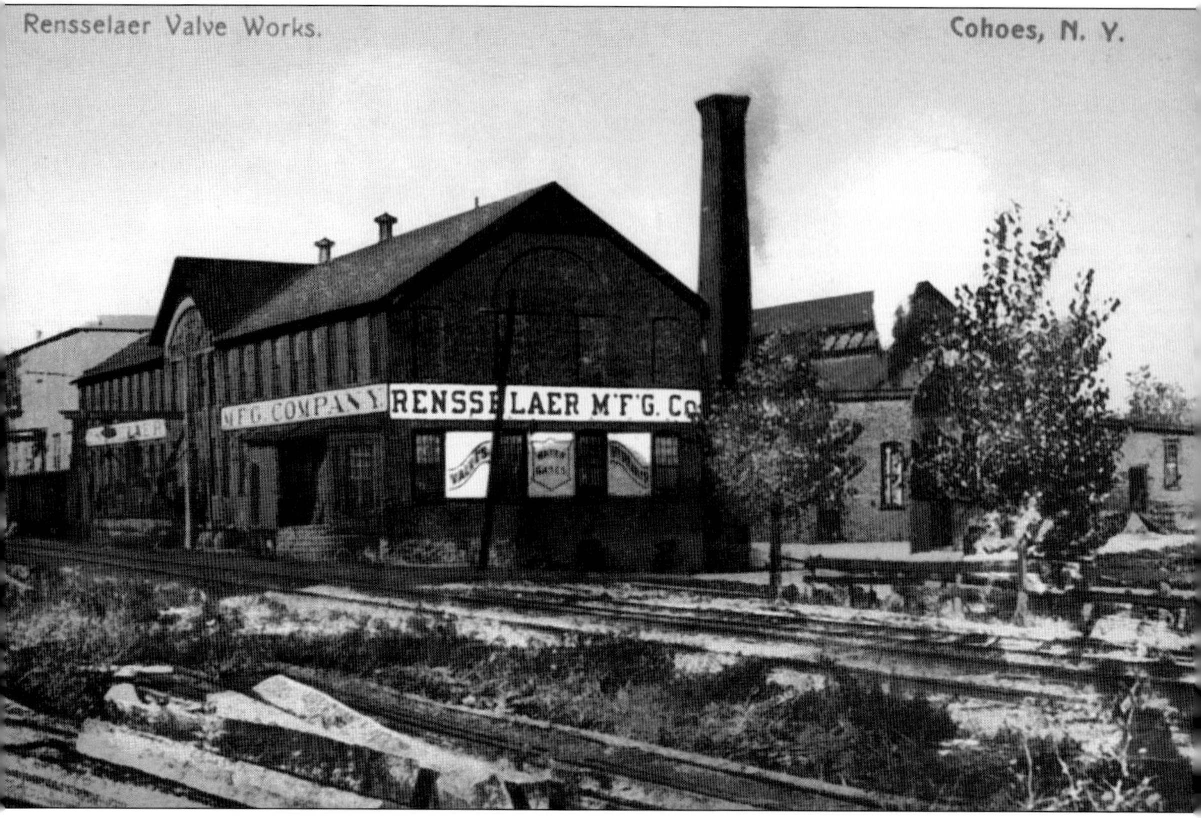


P. Southwick founded the Rensselaer Valve Works in 1853. The Rensselaer Valve Company began manufacturing valves in 1879 at a plant in Lansingburgh, owned by S.V. Arnold and E.L. Rowe. The company settled in Cohoes at 1 Ontario Street in 1887, induced to this location by tax exemptions offered by the city. The factory complex in this c. 1915 postcard was built in 1888. Other sections were added to the factory in 1908 and 1937. The company had patents for fire hydrants and was the sole producer of the Corey fire hydrant in the United States. It was one of the firms that made the region a nationally regarded center for the manufacture of valves and fire hydrants. Rensselaer Valve merged with the Troy-based Ludlow Manufacturing Company in 1954. The Weglarz Machine Shop later occupied this site on Ontario Street.

# *Five*

# The Hill

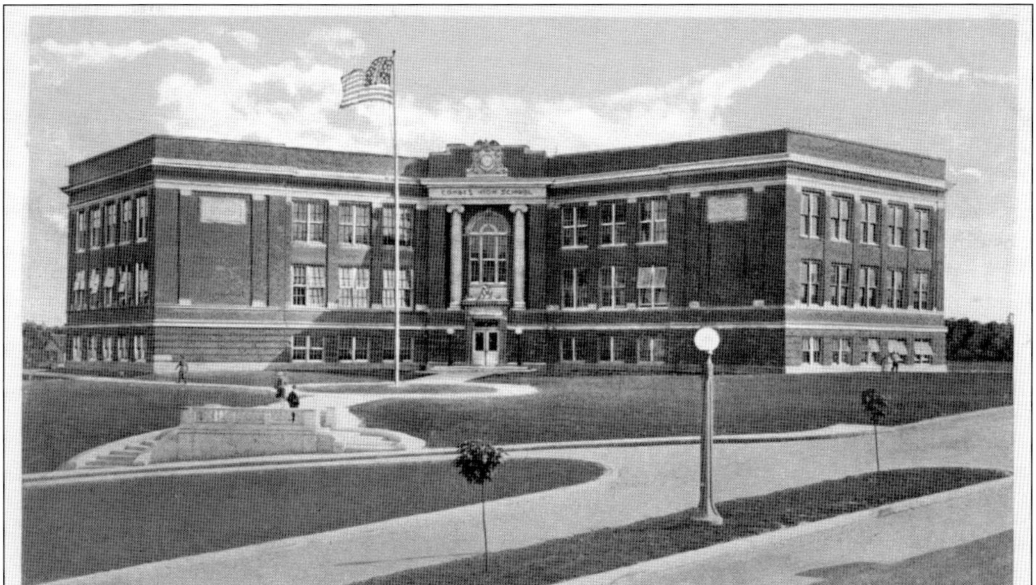


The Cohoes High School on Bevan and Columbia Streets was constructed in 1919. It replaced Egberts High School on White Street. The building became Cohoes Middle School when a new high school was constructed at the western end of Elm Street in 1965. Alumni who attended the old high school have fond memories of principal Madelon K. Hickey and her predecessor, Charles "Pop" Wheeler, both outstanding educators.

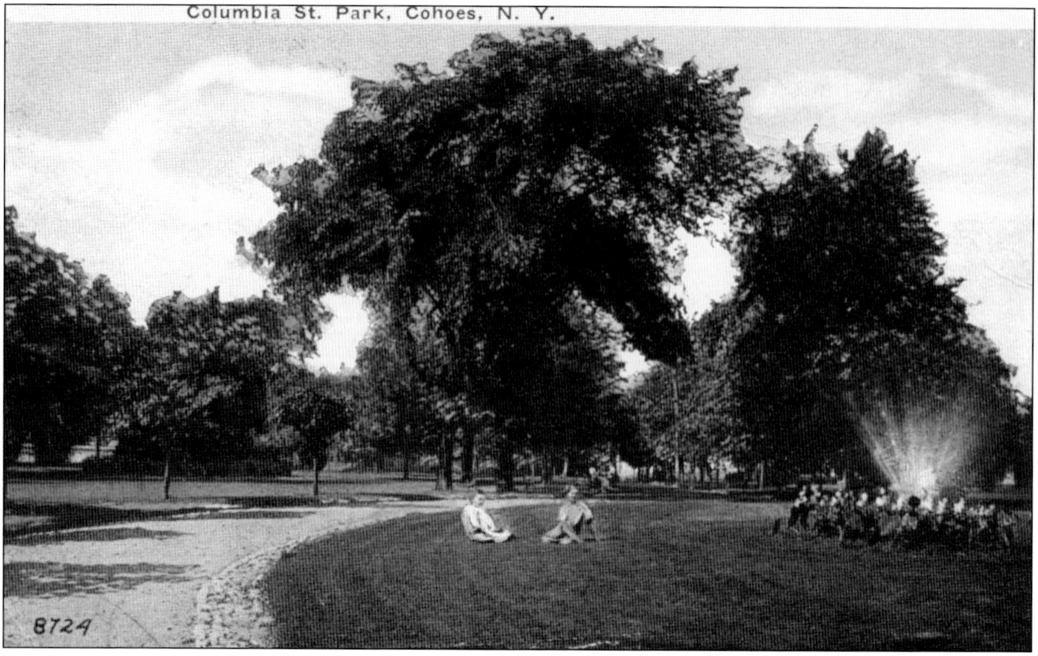


Early in Cohoes's history, a plot of ground that is now within West End Park was given to the Cohoes Company by the Lansing family for use as a burying ground. The Cohoes Company sold the first burial plot for $4 in 1846. In 1857, the Village of Cohoes was given the cemetery by the Cohoes Company for a nominal fee. The old burying grounds were formally earmarked for a park site in 1896. Exhumation of the bodies began in June 1896, but as workmen dug, water held by thick clay flooded the holes. The pine coffins unearthed had disintegrated and the remains were characterized as "black slimy bones." Over 900 unmarked remains were exhumed and transferred to Union Cemetery in Crescent. Thirty-eight identified bodies were moved to Waterford Rural, Oakwood, and Albany Rural Cemeteries.

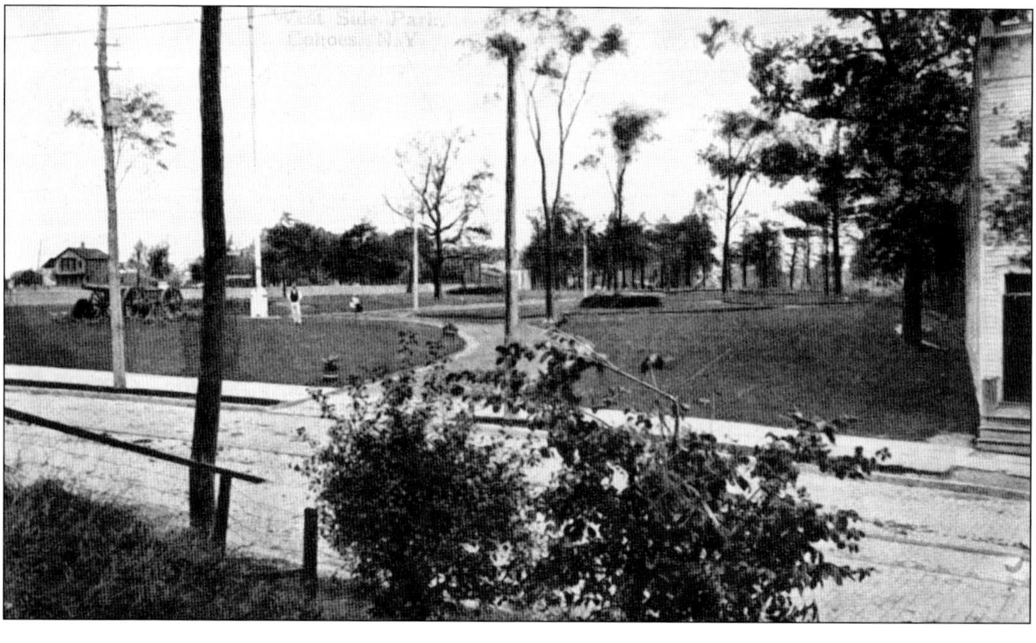

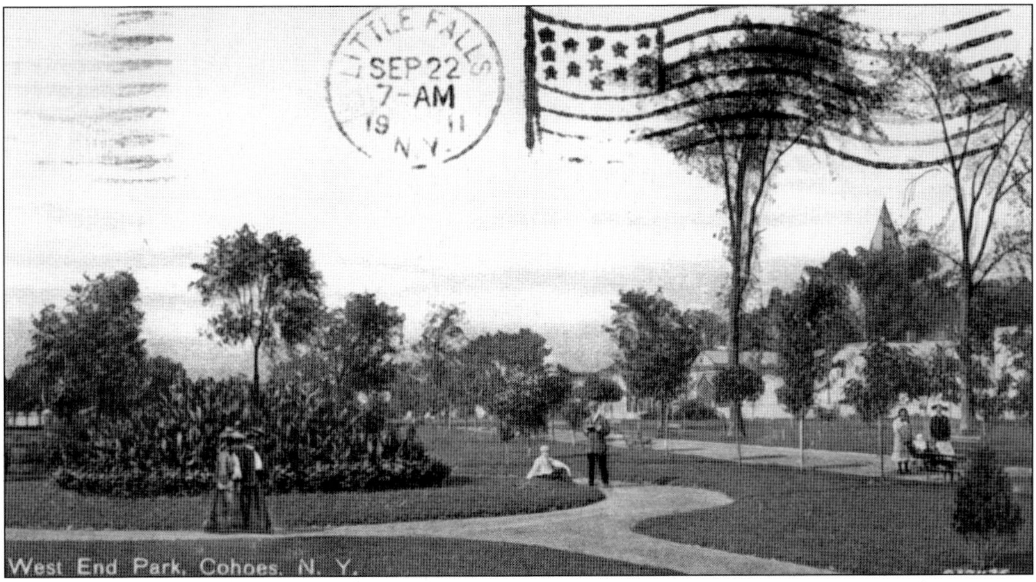


The dedication of the Soldiers and Sailors Monument at West End Park took place on July 4, 1910. The ceremonies were preceded by a parade, with participants including the veterans of the Civil and Spanish-American Wars and the unions of the Cohoes Federation of Labor. Among the unions represented in the parade were jackspinners, mulespinners, loom fixers, shirt ironers, carders, washers and dyers, carpenters, painters, plumbers, coal handlers, clerks, theatrical stage employees, and cigar makers. At the unveiling, speeches were delivered by J.W. Himes, Mayor Merritt D. Hanson, and Rev. T.M. House, chaplain of Post Lyon of the Grand Army of the Republic (GAR). Following the ceremony, a picnic and field day were held. The parade stepped off from the northern end of Remsen Street. The route went from Remsen Street to Mohawk Street, to White Street, to High Street, to Younglove Avenue, to Walnut Street, to Columbia Street, and into the park.

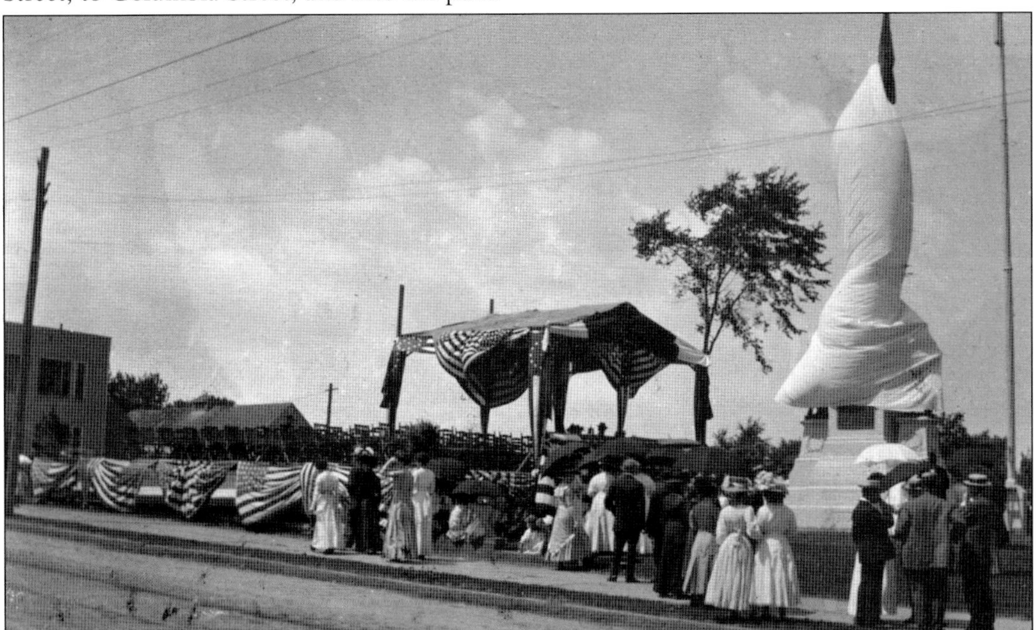

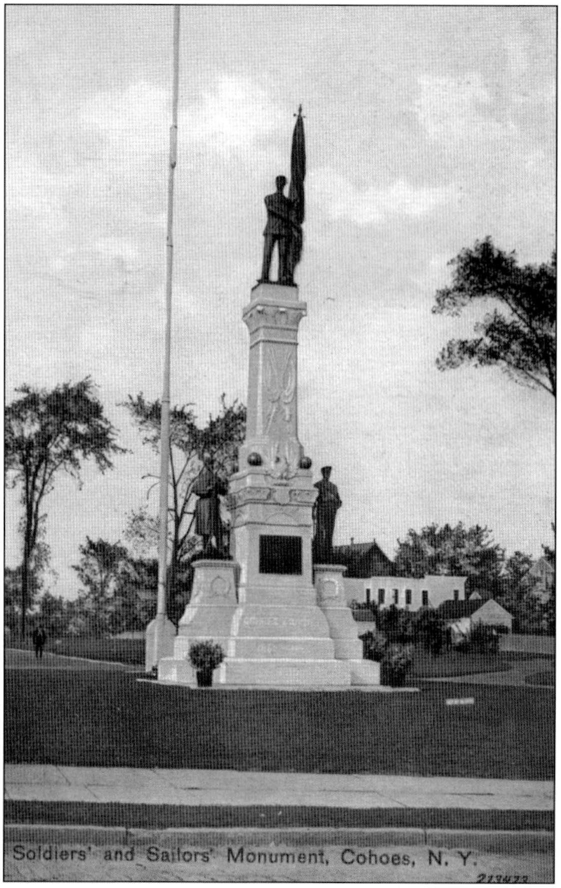


West End Park on Columbia Street was the city cemetery for many years. In 1897, the cemetery committee reported that 981 bodies were disinterred to prepare the site for a new park. The Soldiers and Sailors Monument shown in these postcards was originally near the Champlain Canal east of Ship Street. It was dedicated in 1872 to those who died in the Civil War. The monument was moved to the Columbia Street side of West End Park and was rededicated in 1910, with mortars placed on either side. In the center of the park, there is a monument honoring those from the 5th Ward who served in World War II. A third monument in the park near the Soldiers and Sailors Monument, dedicated on May 24, 1991, recognizes the men and women of Cohoes who served in Korea and the Persian Gulf.

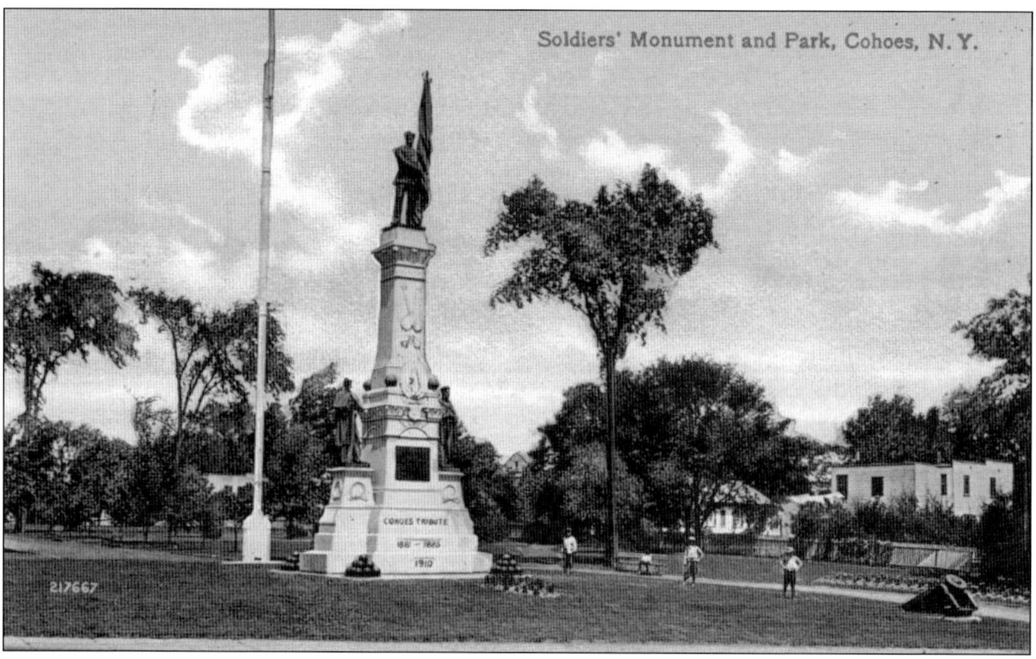

The Park Methodist Episcopal Church, built in the 1870s on Masten Avenue and Cherry Street, was succeeded by St. James Methodist Episcopal Church, formed in 1881. In 1894, the church pictured here was built on McElwain Avenue. It was destroyed by fire in 1962. Of interest is the signature "Charles Spence" on this postcard. A Charles Spence was a steward of St. James Church in the 1940s.

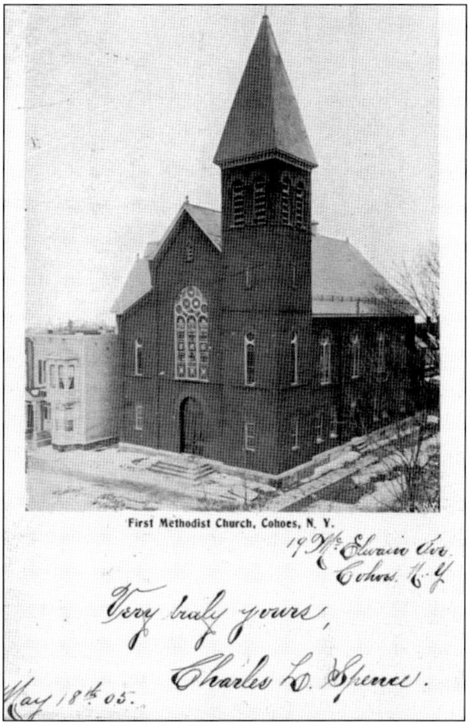


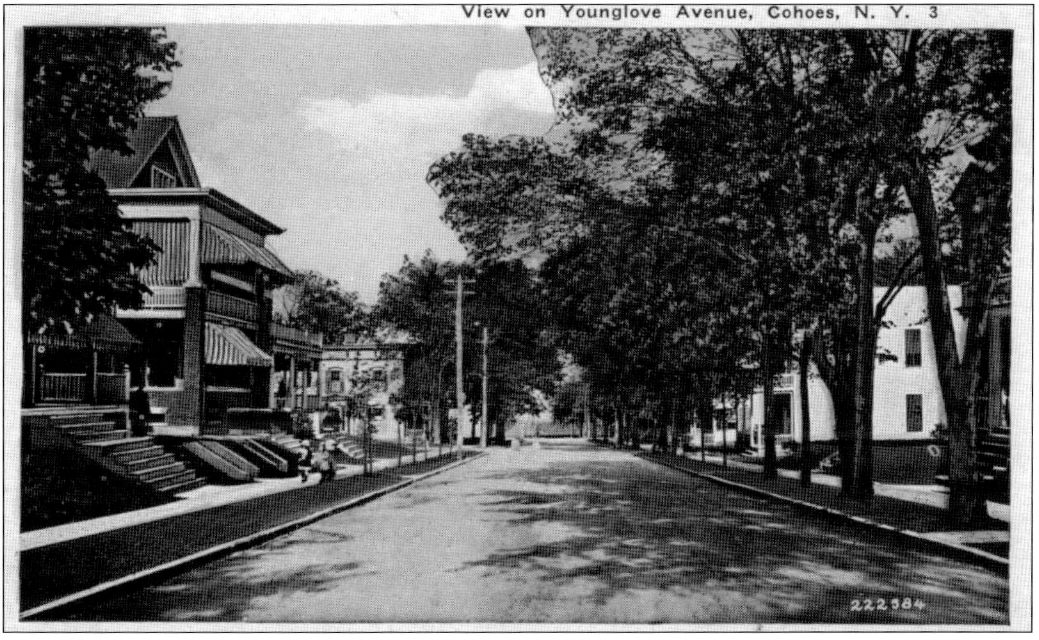


Younglove Avenue was named for Truman Giles Younglove (1815–1882). He directed construction of the dam, gatehouse, and power canal system for the Cohoes Company and supervised construction of Harmony Mill No. 3. He was a trustee of the village of Cohoes, water commissioner of the Cohoes Waterworks, trustee of the Cohoes Gas Light Company, an incorporator of the Cohoes Savings Institution, and treasurer and director of the First National Bank.

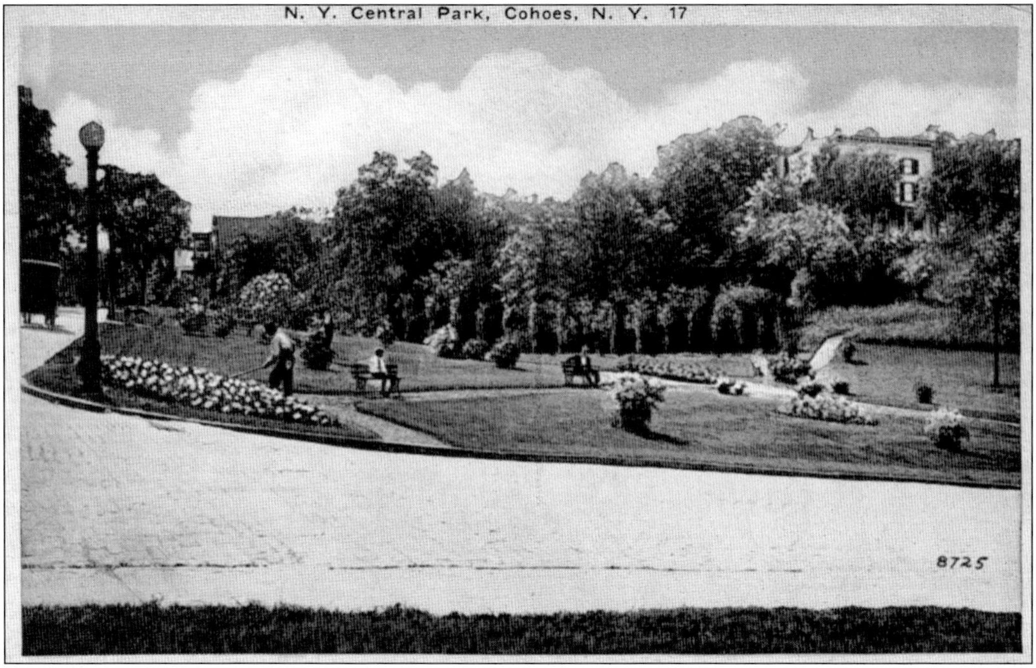


The postcard below shows the depot for the New York Central Railroad on Younglove Avenue, which opened in June 1904. As a result of petitioning to the railroad by the Cohoes Businessman's Association, the depot was built of brick and stone instead of wood. An earlier passenger station was east of the tracks on the south side of High Street but was moved when the railroad bridge was added to eliminate the grade crossing at the street. The project was undertaken as a result of public outcry about frequent accidents at the crossing, where it was necessary to cross the main rail line as well as sidetracks in a busy freight yard and warehouse area. During the grade crossing elimination project, the New York Central Park, shown in the postcard above, was created at the base of Younglove Avenue.

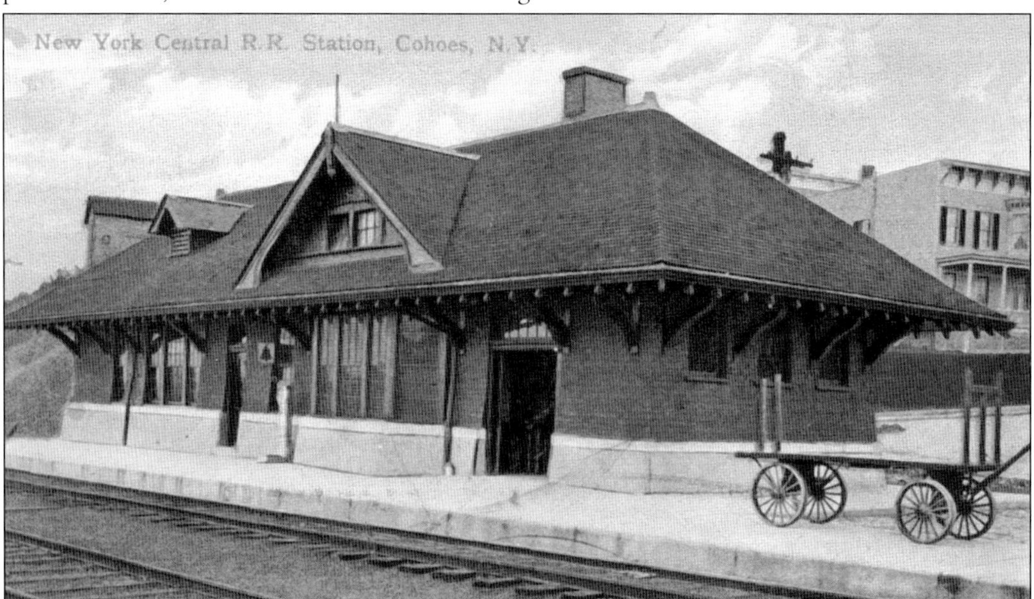

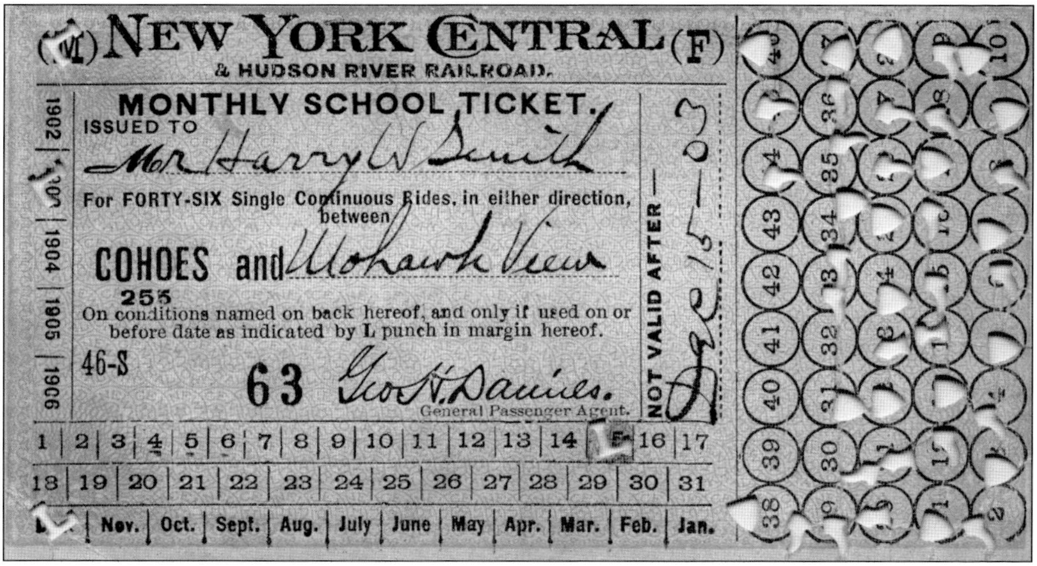


This 1903 school ticket for the New York Central Railroad permits 46 one-way train rides between Cohoes and Mohawk View, northwest of the city in the town of Colonie, along what is now the Mohawk-Hudson Bike Trail. At the time, the extensive network of passenger rail and trolley systems in Cohoes and around the region permitted convenient travel to work or school, shopping, or for a Sunday outing.

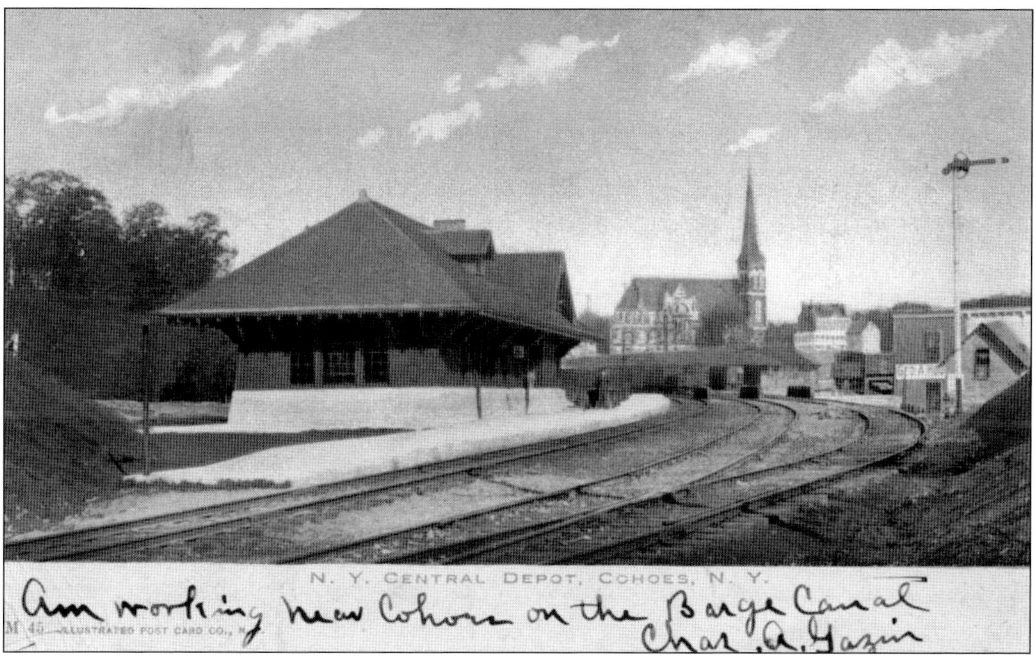


Passenger service continued into the 1920s, and freight service continued into the 1970s on the New York Central Railroad. The original Schenectady & Troy Railroad became part of the newly created New York Central Railroad in 1853. The line served the Harmony Mills warehouses and other Cohoes industries. The New York Central freight house and George House warehouse are along the tracks, with St. Agnes Church in the distance.

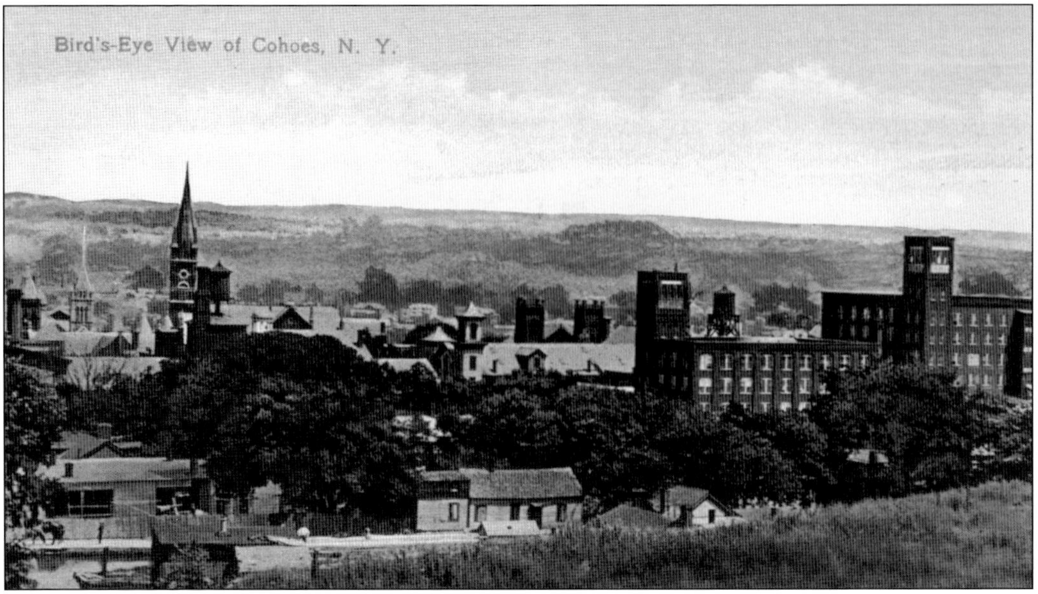


This bird's-eye view looks at downtown Cohoes from the hill at Imperial Avenue, near the childhood home of dancer Adelaide Dickey. In the foreground is Lock No. 13 of the enlarged Erie Canal, now buried under Bedford Street. Note the mule on the towpath. Buildings in the distance include the Silliman Memorial, city hall, St. Bernard's, the Dutch Reformed church, the Troy and Cohoes Shirt Co., and the Victor Mill.

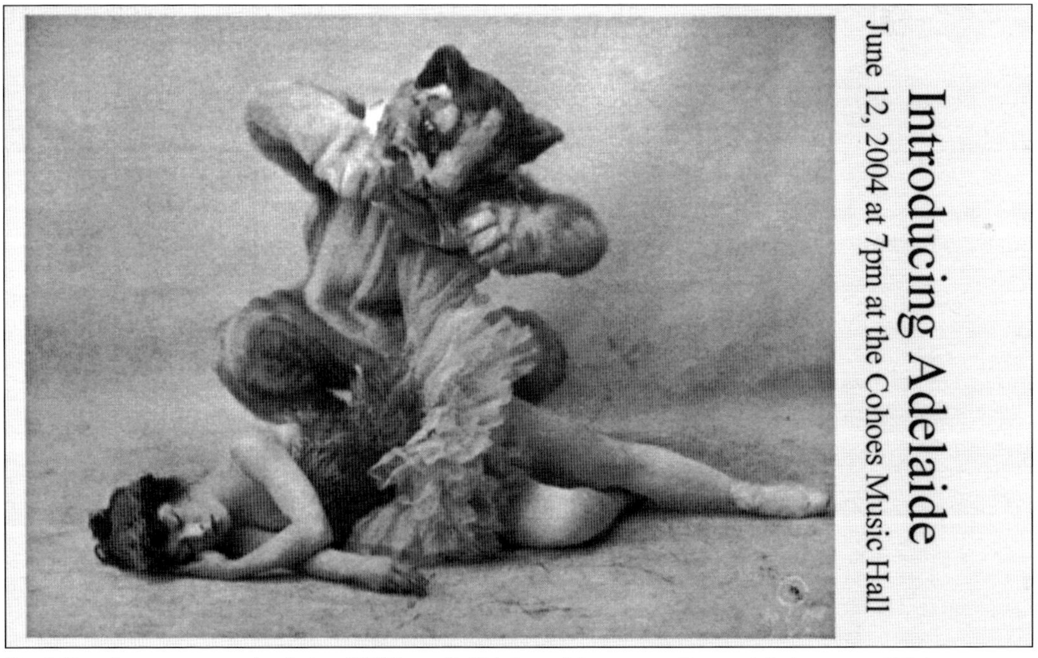


Paul Dunleavy researched the William J. Dickey House on Imperial Avenue. Dickey was a superintendent of the Egberts and Bailey Mill, and his daughter La Petite Adelaide became a vaudeville star, who started at the Cohoes Music Hall. She danced with and married J.J. Hughes. She often spoke of Cohoes and remembered practicing in a room at the Imperial Avenue house. This postcard was mailed to introduce Adelaide to Cohoes.

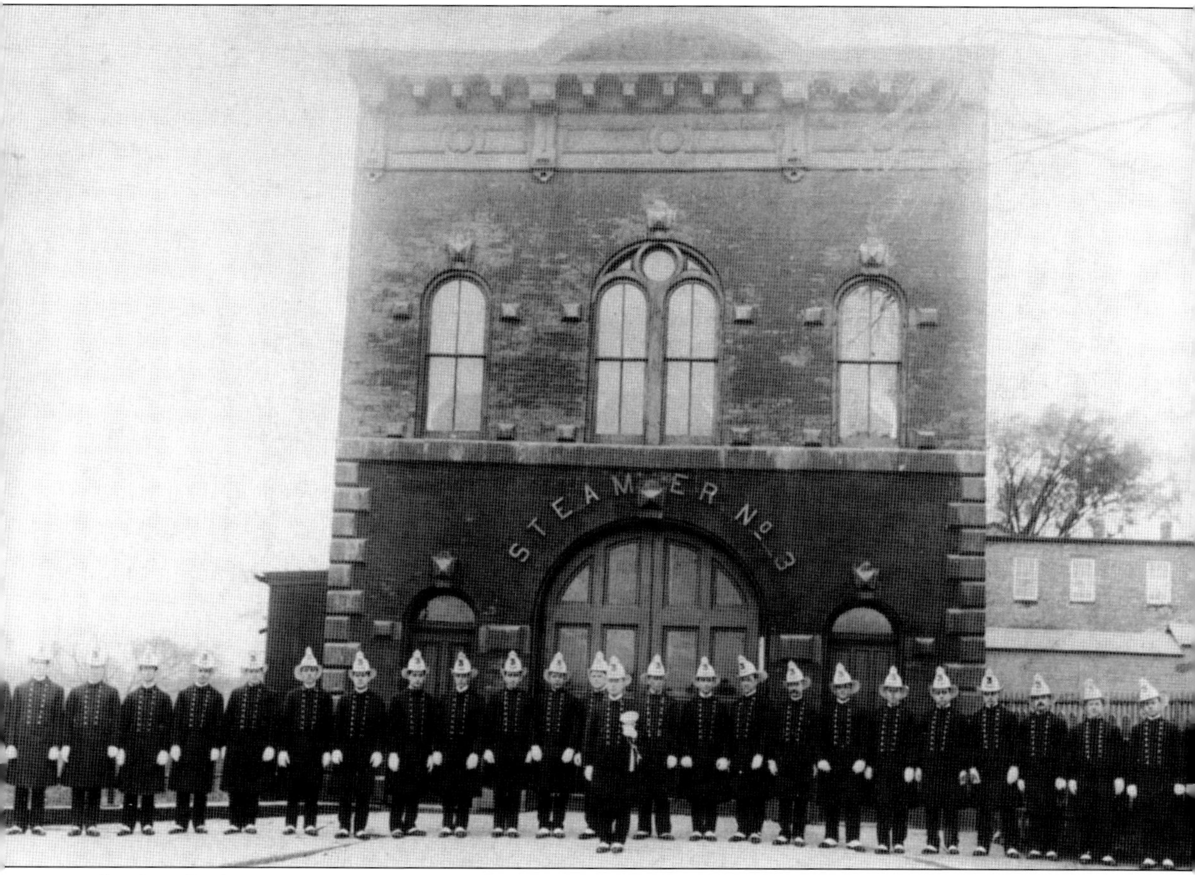


The first firehouse on Johnston Avenue was the Alden Hose Co. in 1865. In 1867, it was named Steamer No. 3, which became the main fire station in Cohoes. The necessity for fire engines at numerous locations was greatly diminished with the completion of the city waterworks and placement of numerous hydrants. Many fires plagued Cohoes in its early years, and standard procedures for handling fires and sounding alarms were established in 1872, with a false alarm subject to a penalty not to exceed $5 for each offense. St. Agnes Church was under construction in 1878 when the new pastor Rev. John Lowery celebrated Mass for his parishioners in the Steamer No. 3 Building. In 1968, the station was closed, and personnel and equipment were moved to the new firehouse on Central Avenue. The Steamer No. 3 Building served for 12 years as a storehouse for the city's recreation department and was sold at public auction in 1981. The former fire station is now a residence.

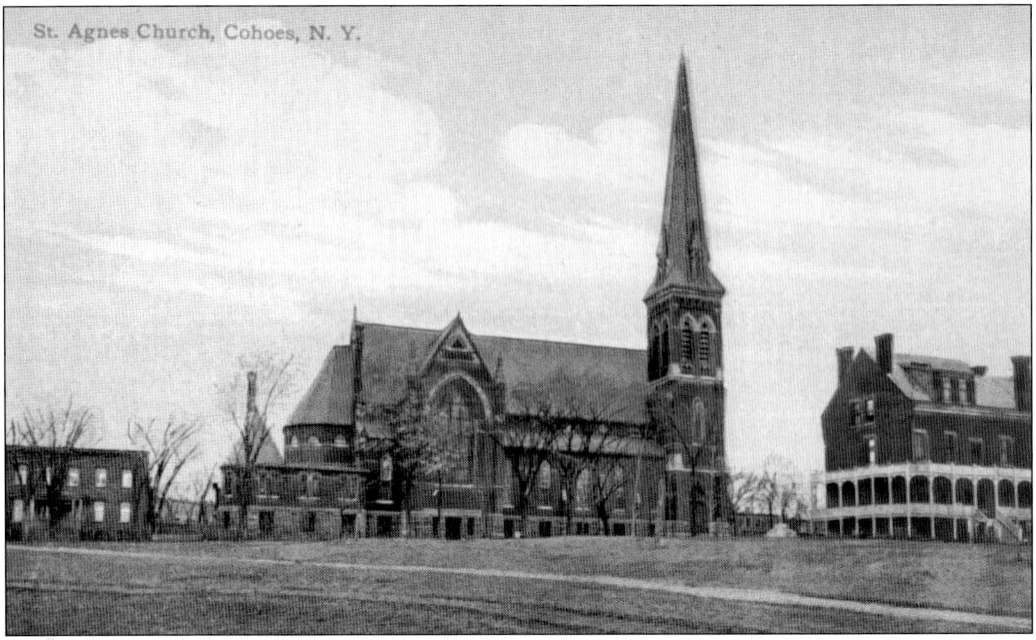


In 1878, Fr. John F. Lowery came to Cohoes to found a parish on the hill. The first St. Agnes Church was a wooden structure, which was destroyed by fire in 1883. The present church on Johnston Avenue was built to replace it. The building is one of the finest examples of Gothic Revival architecture in the area and is a city landmark that can be seen for miles around because of its soaring steeple and location in the hill section of the city. St. Agnes School was constructed during the tenure of Father Gavin, who succeeded Father Lowery. The Sisters of Mercy taught students at the school. Msgr. Joseph Franklin succeeded Father Gavin, and while he was pastor, the parish lyceum was constructed in 1931. The building contained a gymnasium and a bowling alley, and facilities for other parish activities, including dances and church suppers.

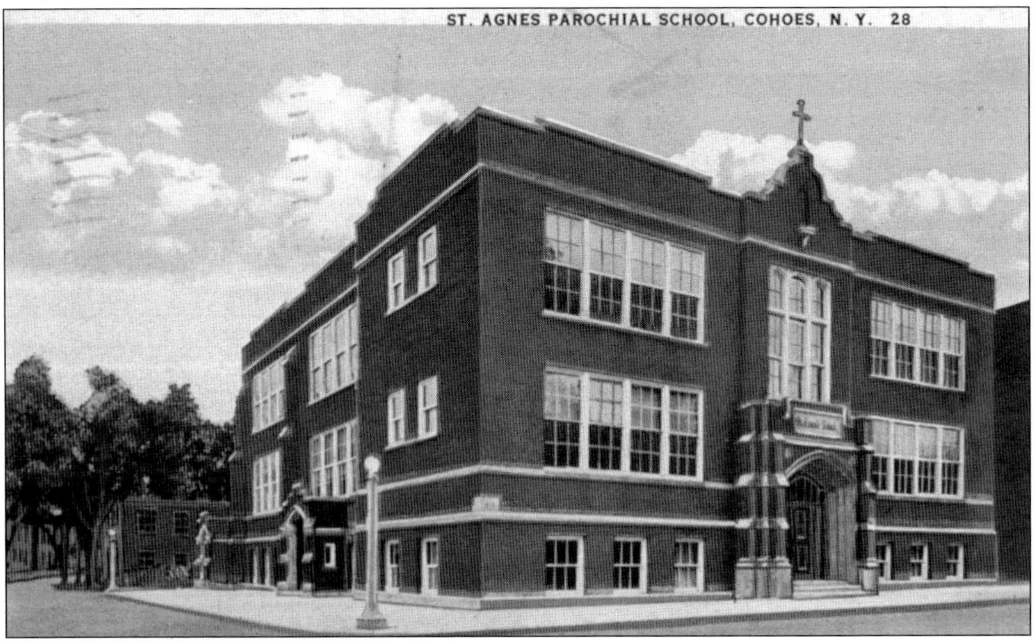

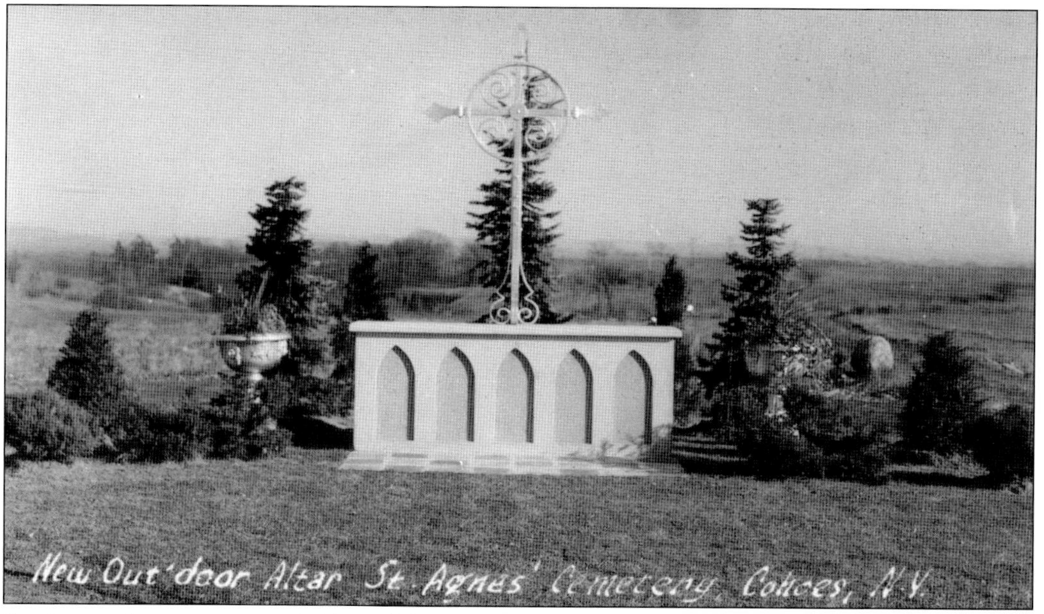


St. Agnes Cemetery was dedicated in September 1883. The altar in the postcard stands at the end of the "Sorrowful Way," the path of the Stations of the Cross, built in 1949 at the cemetery's east end. The metal cross atop the altar originally graced the spire of St. Agnes Church. A replica of Michelangelo's *Pietà* is located on a slope behind the seventh and eighth Stations of the Cross.

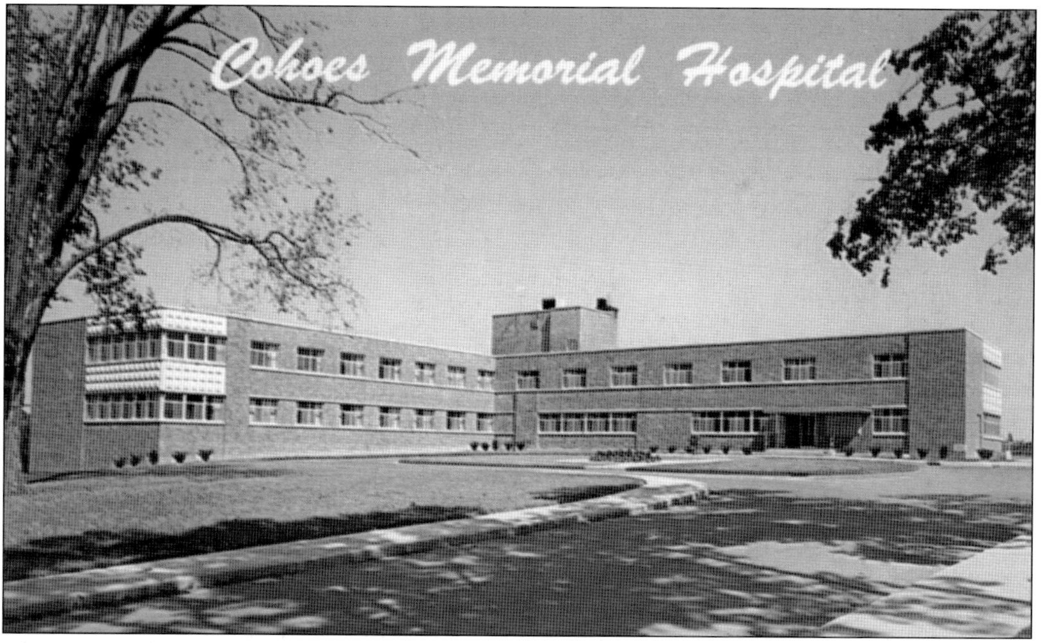


The new Cohoes Hospital on Columbia Street was dedicated in November 1960 with more than 2,000 in attendance. O'Rourke's riding stables was formerly at the site. The hospital chief of staff and president was Dr. James H. Mitchell, whose father and grandfather were also Cohoes physicians. In 1968, Eunice Antonucci became director of nursing. The hospital was closed in 1986. Today, the site houses a short and long-term care complex.

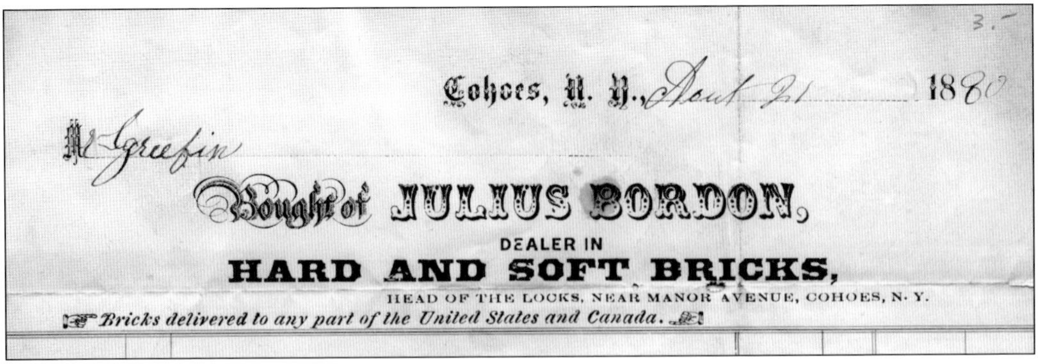

Cohoes, N. Y., Aout 21 1880

M Greefin

Bought of JULIUS BORDON,

DEALER IN

HARD AND SOFT BRICKS,

HEAD OF THE LOCKS, NEAR MANOR AVENUE, COHOES, N. Y.

*Bricks delivered to any part of the United States and Canada.*

Julius Bordon's brickyard was located at the "head of the locks" near Manor Avenue, just above the flight of locks ending with Lock No. 18 of the enlarged Erie Canal. The proximity of the canal permitted bricks to be shipped all over the United States and Canada. During the 1880s, construction in Cohoes was at a near standstill due to a lack of bricks, as local brickyards could not keep pace with the city's growth during its industrial boom. This demand for bricks led to the establishment of several brickyards in this area near Manor Avenue and the canal. Brickyards included those of John Murray, Bleau and Dupuis, Marais and Berube, and John Baillargeon Jr. On June 8, 1888, one of the new brickyards, owned by Nelson Gadeau, turned out its first batch of 250,000 bricks.

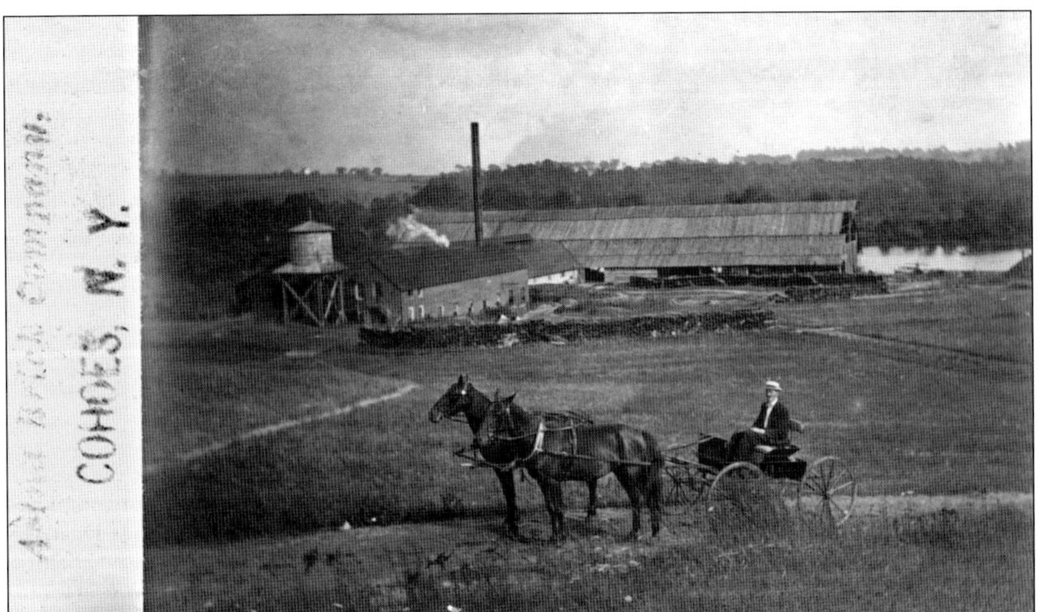

# *Six*

# All Around Town

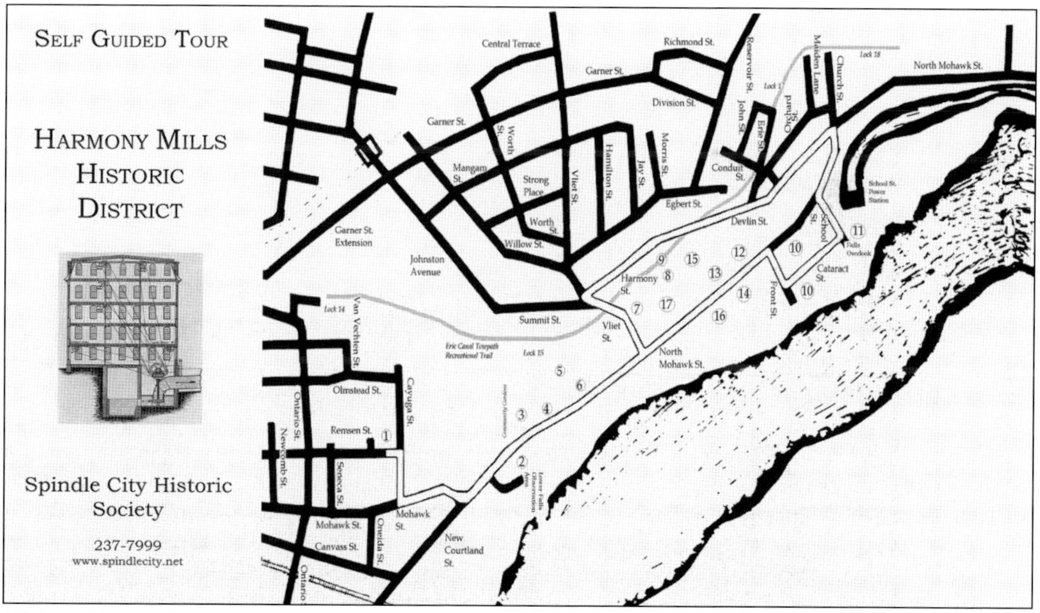


This guide to the Harmony Mills Historic District is one of several self-guided tour brochures created by the Spindle City Historic Society. The brochures are available at various locations around the region, and can be downloaded from the websites of the Spindle City Historic Society and the City of Cohoes. They are an important component of the society's mission to educate people about the rich history of Cohoes.

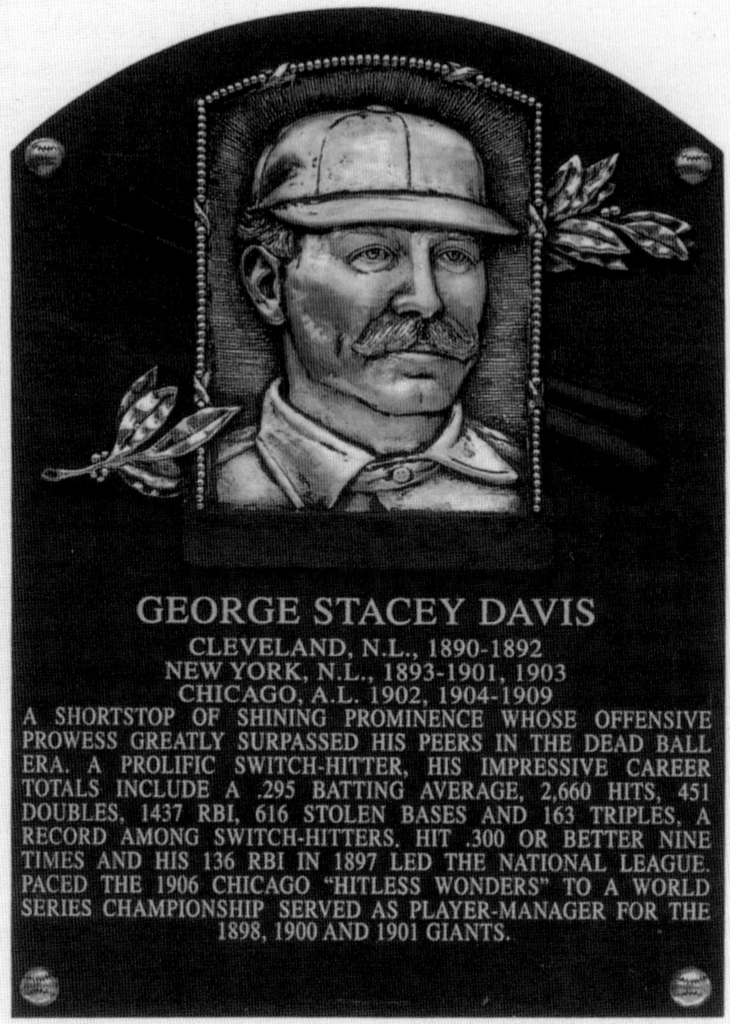


NATIONAL BASEBALL HALL OF FAME & MUSEUM®
Cooperstown, New York

George Stacey Davis was born in Cohoes in 1870 to an Irish immigrant family. As a teenager, he worked in his uncle's teamster business and developed an interest in baseball. He signed a contract with the National League's Cleveland Spiders in 1889, and was touted as "the greatest all-around player living" by Cleveland fans by his third year on the team. Davis went on to play for the New York Giants and the Chicago White Sox, amassing statistics in fielding and at bat that place him among the top five shortstops ever to play the game. Throughout the 1890s, he regularly ranked among the league leaders in doubles, triples, RBIs, and stolen bases, and on June 14, 1893, he became the first player in major league history to hit a home run and a triple in the same inning. Over his baseball career, Davis enjoyed a reputation as an intelligent and hardworking player and was known as "Gorgeous George" for his graceful play and blond locks. He was inducted into the National Baseball Hall of Fame in 1998.

The flag with a harp in this postcard is among the oldest symbols of Ireland, dating to the 1640s. It is crossed with the US flag, with friendship symbolized in the clasped hands. Irish immigrants escaping hardship came to Cohoes to work on the canals and mills, and citizens of Cohoes assisted their families through the Irish Relief Association, which sent provisions to those in need in Ireland.

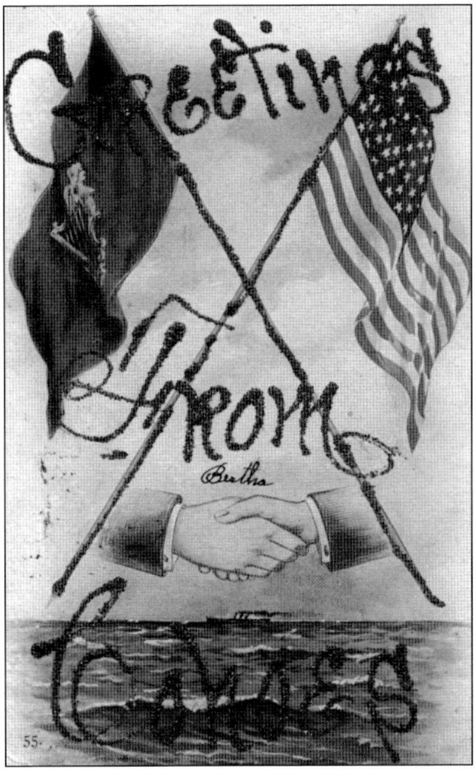


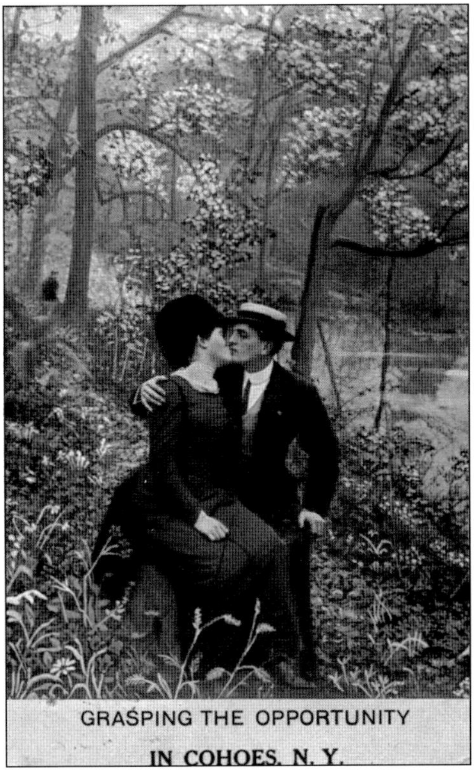


Postcards were first used to send quick notes. They first appeared in America in 1873. Penny postcards were introduced soon thereafter. Postcards that acknowledge an event or a place were printed after 1893. Before 1907, messages were written on the front, with the address on the back. Postcards with a message like this one used stock artwork and a generic message; the geographic location was added as needed.

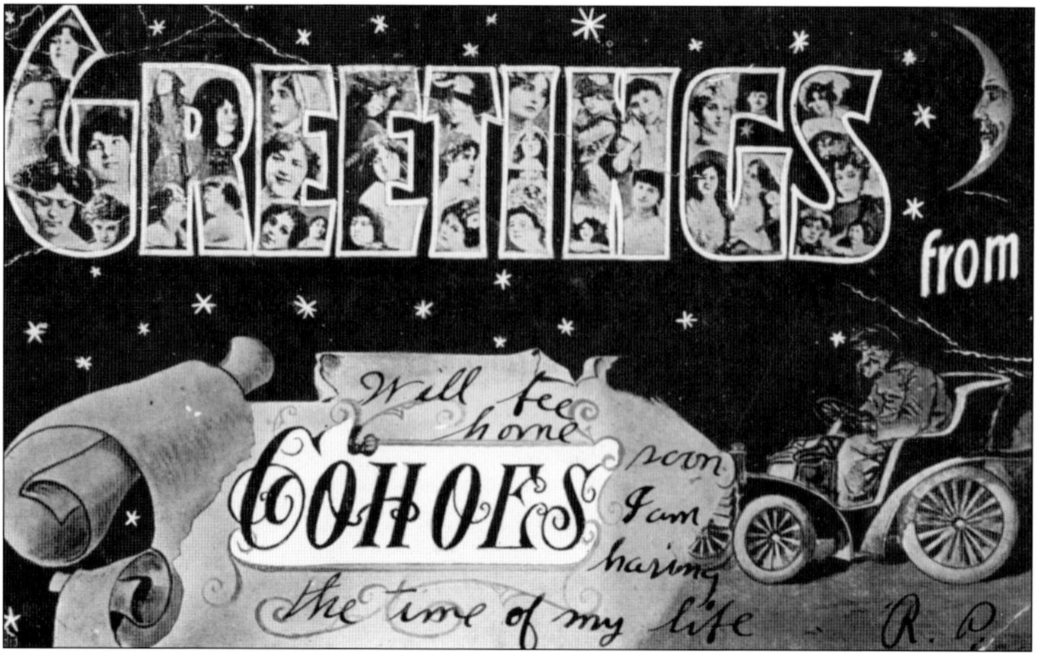


This generic postcard is labeled with "greetings from Cohoes," but could be inscribed for any number of places. Second only to "wish you were here" was the message "having the time of my life." Cohoes was an important destination for many, whether it was to see the Cohoes Falls, to visit a family member, or as a stop on an Erie Canal or rail journey.

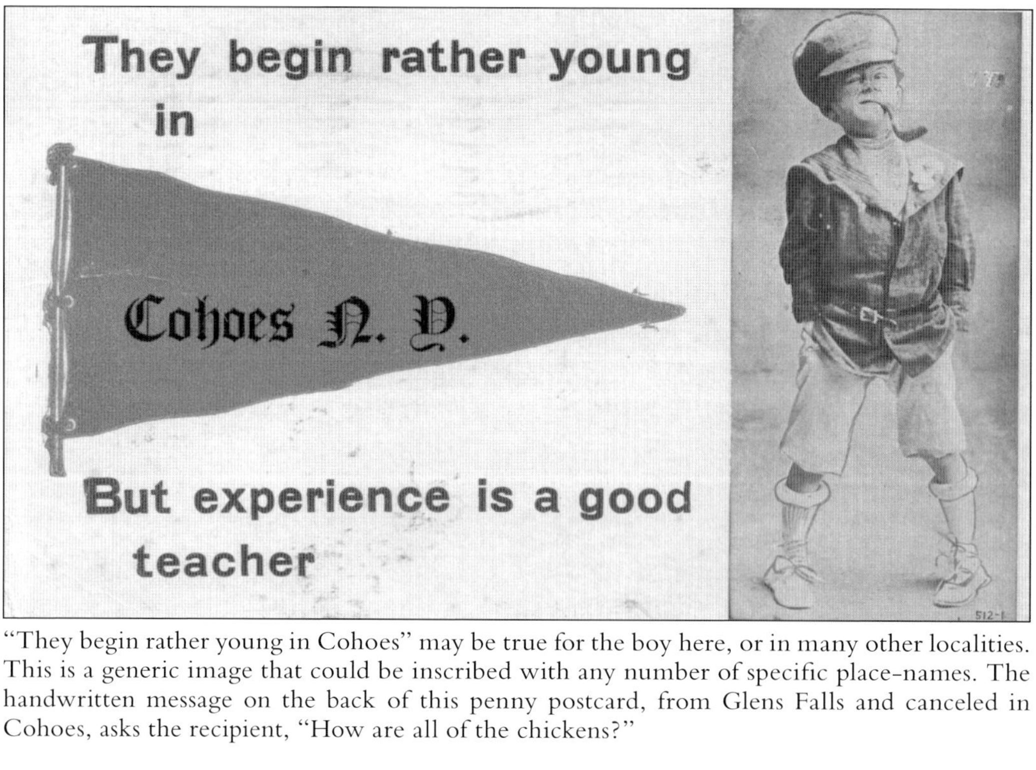


"They begin rather young in Cohoes" may be true for the boy here, or in many other localities. This is a generic image that could be inscribed with any number of specific place-names. The handwritten message on the back of this penny postcard, from Glens Falls and canceled in Cohoes, asks the recipient, "How are all of the chickens?"

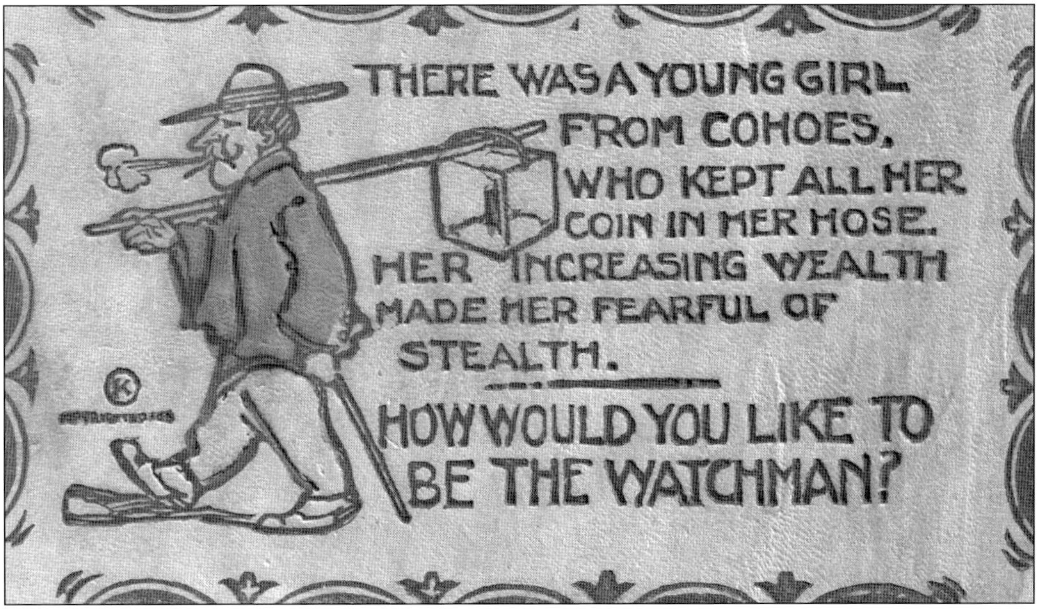


Leather postcards, like this example with a limerick, were produced between 1903 and 1910, despite a ban by the post office in 1907 because their thickness would jam the postal machines. Most were made from deer hide and engraved by pyrography, which became popular again in the 1950s when people were burning designs into wood. Postcards such as this are rare and are second only to real-photo postcards in collectability.

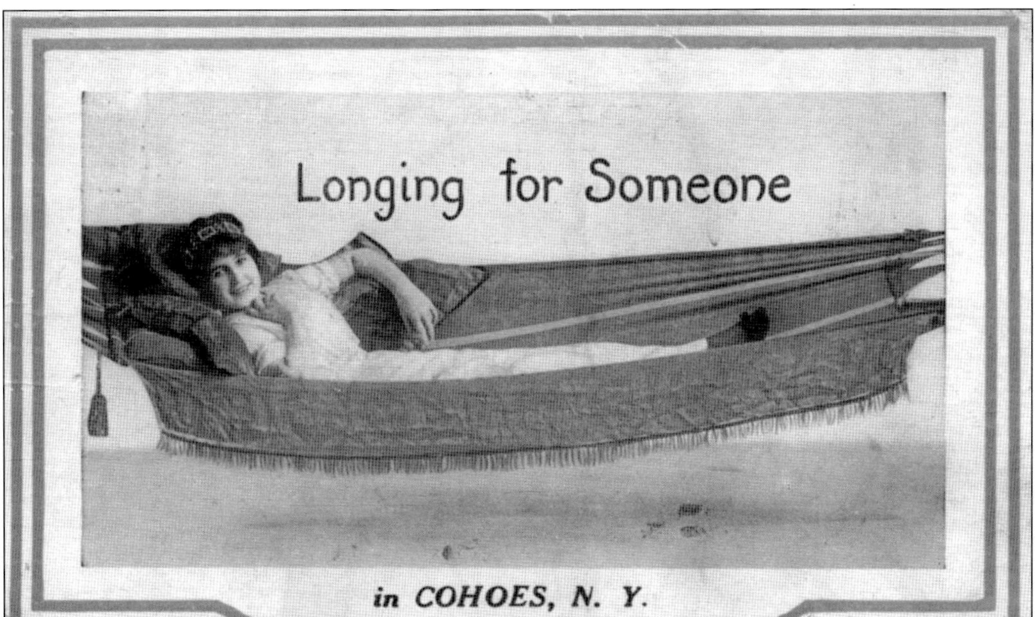


This is another stock postcard, yet the message on the back is quite compelling. One can only guess of the interest the writer had about the recipient, as the card reads: "Longing for someone, can you guess who? Write me a long letter just like I do." It was not until 1907 that the post office allowed people to write on the back of the postcard.

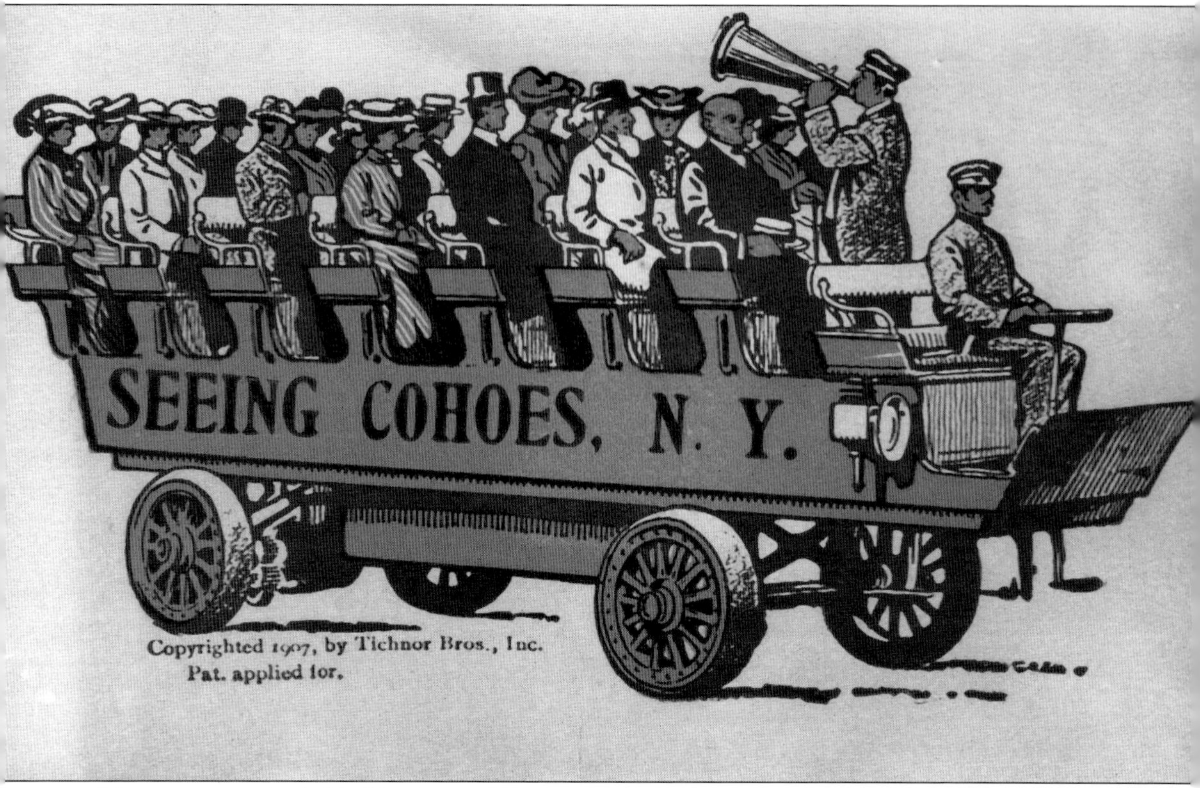


If a person received this "Seeing Cohoes, N.Y." postcard as a gift, he or she might have made a visit to Cohoes and used it as a tour guide or destination map to the city. To do so, the person would open it to an accordion fold of then current images of Cohoes. Due to the complexity of manufacturing cards like this one, not many were produced. The tour would take the traveler past many sights and locations that were considered the showpieces of the city at the time. Today, many people take directions for granted, as there are Global Positioning Systems (GPS) built into vehicles, mobile phones, or other devices. In 1907, everyone relied upon handwritten directions, oral directions, paper maps, or navigation by the "seats of their pants." Postcards like this, with thumbnail "tours" of the community, were mass-produced for resale in many localities.

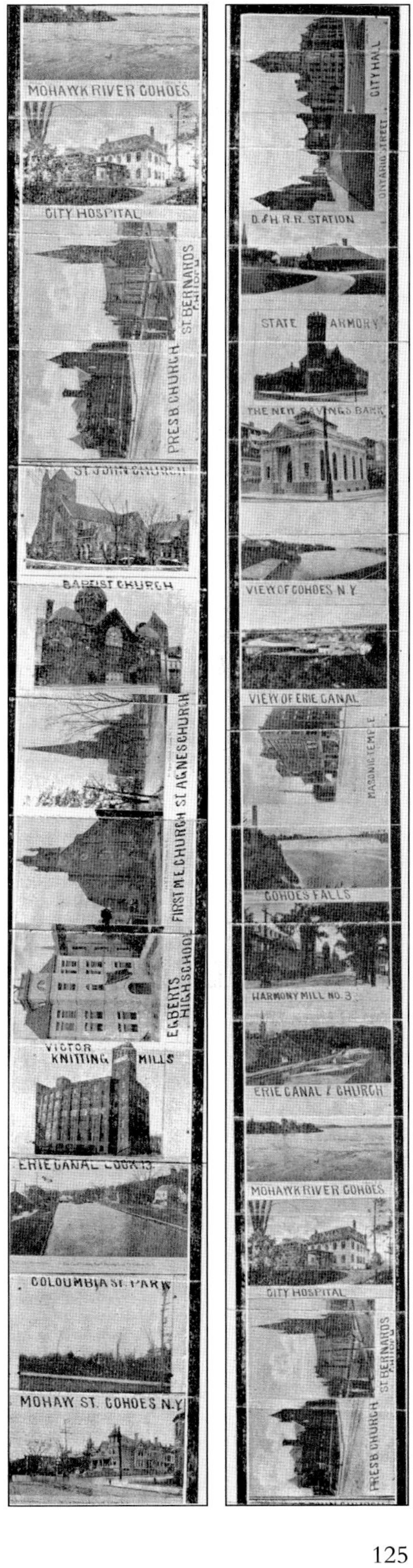


This 1907 foldout contains a total of 24 miniature images, of which there are six churches, street views, the railroad station, and other points of interest. Many of these miniature images were reproduced from full-sized postcards shown in this book. For example, the traveler is encouraged to look at Mohawk Street, Columbia Street Park (West End Park), Erie Canal Lock No. 13, the Victor Mills, Egberts High School, the First Methodist Church, St. Agnes Church, the Baptist church, St. John's Church, Silliman Church, St. Bernard's Church, Cohoes Hospital, the Mohawk River, the Erie Canal, Harmony Mill No. 3, Cohoes Falls, Masonic temple, Cohoes Savings Bank, Cohoes Armory, D&H Railroad station, Ontario Street, and city hall.

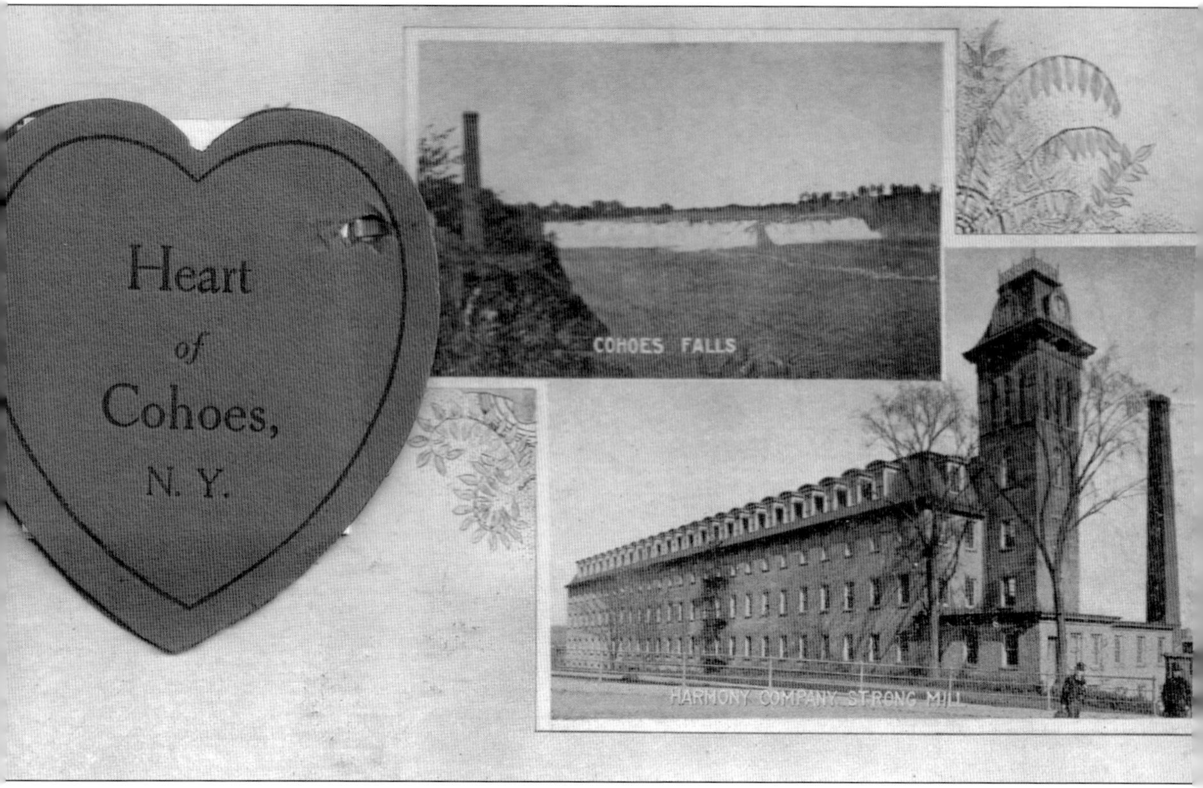


Postcards made with foldouts of multiple images were the exception to the rule, undoubtedly due to the increased production cost of hand-assembling their components. More common were double postcards that were folded in the middle, as these were less complicated to produce. They involved a larger image spread over a greater amount of card stock. However, it was not unusual to see postcards like this "Heart of Cohoes" postcard that included an envelope containing a set of images showing views of the city's major thoroughfares and other places of interest. The envelope is heart-shaped and was hand-attached to a double-thickness postcard that held the binding tab in place to keep it out of harm's reach on the address side of this card. It seems unlikely that a machine could have assembled these delicate embossed pieces of paper without damage.

The heart is made with typeset printing that looks embossed, due to the soft texture of paper that was used. The locality identifier was likely run in batches and then stitched to its accompanying postcard to complete the production process. The printer would have reset the type carriage as different batches for towns or other areas of interest passed through the printing press and the assembling process. With all of this labor, these cards still mailed for only 1¢. This postcard represents the "Heart of Cohoes, N.Y." On the front of this fancy postcard are pictures of the Cohoes Falls, which powered the Harmony Company's Strong Mill. Opening the heart leads to an accordion set of images of the Cohoes Savings Institution, Mohawk Street at Ontario Street, Silliman Church, Masonic temple and opera house, D&H station, city hall, the Erie Canal, the city hospital, Harmony Mill No. 3, and the Mohawk River and dam—places that Cohoesiers hold dear and that give the city its unique identity.

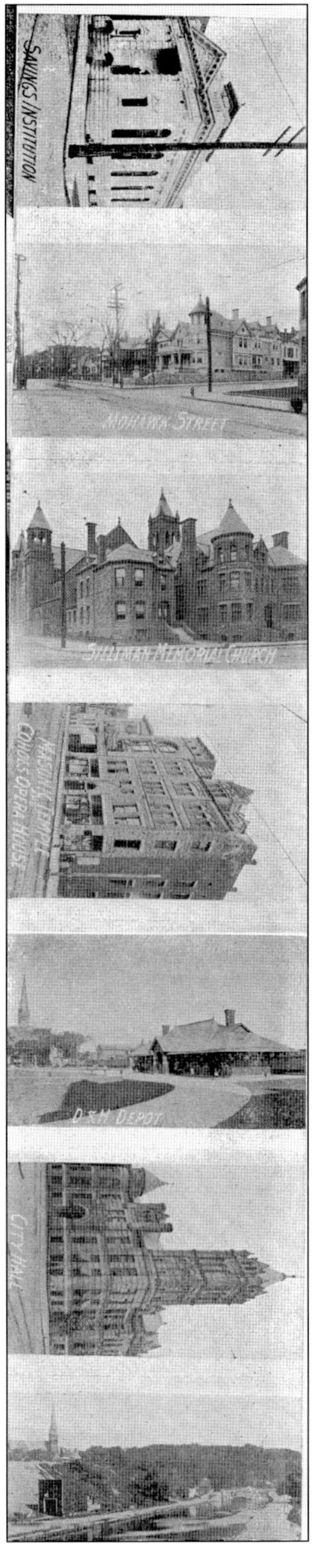


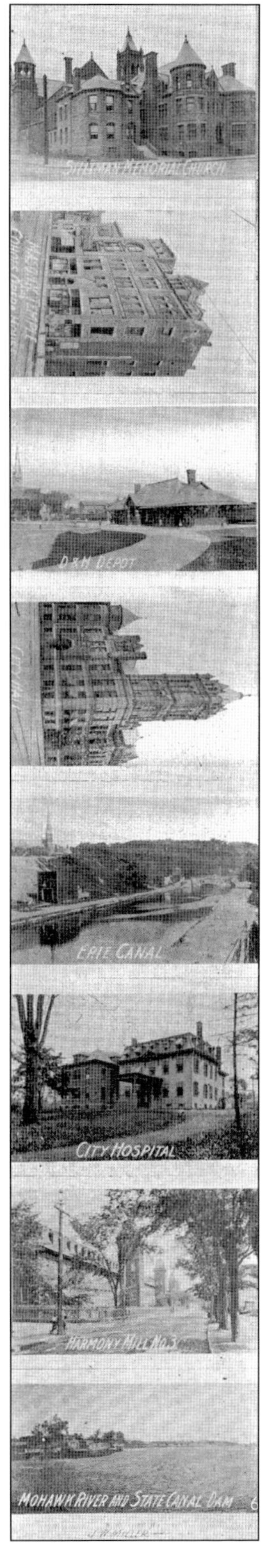

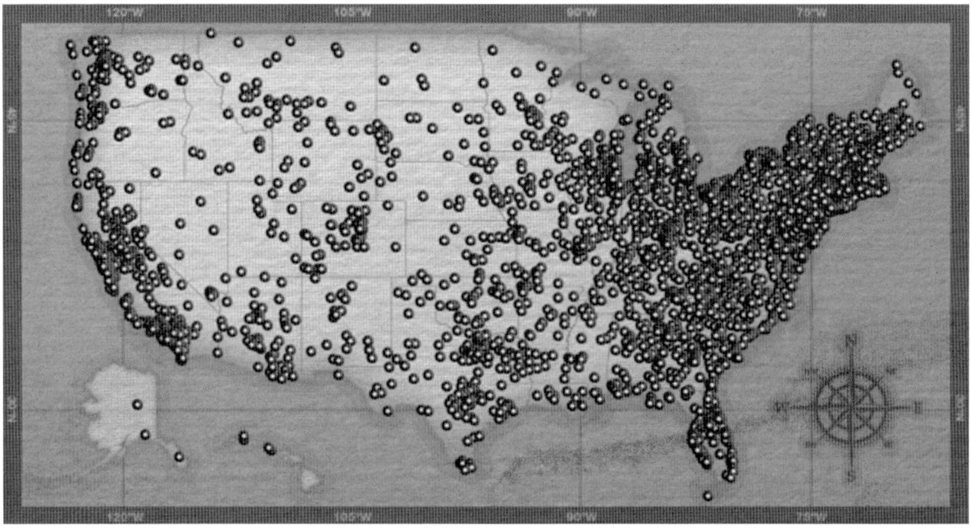